User.

Fivos Panayiotou

Published by MMH Press, 2020

Copyright © 2020 Fivos Panayiotou

All Rights Reserved. No part of this book may be used or reproduced by any means, graphic, electronic, or mechanical, including photocopying, recording, taping or by any information storage retrieval system without the written permission of the copyright owner except in the case of brief quotations embodied in critical articles and reviews.

This book is a recollection of true experiences over time. Some events may have been compressed, and some dialogue has been recreated.

The author has gone to great lengths to ensure that all identities are protected by changing the names and claims his rights to share his story to help others.

Because of the dynamic nature of the Internet, any web addresses or links contained in this book may have changed since publication and may no longer be vaild. The views expressed in this work are solely those of the authors and do not necessarily reflect the views of the publisher and the publisher hereby disclaims any responsibility for them.

National Library of Australia
Cataloguing-in-Publication data:
User./MMHPress
ISBN: (sc) 978-0-6489519-9-5
ISBN: (e) 978-0-6489519-8-8

"Debut novelist Fivos Panayiotou shares this gripping account of one man's journey as he finds himself trapped in one of the most shocking manipulations and case for domestic and violence and psychological abuse. The fact that he is able to withstand such tortures and crimes against the soul is not only a testament to the strength of the human spirit, but an example of the potential that lies within each and every one of us to survive in the face of adversity. This riveting and gut-wrenching body of work is the embodiment of triumph over the human condition."

Susan Wakefield, Editor

CONTENTS

Chapter One: Alone	7
Chapter Two: New Beginnings	15
Chapter Three: Sheena Baxter	19
Chapter Four: Close Calls	29
Chapter Five: Blown Out of the Water	36
Chapter Six: Meet My Family	58
Chapter Seven: Scarborough	71
Chapter Eight: Maxed Out	83
Chapter Nine: True Colours	99
Chapter Ten: Harsh Truths	111
Chapter Eleven: Connect The Dots	125
Chapter Twelve: Rock Bottom	136
Chapter Thirteen: A Fraudulent Life	159
Chapter Fourteen: Abort Mission	176
Chapter Fifteen: Brutal	189
Chapter Sixteen: Bianca Brady	204
Chapter Seventeen: Drifting	215
Chapter Eighteen: Heartbreak Hotel	226
Chapter Nineteen: Redefined	247
Epilogue: God Awaits	278

CHAPTER ONE
Alone

1 Kings : 19
When Elijah said 'Lord I want to die,'
God gave him strength to live.

It was a muggy Monday night in Melbourne, late summer of 2008 and the rain was falling hard. Brondo Violaris sat alone in his bedroom, recalling his life and childhood and wondering how he had gotten to this point in time. Time, he was learning, was that strange thing that was neither friend nor foe, except for today, because today he felt time was against him, and he could feel the pressure building and constricting in his veins. Brondo was twenty-nine and living with his grandmother and uncle and working as a two bit security guard driving around in a gold Commodore that was well past its use by date, ready to hit the scraps. The car was pretty much unroadworthy and in need of several mechanical parts that Brondo couldn't afford. On top of that, he was going nowhere, falling in a heap of depression. No prospects, no dreams of further bettering himself; just lost and alone in a slump that was a mixture of anxiety and loneliness.

He had gone from job to job feeling never good enough, insecure and inferior, always lacking self-confidence and the self-belief he so desperately needed to be able to forge ahead with things in his life. Every day was the same; he would get out of bed, go to his job or whatever job was lasting in the moment, make it though the day and return to his bed, exhausted and empty. Every day was an effort for him.

He had been on a date, his first date in forever, just the week before, only to be given a rude awakening. The girl was pretty, but blunt; the dinner couldn't have lasted even an hour as they sat and ate pizza at a hole in the wall in Brunswick. She bragged for a few minutes about having her own job and business and then stated that she felt she and Brondo were headed in two different directions; this was a body blow to Brondo, who was super keen to date the girl and so far had only mentioned his love of fast cars and Space Invaders, which he jokingly said got on his grandmother's nerves sometimes, and with whom he lived. The girl had grimaced, tried on her best cheesy smile and made the fake excuse that she had to go because she was meeting someone else. She even offered to pay the bill, which Brondo thought was nice, but he did not appreciate her fast and very abrupt exit.

Brondo left the pizzeria feeling deflated; at this point in his life he felt that the restrictions of home life and the isolation he felt, plus the lack of family support was overwhelming; he was constantly being treated like the black sheep of the family and was never given any respect, despite the fact that he knew they loved him. It was the continual passing of judgment and presumptuous attitudes that were a painful and frustrating thorn in Brondo's life.

How could he ever break free of this stranglehold that his

family reigned over him? Sometimes the only option seemed to be giving up because he just couldn't cope anymore.

Eight months later, Brondo was considering his reflection in the small bathroom mirror; in a week he would be turning thirty and he could already see train track lines forming on his brow, around his eyes; he was dreading turning thirty. He felt that everyone around him was already successful, in great relationships, lots of friendships, connections, marriages, careers, businesses, travel, properties, kids etc. etc., the list was endless. And depressing. Because Brondo had none of that. All Brondo had was the ability to dream, to fantasise about those things, the wants, needs, desires. It all just felt like an unattainable illusion to him.

Growing up, Brondo had had a tumultuous relationship with his mother, Maria; she was the strong matriarch, the dominant, aggressive type with a stern demeanour and a cast iron will. It didn't help matters that his father Bill had been an absent father, and the complete opposite to his domineering mother. His father's absence meant that most of the time he was left in the care of Mother, and, more often than not, he had to submit to her will, be a good boy and behave. When Father did come home, Brondo resented him more and became more angry for the fact that he was never around. He fantasised about offloading, blasting him for not being a better father and husband; however in reality when they did come into contact his anger became tempered, muted, though you could cut the air with a knife. Instead, there would be a controlled exchange of cold, harsh, rude or judgmental words and his father would up and leave again.

The problem with Brondo was, he'd been raised a good Greek Orthodox boy in a strict family, which meant he naturally had a high level of respect for his parents yet a low opinion of himself, and this permanently held him back from standing firm and defending himself in his own life.

As time wore on and things became more and more tense around the kitchen table, Brondo decided it was better to go live with his grandmother. For the next twelve and a half years he had an on and off relationship with Yaya, as they too clashed, mainly because many from Brondo's church spirit house passed judgment on a grown man living with his grandmother. He was constantly barraged with snide laughs, sneers and sarcastic judgment calls about his living arrangements and inability to hold down a job. Being a people pleaser and looking for everyone's approval inadvertently fed a growing resentment within him. Brondo had had enough.

On January 14 Brondo went to bed wishing he would never wake up again. He had had enough of life and couldn't bare feeling like a failure anymore; he was angry at life and at God for he didn't believe he could overcome the obstacles that lay in front of him. It all seemed useless.

Brondo's younger brother Vito came to visit one evening. Vito was married to Sonia, a lovely traditional Greek woman; he was a successful builder who owned his own home and was going places. He had been secretly organising a party for Brondo for his thirtieth birthday; a hunting trip with him and his friends and Brondo's one friend, Juan. He told his brother of the plan, hoping it would lift him out of the funk he was in.

"Hey man, what's up?" Vito said, greeting his big brother in the kitchen. They embraced in a slap bear hug; Brondo was a much more burly build than Vito, broad shoulders, long arms.

"Not much, the usual," Brondo muttered, sitting down to eat Vegemite toast.

"Look, man—I'm just checking in that we're still cool on the trip for tomorrow, yeah? I gotta pick up da boyz around nine, so I'll be at yours around ten, ok? We got a big trip ahead of us tomorrow, so the sooner we get out on the road, the better. Hey—and no backing out. Now, where's Yaya? Just wanna say a quick hi before I get going. Remember—ten sharp, man." Vito pointed a finger at Brondo all dude like and Brondo just sat and looked at him with a half eaten slice of cold toast.

Tomorrow. Ugh. Why did Vito always push him into these things? He was having real trouble with the thought of shooting an animal—how could that possibly feel like a birthday trip? It wasn't his kind of idea of fun. He began to secretly fantasise about his own demise; there'd be an accidental shooting and he'd wind up dead—it would make for a great and dramatic ending, he thought. What better way to leave this earth than with all the noisy Greek relatives standing around sobbing at his funeral?

He kept his thoughts to himself and figured that if the occasion arose and he just couldn't bear life any longer that he'd have to pull something off by himself; but he couldn't tell Vito or anybody this, because they'd all just think he was nuts.

Brondo awoke in the early hours of January 15; he had all of his packing all ready to go on the floor of his room so the only thing he had to do was get up and shower. Their hunting trip to Mount Hope in the outback of New South Wales was a good 700 kilometres away, and the boys would be driving the most part of the day just to get there. The guns were already packed in the back of Vito's Hilux; they had the tents, food, blankets and other necessities all piled in the back when Vito showed up to pick up his brother. Brondo was nervous about meeting the rest of the crew. They drove out through the outer suburbs of Melbourne, the boys all introducing themselves, making nice in the cab. Brondo listened for awhile but small talk always made him feel like he had nothing interesting to say, so he dozed off in the back seat to the drone of men swapping hot chick stories. His life was so boring compared to these guys, he just never felt like he fit in anywhere.

Mount Hope appeared in the distance just as Brondo woke up in the back seat. The boys were eager to get out of the car and hunt right on cue, even before setting up for the night. Brondo was too busy rubbing his eyes to care, he felt sleepy, detached.

"Come on, Bro, you can't be tired, you pretty much slept the whole way—we was gonna wake you when we stopped in Gundagai for Maccas, but you were so out of it we just let you be," Vito said, knocking back a Vic Bitter. Brondo said nothing; he watched the boys as they loaded their guns and prepared to drive off to the hunting site. Deer and goat were on the menu tonight.

Brondo felt his depression worsening as anxiety crept into his throat. He was out in the cold darkness, out in the middle of nowhere and the closest thing to civilisation was at least a good thirty kilometres away. Now, he thought; now was as good a time as any for him to throw his life away, he just needed the right opportunity. He waited for Vito to start walking back to the Hilux, then he began praying in secret, asking God for help to end his life.

Except, Brondo didn't end his life just then. He only thought about it. The moment passed and to his own surprise Brondo found himself encountering snakes and spiders and going on adventures under the intense heat of the Australian sun. He and his brother and his brother's mates would kill goats, wild pigs, deer and Goannas. On the fourth day, Brondo and his brother were sitting in the outside cab of the Hilux pointing their guns, waiting for anything to shoot at, when, without warning, George, one of the crew, hit a bump in the road pretty hard, which caused Brondo and Vito to bounce off the Hilux and go flying. The brothers turned and screamed, hoping their men would turn around and come back, but the others just kept on driving, not realising they'd just lost two of their men.

Brondo followed his brother in the opposite direction a couple of kilometres then Vito stopped and fired a flare shot.

"Goddam fuck it, I've run out of flares," Vito called out to Brondo. "You need to shoot your flares as there are goats in the vicinity! If they don't see us they might start shooting in our direction!"

Brondo silently smirked at the realisation his prayers for his death wish might finally be answered; what a relief it would be if someone else could pull the damn trigger for him and have done with it because he was too chicken shit to do the deed himself. Without warning and just seconds later a couple of shots rang out and bullets came flying in their direction.

Shoot out a fucking flare! Shoot out a fucking flare, man!" Vito screamed.

Brondo was secretly glad now that he had decided to come on this trip. He did nothing. Vito yelled out again.

"Shoot out a flare, bro! For God's sakes! Please!"

Brondo, still stuck in his death wish fantasy suddenly felt fear strike; the sudden realisation hit that the pain of death might be too unbearable—and what if he wasn't hit in the head directly enough to die instantly? What if it went all wrong and he lived, and suffered with some horrible facial disfigurement instead? He couldn't believe God was answering his prayer this way; yet he was grateful all the same. The answer was no. He was not going to die. Not like this. Not today. Vito's blood curdling scream broke through his haze.

"What in God's fucking name are you waiting for? Shoot another flare!"

Now Brondo was awake again; his love for his brother engulfed him finally and he raised his arm and quickly fired five warning shots. The men stopped firing and Brondo looked beyond the clouds to see Mount Hope faintly in the distance, realising there might just be hope after all.

CHAPTER TWO
New Beginnings

Revelations 21: 4-5
He will wipe away every tear from their eyes, and death shall be no more...for the former things have passed away. Behold, I am making all things new.

Brondo returned to Melbourne, but he continued to feel distressed about the brutal slayings of the animals in the outback. He could feel his depression and anxiety worsening at the sick thoughts. He loved animals and he couldn't comprehend how he could have allowed himself to go on this trip; maybe the constant pressure of never feeling like a man had been part of it, wanting to restore his manhood on some level.

Coming back home was no better than before; if anything his family was just as selfish and controlling as they always had been. What bothered Brondo the most was that they never offered any support or compassion; they just seemed content to watch him struggle and sink, without ever the offer of an olive branch. It seemed they revelled in their righteousness, were always too quick to gossip and run him down, compare him to Roberto's son or someone else's brother, make him feel like he wasn't good enough. Why couldn't they just see him as he was? The internal anger and rage was building in him, and he dreamed of breaking away and alienating himself, getting away from them as quickly as he could. He realised that separating himself from them couldn't possibly hurt anymore than it already did, the alienation he already felt, at their hands.

Brondo found places of peace and quiet where he could just be; he would venture off to the local internet café, where he could spend time on social media, mainly Facebook and playing video games, to bide his time between work and the gym. It was an escape, and he began conversing with several girls online who took a liking to him. He started to feel small shifts in regaining his confidence, and he started believing in himself again, believing that he had what it took to find a partner who would love him and find him enjoyable. He would talk with a great many girls, but it was the deep, meaningful conversations with one girl, the lovely yet mysterious Sheena Baxter, who triggered and fascinated him the most. The more he thought about the lonely figure of Sheena, the more he found himself losing interest in other women and other chats. Sheena's similar stories of strained familial relations with her parents and siblings lured him in; they quickly became each other's life support in facing the abusive nasty stepfathers who had treated them like dirt for years.

They both supported the same AFL team and had a love for Roger Federer in the tennis. They both found they had shared interests too, in Scrabble; Brondo thought he might put it to Sheena after a month of non-stop messaging that they get together and watch the mighty Blues play football and end the day on a game of scrabble.

"What do you say? Sound like fun?" Brondo messaged, trying to sound cool, nonchalant.

"Well, that sounds like a great idea—but I have to tell you something...I'm married."

Sheena's words floored Brondo; he had no idea that Sheena was a married woman. Where were the photos in her profile pictures, her married status? Brondo suddenly felt misled, deceived and deflated. His stomach felt like a punching bag that had just gone ten rounds. She broke the silence first.

"Look—if I spend the night and day with you I will end up leaving my husband," she muttered sheepishly.

Brondo was horrified and humiliated; he had never been in this position in his entire life; he felt quite nervous, and thought that, from that moment, he should steer himself clear of Sheena. Sheena, on the other hand, had other ideas, and grew annoyed and frustrated that Brondo wanted to distance himself suddenly from her, after a month of messaging on Facebook. She couldn't let go of him, though he tried to cool things off.

"Look, I know I probably should have said something, but I was afraid I'd scare you off. My husband abuses me, he hits me, has given me black eyes; Seedy is a brute, he's played up on me too—I've never loved him and the only reason I've stayed with him is because after one stupid, drunken, one night stand I fell pregnant with my twins."

Brondo could feel himself buckle; he felt obliged to rescue this woman, which instantly renewed his sense of purpose and mission in life; now he felt he had a reason to go on. He couldn't turn his back on her. He was about to reply, but Sheena was already messaging again.

"I've contemplated suicide but I can't leave my three kids, Brondo! Max, Thomas and Ally—they need me—they are my world. Look, I have been developing feelings for you these last few weeks; we have so much in common—I know that this isn't what you asked for, but—" she paused for effect, "I need you."

"I need to see you—at any cost, right?" Brondo sighed. He re-read her words. Sheena explained that with a bad back and sciatica she would need to be at Epping hospital the following week; she could create a motive and an alibi to set the wheels of her plan of action into motion; she would organise to stay with her brother the night leading up to her visit, with the excuse that her brother lived much closer to the hospital; and then she would tell her brother Nixon that she had arranged to meet a new man, news which thrilled her brother to no end. Nixon was only too pleased that his sister was getting out to meet someone new; he had no respect or love towards Sheena's husband for the way he had been manhandling and abusing his sister for years.

So it was sorted: Brondo would meet this woman, the one he had connected with most. Maybe it would all just come down to a night of pleasure and happiness, even if it was just one night. Lord knew he needed it. It felt exciting, it felt exhilarating, too, to feel needed again. It would boost Brondo's confidence, lift his game in the desirability stakes. A new beginning. Somewhere in the distance, deep in the back of his mind, floated the dangers and risks, but they didn't feel real; and in weighing up his options, Brondo felt like opportunity was knocking. Instead of always putting himself last in line, maybe it was time to finally put himself first. Just for once. And now he had a real purpose, too: this woman needed saving, and he was good at saving people. Just not himself.

CHAPTER THREE
Sheena Baxter

I Peter 4:8
Love covers a multitude of sins

The wheels had been set in motion; two star-crossed lovers were to meet at the Epping hospital after Sheena's back appointment on Monday, the last day of March; from there they would drive to the nearest motel where they could gaze into each other's eyes and live out a night forever to be remembered. It would be a night of lust and passion and mutual admiration; it was to be an affair of the heart. Brondo felt nervous as he left the motor running; would look away daunted by the older woman as she approached his suffering Commodore on its last legs. She climbed in the passenger seat, and, picking up on his nervousness, served up her best smile just for him.

"Are you intimidated by me? God—you can't even look at me!" Sheena said, laughing out loud. Brondo felt like his face was stuck; it was like when he was a little boy, when he would become so shy, lost for words and his parents would make fun of his stammering. He worked hard to hide the stammer right now, he tried as best he could. He gave her a sidelong glance. The short skirt. The slit. The legs.

"No um, I'm just thinking where to go from here."

However Sheena knew better; she took this as her cue to take charge, advise him to drive to the nearest suburb Brondo was familiar with; from there they could drive to the Coburg Motor Inn off Sydney road and get a room. Sheena asked him if he could perhaps stop by the shops on the way and buy them some food and drinks whilst she prepared herself.

Brondo pulled into the Coles parking lot and sprinted to buy plenty of alcohol and food and sweets; he couldn't believe his luck, man, he was going to get lucky with this girl!

Upon returning, Brondo found Sheena already splayed across the bed, all seductive in a puffy sky blue outfit; she patted the bed teasingly, prompting Brondo to come sit with her. Brondo was unusually nervous as his head went swimming in the situation he now found himself in. An older married woman with kids from up the countryside of Scarborough and his first sexual encounter in over two years. What was he thinking? He sighed as Sheena took his hand and placed it on her thigh. She kept looking at him, gazing into his eyes and chatting flirtatiously; his head was spinning and he could barely keep up with her words. It was all moving so fast. Where was the football? The scrabble? Sheena became restless and impatient; her breathing became more rapid as she placed her hand on Brondo's hair and face, stroking his hair, his cheeks. Before Brondo could take hold of the situation, Sheena was pulling him into a kiss; Brondo let loose and took over, planting the deepest kiss on her plump red lips, his tongue ravaging her. Then they were kissing and pulling each other's clothes off.

Throughout the night they would drink and have many sexual encounters, Sheena bragging about his sexual prowess, calling him a stud, an unstoppable machine. She stroked him lovingly and made him feel like a king until they were both too exhausted and fell asleep in each other's arms.

Sunlight streamed through the cheap motel curtains at dawn; the room was a mess, littered with bottles of alcohol, spilled wine, crumbs and food and bras and underwear lying about. They barely spoke; Sheena excused herself to the bathroom and Brondo lay there butt ass naked watching the television set flicker. He knew he had to drive Sheena back to brother Nixon's house in Thomastown in an hour; as usual he could feel his old worrywart self slowly creeping back in as reality set in.

What was he thinking, with a married woman, of all things? And unprotected sex? He could feel his anxiety rising; what if he had just made himself vulnerable to the possibility of Sheena's falling pregnant? What if she was carrying sexually transmitted diseases? What if she fell pregnant, and her husband found out? He was becoming more and more apprehensive by the moment, so he decided to ask her.

"You know, I hardly know you, and I'm sorry I'm feeling a little funny, a little guilty about not using a condom, and about catching sexually transmitted diseases, you know?" He hinted at all this, hoping she would not be offended. "I mean, last night you also said your husband knows outlaw bikies etc. and that his family is connected to mobsters." Sheena sat down on the edge of the bed, eager to dismiss the whole thing.

Oh, I'm sorry Brondo, that probably freaked you out a bit, huh? Don't worry, that was just the alcohol talking!" She giggled lightly. "Forget it—he doesn't know anything, and he's too stupid to work it out."

"But, what about diseases?" Brondo pressed on.

"My, you are the worrier type, aren't you!" Sheena glazed over him, non-rhetorically. "Look, I'm clean, if that's what you're worried about—and I can't get pregnant, 'coz I've had my tubes tied. Three kids is enough!" She laughed and lit up a cigarette.

Over the coming days Brondo would constantly think of Sheena and she would think of him; Sheena had decided to throw the affair away as a fling, believing she had been nothing more than a conquest to him. Deep down she secretly wanted and longed for more, but she didn't hold her breath when it came to men; she'd given up dreaming a long time ago.

Sheena's husband demanded sex when she got home; he was a brute and things could get ugly if she refused. So she lay there in all of the ugliness of the event, going through the motions until he was finished, closing her eyes and fantasising the whole time that it was Brondo instead making love to her.

Her eyes brightened and her lips formed a smile the next day when she checked her messages and there were a dozen in her inbox from Brondo. He asked how she was doing and when could he see her again. Their encounter had not been a fling after all, she thought. Sheena couldn't believe her luck and quickly texted back that she longed to see him again, too. Dare she see this man again, this man she could not stop thinking about? She lay in bed quietly next to her husband and messaged Brondo again and again, careful not to wake the brute.

Brondo finally confessed his love for Sheena in his last text message, and Sheena in return admitted and confessed her love for Brondo too, and the pair decided they would go to sleep after laying all their cards on the table. It was a huge relief to show each other their hands, Brondo thought. Brondo had taken a huge risk in revealing his feelings to Sheena; he was careful with who he trusted these days, as he'd been hurt enough. He smiled into his pillow, thinking that things were finally falling into place.

"Sheena Baxter, Sheena Baxter," he whispered to himself, drawing curly cursive script, scribbling her name over the back envelope of an electricity bill. Just writing her name sent electric shocks up his forearms, down his spine. Brondo was such a sucker for romance; unlike his brother, he loved nothing more than to write sweet love notes, or light candles and buy flowers. He was a dreamer, and he fell into a sweet slumber full of hope and happiness for his future with Sheena. God, and to think that only a month ago he had been contemplating suicide.

That night Sheena would deliberately pick a fight with her husband, and after much provoking, she would grab her daughter Ally and race out the door to her mother's house for refuge. Her son Max stormed out the front and glared at her telling her to get back inside.

"If you don't come back inside I'm going to kill ya!" he yelled, crazed with anger. Sheena, however, was undeterred by his words. She'd heard it all before.

"I'm leaving, Max—I'll see you later," she said, and with that she was gone.

Five short months earlier Brondo had depression and had been contemplating suicide; now he had more than he bargained for, as he found himself falling in love with an older married woman with three children in tow and a husband with mob and criminal connections. He knew he was getting in too deep with Sheena, but he couldn't help it; now they would sneak around to and from Scarborough, wary of Sheena's son Max, constantly dancing around and dodging his anger and wrath. Max was insistent that his mother was sneaking around and wouldn't leave the situation alone, and though Brondo had never met Max in person, he sensed there was more to her son than met the eye.

One night while Brondo was in Scarborough with Sheena after visiting her mother Varma, they had gone to bed when Sheena placed her foot on Brondo's chest, rubbing it and taunting him, saying how she liked being in control of things, and that he brought her dark side out of her.

"What do you mean?" Brondo responded, feeling a little ill at ease by Sheena's comment.

"I just love a little bit of voyeurism, that's all," Sheena beamed naughtily.

"Oh, is that where you have sex on ships?" Brondo asked.

Sheena laughed and teased him, explaining that voyeurism was just what it was: watching other people sexually and getting turned on by it.

"I've never had control over a man, Brondo, and it kinda excites me to have control over you, in a playful way of course; you're such a big puppy dog! Even my son Max has control over me—he's like, a big strong boy, a Taekwondo black belt; six-foot-four and a hundred and twenty kilograms, covered in tattoos, he could crush the life outta both of us, if he wanted, haha," she laughed.

Brondo felt vulnerable, small and humiliated; was Sheena mocking him? He was by no means a small guy; he had a fairly large build himself and broad shoulders, manly enough he had thought to be a match and hold his own in any contest. But he had a softness too; a kind heart and a sensitivity all his own and did not have it in him to be a brute. A mixed wave of emotions came over him at this moment, that a woman would want to make him feel so vulnerable, yet truth was he enjoyed it; he enjoyed the humiliation though he never truly understood it himself, he was just used to being mocked and played.

Call it women's intuition, but Sheena's wisdom and experience with men led her instantly to take full advantage of Brondo; she sensed his weakness the way a wild cat seeks out its prey, and she began to rub her foot across Brondo's leg and chest, finally resting it on his shoulder as he sat down digesting all of her voyeuristic revelations and sexual desires.

"There *is* something you should know about Max, Brondo; he suffered a brain tumour when he was just thirteen," Sheena explained, looking down at her chipped nails. "It was a horrible time and put a lot of stress on the family—and he's going to need to go back again soon, for checkups and stuff. We've been battling this for years, since he was just two years old—I guess I have played favourites over the years; I did spoil him more than the others, but it was only because of what he was going through, because he was so sick," Sheena said, her voice trailing off into memory dust.

Brondo couldn't find much to say as Sheena continued rubbing her foot over the side of his face. He felt sorry for the kid, truly he did, and right now he felt strangely turned on by Sheena's foot in its stocking, taunting him relentlessly.

"Finally shut you up, haven't I?" Sheena bragged playfully, and the normally chatty Brondo realised he was at a loss for words with nothing to say. She just had this *way* with him, and he became a slave under her spell, unable to walk away.

They would stay the entire weekend in Scarborough, though Brondo felt like they were playing with fire the whole time, as Sheena would duck out here and there to take her daughter's homework to her, or to pick up food; Brondo made sure to only visit Sheena at her mum's house when he felt assured that Sheena's daughter Ally would be at her dad's house on the weekend, or while at her girlfriend's house, depending on the situation at hand. On multiple occasions Sheena would duck out and leave Brondo alone while Sheena's mother would go to work, and Brondo would feel naked and vulnerable, worried that someone might show up.

One night when he was alone at Varma's house, Brondo heard a knock at the door, and, not thinking, he called out to Sheena to ask why she wasn't using her key. When Sheena didn't answer Brondo panicked and jumped in the wardrobe where he lay, deathly still, hidden under the rack of clothes until either she returned or he thought the coast was clear and he could call her or message her to get her to distract whoever it was at the door.

One time Brondo's phone started ringing when he was hiding out in the closet. It was his cousin in law, Steve the Ox. He had no choice but to pick up the call in order to stop his phone from ringing.

"Look, Man, this is a really inconvenient time to be calling me; I'm umm, I'm, well, I'm at Sheena's and there's someone at the door, and it could be her husband or her son, so I can't talk right now...'coz I'm in a closet, " Brondo said, feeling stupid.

"Jesus, Man! Don't get stabbed! Don't get stabbed!" Brondo could hear Steve yelling in a panic. Brondo quickly hung up and curled himself deeper into a ball in the closet. He could feel his anxiety rising, and he felt out of his depth as he realised there wasn't much he could do about the current situation; he was far out in the countryside and he knew he had to continue to play it safe, though his heart rate was going at a hundred miles an hour.

The knocking came again, more forcefully this time. In the darkness of the closet, Brondo texted Sheena.

"Is that you knocking?" Sheena was horrified and quickly

texted back.

"No—I wouldn't need to knock, I've got a key—it's probably Max—wait a minute, I'll text him and tell him I'm over at the supermarket...that'll distract him to come and find me over here." Sheena then hung up right away in a panic herself; things were getting too close now, things were getting harder.

Brondo could hear Max's voice grumbling and becoming more faint as he left the property. Brondo felt that Max was a sinister type, on a mission to catch his mother out, exhibiting similar abusive traits to what his father had modelled. It seemed that sadly, the apple did not fall far from the tree and Max would continue to repeat the cycles of possession, domination and control that held his father transfixed in a history of abuses with their mother.

Luckily enough, Sheena did call Max and was able to divert him to the supermarket.

"Oh yeah?" Max quipped. "Well, who's home, I can hear the TV?" Max challenged.

"Maybe that's Grandma, she might be home," Sheena said, trying to remain nonchalant.

"Why didn't she answer the door then?" Max continued questioning her adamantly, determined not to let her off the hook.

"Maybe she's in the shower most likely—let it go Max—I'll be home later," Sheena groaned, feigning disgust.

Eventually Max left his grandmother's place, pleased enough with his mother's explanations. Sheena returned home and when she opened the door Brondo jumped out of his skin. The two immediately hugged in relief, realising what a close call it had been.

Both Sheena and Brondo knew the gravity of the situation,

and that things were getting more dangerous; but it seemed the more tense Brondo became, the more Sheena was enjoying it; the element of danger, the thrill of having a younger man, a secret lover who was willing to put his life on the line for her. That a man would risk his own flesh and blood for the possibility of loving her in that way that all women dream of—a man who would give it all up, sacrifice it all, just to have her. It gave her life new meaning and purpose; it made her feel great, worthy and alive—not flung to the side like a piece of trash but valued like an exquisite diamond.

A wife of noble character, who can find?
She is worth far more than rubies.
Proverbs 31: 10

CHAPTER FOUR
Close Calls

Proverbs 6: 32
But the man who commits adultery is an utter fool, for he destroys himself.

They made love in the night and upon the days and weeks that followed Brondo and Sheena became like two inseparable lovebirds, flying from nest to nest, flitting from text to text. Brondo would drive back to Melbourne and within a week he would be back in Scarborough again, whenever she had the weekend, kid-free. Every free moment was a chance to be together, and they took it.

By this time, Sheena's daughter Ally was fast becoming suspicious of her mother's behaviour as she could hear her mother every night, late at night; the secret phone conversations coming from under the bathroom door, the intermittent giggles, the way her voice went into a higher octave, a light, flirty pitch whenever she got excited.

After much discussion, Sheena decided to confide in her daughter Ally; she knew she could trust her daughter not to say anything. Ally was intrigued, pleased to see her mother finding the happiness she had been so starved of. Sheena was pleasantly surprised by Ally's positive and mature reaction and decided her daughter should meet the great mystery man who had managed to put the smile back onto her mother's face.

Ally and her grandmother discussed Brondo, and Varma was keen to voice her approvals too.

"Brondo's amazing, Ally—he's really making your mum so happy, it's the best and happiest she's been in the twenty plus years I've seen her, since having you kids."

"Wow, Grandma! That's amazing! I can't wait to meet him!" Ally squealed.

That weekend in May of 2009 it was around Mother's day weekend when Brondo went to Scarborough yet again; it was the most traveling he had done with his car ever in his lifetime. He stayed the night at Varma's house, and the following day after school Ally came home to meet him. Brondo was immediately impressed by Ally's maturity, compassion and love for her mother.

"Wow—you even look alike, both beautiful girls, you are," Brondo said, admiringly. Sheena and Ally both giggled and blushed and Brondo couldn't believe how easily and naturally he seemed to fit in with Sheena, her mother and now her daughter. It felt like a dream; how he had stumbled into this most unexpected relationship with an older married woman was beyond his comprehension. That she had twin adult boys and a daughter whom he had now met was mind boggling, because it all just seemed to happen so fast. Brondo had to catch his breath; he had never been in a serious relationship like this before in his life. And he had really hit it off with Ally; the two connected instantly, playing a game of words with friends and joining Varma and Sheena for curried sausages for dinner. Brondo had found himself an instant family, and he loved it.

Ally's friends came over the next night and met Brondo too; they immediately were taken by him and very impressed with Sheena for finding someone so attractive. Brondo felt his head swirl as he wondered how he should act; was he like an uncle now to Ally, or should he behave more like a father figure? Ally could not get over how cool Brondo was; he wasn't mean and grumpy like her father; he was friendly, easy going and listened to her talk about school and wanted to hang out and play games with her and her friends.

"Mum, he's just sooo cool—and nice! Can we keep him, pleeeeaase?" Ally joked and fell into fits of giggles.

The next afternoon when Ally and Varma went out, the couple showered together and afterwards Sheena wrapped herself in a robe and took her time drying off Brondo's body with a towel while he shaved. They were living inside a cocoon of bubble bliss, and the outside world didn't matter. Suddenly they could both hear what appeared to be a knock at the door. Brondo stopped shaving, his muscles tensed, and he alerted Sheena.

"I think I can hear knocking at the door; Sheena—is someone at the door?"

Sheena looked at Brondo and her face went pale and white.

"Stay here, don't move—and whatever you do, don't come downstairs, I'll take care of it," Sheena said sternly and left the room to see who was there.

Brondo continued shaving but his whole body was tense now wondering who was downstairs. He finished in the bathroom, and, not knowing what to do next, got himself dressed and then sat down on the edge of the bed waiting for Sheena to return. After about twenty minutes Sheena returned and burst through the door in near tears, heart pounding; Brondo rushed to her and wrapped her shaking body up in his arms; she had the fear of life in her.

"Babe what's wrong? Are you Ok? What happened?"

Sheena looked up into Brondo's expectant eyes but she could not respond with words; instead she gave him the most frightened look of fear and horror.

"Who was at the door, *Sheena*? What's wrong? Please talk to me, please say something—you're scaring me."

"Seedy. Seedy was at the door," she uttered again, in almost a whisper.

Brondo was in a daze; what was he supposed to do here? He was in too deep, and he couldn't just walk away from the situation; too many people were involved now.

"What did he want?" Brondo asked coolly, trying to keep his voice from wavering.

"I don't know, but he's suspicious—Seedy's always nosing around, being his usual controlling self I guess; I just kept praying that he wouldn't go upstairs and find you. Thank God he didn't—I think he grew bored when he couldn't find anything, then there wasn't any reason to be here, so he left. But before he left he kept asking me why I was here, and I just kept saying I wanted to spend some time with my mother. Which is true. But—close call, huh?" Sheena wrapped her arms around Brondo and nuzzled into his neck.

"I think it's best if we head to Melbourne and spend the night in the motel there babe, what do you think? We can't have him lurking around here—it's not safe."

Luckily for them that they'd decided to leave, because later that night Sheena would get a call from her mother, Varma, all shaken and upset.

"Mama, tell me again what happened?" Sheena said, anxiously.

"It was Max, darling—he came here all angry to find that you were not here—he was outraged, banging things, demanding to know where you were when you had told him you were staying here. Then he demanded I loan him some money—me, his poor grandmother! I tell you Sheena, he is out of control, that one," Varma sobbed.

"You didn't tell him where I was?" Sheena cringed.

"No dear, I just keep saying 'I don't know, I don't know. You did the right thing by leaving."

Sheena relayed Max's outburst to Brondo. All he could feel was relief that they had left in time.

"Sheena—can you imagine what would have happened if we had stayed in Scarborough? What would have transpired? Think about it. It would have been the mother of all blowups! Your husband I think I can deal with, but the boys are my greater concern—they're young and they're angry and they're strong, and their capabilities to do serious damage are far greater than mine. You've said so yourself."

Sheena felt very uncomfortable by Brondo's words and tried to deter him.

"What are you worried about, what's scaring you? You seriously think I'm going to let them hurt you? I will protect you no matter what."

"It's only a matter of time, Sheena. I'm not scared—but you are. Tell me what you're scared of?" Brondo asked, looking deep into her eyes. Sheena looked back at him with an emotional look of genuine love and concern.

"You, Brondo. I'm scared for you," she said and shivered.

Brondo knew Sheena was more concerned for his safety than her own; what he couldn't know was how far and at what lengths her husband and boys would go to, to harm him once they knew the truth.

"I can only hope that if the boys do find out about us that they will have enough respect for you not to cross that line, as their mother. Maybe in some ways it would be better if you just came clean with them now, like you did with Ally. And look how that turned out? Pretty well, I think. And look; you've already told your mother, your sister, friends—the only people who don't know about my existence now are the two boys, and Seedy. And since they're sniffing around and getting closer, don't you think it would be better to just come out with the truth?"

Brondo felt his words made complete sense; after all their sneaking around, and the boys sneaking around, maybe it was better to just come out with it all about their relationship, maybe it was just time to put the issue to bed.

"Let's let sleeping dogs lie, for now. We can't go getting ourselves all worked up constantly over all these 'what ifs' when we could be getting all worried over nothing," Sheena said, brushing off his suggestion.

"But, surely the boys would back you, be in support of our relationship, if your allegations of your husband beating you and giving you black eyes and cheating on you is true," Brondo ventured gently. "After what you've been through, don't you think they'd be in support, give us their blessing, after all you've had to endure, staying with that pig of a man?"

Brondo saw Sheena's face turn a strange shade as he saw her expression change.

"What do you mean '*if*' my allegations are true? Of course they're true—I just know what my sons are capable of—and at the end of the day they are my sons and it *is my decision*," Sheena said firmly in that non-negotiable tone of voice she was good at.

But Brondo could tell Sheena wasn't being rational, and whether she just couldn't see past her own people pleasing mentality or not, he didn't know. What Brondo did know was that things were going to end badly should the boys find out any other way. But Sheena wouldn't listen; she brushed it off and told him not to focus on it. And Brondo would go against his better judgment again and listen to her words rather than his own thoughts.

CHAPTER FIVE

Blown Out of the Water

Luke 12: 2
Nothing is covered up that will not be revealed,
or hidden that will not be known.

The affair had now been going on for the better part of three months and Brondo made the trek from Melbourne out to Scarborough on a cold June afternoon to see Sheena, as had become typical for them on Wednesday nights. The Queen's Birthday long weekend was fast approaching and Brondo couldn't explain why, but he had an uneasy feeling in the pit of his stomach and told Sheena he felt so.

"Babe—I got a bad feeling we're gonna be blown out of the water tomorrow, not sure why, but I've just had a weird feeling about it all. I can't even sleep."

Sheena hushed Brondo over the phone, gently telling him that he was over thinking things and being too negative, suggesting perhaps that was even what he had wanted. Still, Brondo knew that he felt these things all his life and that what he was saying should not be taken lightly; it was always his sixth sense at work. Still, Sheena chose not to listen and instead told Brondo they were going to have a magical weekend and to stop worrying. That night Brondo went to sleep full of anticipation and concern as he knew better than to go against his feelings; he could only hope that tomorrow would not turn out to be a day of dread the way the spirits had warned him.

The next morning Brondo awoke and looked out the window upon the drizzle of rain falling; the feelings of uncertainty and fear hadn't left him and now he could add more feelings like confusion and déjà vu to the mix. He jumped out of bed and showered and went to work; he had a short shift working security this morning. Some days were longer shifts than others, but this morning's shift would be over by nine, and if he got straight on the road afterwards he'd arrive in Scarborough as early as 10.45am, which suited him fine. Brondo turned up the radio; the songs were all 1989, the year Sheena's boys were born, a sign which he immediately took as a bad omen. If only Brondo could have predicted that today would be the day his life would be put to the point of the sword in the most unimaginable of ways...

But, for a man who usually had good instincts and intuition, Brondo often felt things that others couldn't at times, even though sixth sense was never taken seriously, least of all by himself. He would be brushed off as a worrier, cast off as weird perhaps. But Brondo *was* superstitious; he felt that numbers represented omens for him, and he was very numerical about everything that happened in his life. It was without doubt one of his most annoying traits, and if he carried on about such things his brother would be quick to shut it down as nonsense. But more often than not, Brondo always knew he was right on the money.

The day started off badly; Brondo had had a run in with some middle eastern boys at the local Hungry Jack's before losing a hundred dollars, and he'd rung Sheena to tell her that he'd lost the money for the motel room they had booked at the Tudor House. When Brondo tried to pay for the room with his card that had been declined too, and Brondo felt more even bad energy envelop him. The signs were everywhere; yet he would push past all of these feelings, driven by his burning desire for Sheena. Sheena insisted that he stop worrying, that she would pay for it and that she wanted two nights with Brondo, not just one. Brondo informed the manager he would return and pay the rest in full upon their arrival and went to collect the money from Sheena. Sheena was to meet Brondo out the front of Sheena's work, where she would give him the money.

"I'm not sure this is a great idea after all—" Brondo messaged her when he was on his way. "It'll be in full view of the main hospital," he squirmed.

"I don't see the problem, I mean it's a public place, we can cover and pretend I'm a client for future family members, or something like that—" Sheena said breezily.

"Sheena, babe, I'm feeling scared—I mean, we are out the front, and it's easy for anyone to spot us; I don't even want to entertain the idea of us getting caught…I'm sick even thinking about it, Oh God."

Brondo looked around the parking lot feeling uneasy. Strange how it was always Brondo getting cold feet while Sheena never worried enough about things.

"Hurry up babe, hurry up, 'coz I'm out here now and I can't

wait long—just give me the money and I'll go back to the motel and wait for you there."

Sheena ducked out the side door and ran to Brondo's car; he pulled his window down just long enough for her to hand him the money and she leaned in for a quick kiss before bolting back inside the building. They had managed to avoid being seen by passersby, and Brondo started his engine and drove back to the motel. Maybe all this sneaking around was just getting to him, making him paranoid; he needed to be more like Sheena, he thought, and just shake it all off.

Brondo settled into the cheap hotel room with striped, 70's curtains and dusty quilt cover. He lay down on the bed and turned on the TV. A movie was playing by lunchtime; it was 8 Mile starring Eminem. Brondo lay back into the pillows and gathered his thoughts; he tried to forget all about the feelings he had had earlier that morning and night before and focus on the excitement that was to come instead. Sheena was right: they would have a magical weekend together. Brondo just needed to learn how to relax.

He was lying there on the bed watching 8 Mile when his phone rang. It was a call from a private number; he toyed with the idea of not picking up, but what if it was Sheena, and she needed him? So he picked up. Upon answering was a girl's voice he wasn't familiar with, but he needn't have worried because the girl never introduced herself, and instead got straight to the point.

"Hi—I'm a friend of yours on Facebook, but I couldn't remember your name," she said abruptly. Brondo could immediately feel his intuition and better judgment kicking in, but as usual he ignored it. It was even screaming at him not to reveal his identity, but foolishly he would answer the girl, because Brondo's good nature and pure heart always overrode his common sense.

"I'm Brondo, who are you again?" he asked the girl politely, but she quickly hung up.

Brondo went back to the bed and lay there all confused. What was that phone call all about? Who was it? and why wouldn't she know my name, when my name is on the Facebook page? he thought. It just didn't make sense, but he was too puzzled by it all so he decided to ignore it and continue watching the movie.

A few minutes later his phone began buzzing again. This time it was Sheena.

"Hey babe, you can't wait to see me, can you?" Brondo poked playfully. Sheena was very serious sounding and quick to the point.

"Did you just get a weird phone call earlier, I mean just now?"

"Yes, yes I did," Brondo replied, even more puzzled.

"Ugh. It was Max, Max put his girlfriend on the phone to pretend she was one of your Facebook friends—he was trying to catch you out," she groaned.

"What? It was Max?" Brondo said, disbelievingly. "But...how, why, how did they find out my number?"

Sheena was surprisingly calm. "Well, long story short—my phone bill went to my old address and they opened it—they've seen the number I've been calling most was yours—so they put two and two together, as I have called you close to two hundred times in the last four months..."

Ugh. Fuck, was all that Brondo could think.

Sheena went on. "Max rang me earlier and asked me 'who's Brondo?' so I played dumb and told him you were just a friend, and he said 'you're dead to me and don't talk to me anymore.'

Then he hung up."

Sheena could hear Brondo's breathing becoming heavier and implored him that now was not the time to panic, and that, if anything, now was the time to keep their heads cool and think straight about how to handle it. But Brondo was not having anything of it, because he knew better, and for once he was listening to his intuition.

"Listen babe, I *told* you I had a bad feeling about today—if anything happens I know you're safe; they won't hurt you, but they will try to come after me—the man always cops it in these scenarios. That's just the way it goes. And they know that I'm in Scarborough too, like an unarmed sitting duck; they will come looking for me, I know it."

Sheena was still calm. "No they won't, babe—I will handle it, do you trust me? I know how to handle the boys and I know that with baby steps the situation will resolve itself and they'll eventually come to accept you; you just need to do as I tell you and stay put."

Brondo was trying to remain calm but he knew there was no way out of this, and in his growing frustration he began to read her calmness for ignorance instead, which only made him all the more angry. Brondo was like a fuse just waiting to be lit.

"I TOLD YOU LAST NIGHT THIS WOULD HAPPEN!!" he yelled in frustration down the phone line, immediately regretting it.

Sheena was undeterred though and ignored his outburst, calmly stating that she had already thought about it all and had a plan; when questioned, Brondo was to state that they were Facebook friends, nothing more. Brondo, although slightly offended by this, quietly agreed to it. But something bothered him about it: that now, even in the face of adversity, Sheena would deny that they were lovers, whereas Brondo in reverse would do anything to prove his love for her. And something about that felt off. Could Sheena not see that half the world already knew about them anyway? What was the point of prolonging the lie? Yet Sheena was adamant that they could lie their way of it, so Brondo reluctantly agreed.

At this time his phone would ring again within minutes of hanging up on Sheena. Brondo didn't know whether he should answer it or not. Reluctantly, he answered and was met with an angry voice that came barreling down the line. This time it was Sheena's sister in law, Michelle, and upon answering Brondo met with her wrath.

"This is Michelle, and I'm Sheena's sister-in-law; I don't know who you are, mister, but we all know what you've been up to—the both of you!" She screamed. Now it was Brondo's turn to yell.

"You don't know shit, Michelle—you are wrong as I am not seeing Sheena but we are more so friends," he said, trying to keep up the act.

Finally Brondo heard her say, "Look, I'm not going to argue with you—but I know what I know, there's no use in lying."

"Well, you're as presumptuous as all hell, because you don't know me and you don't know much about anything, or about me, or what you think you know. If anything, I'm friends with Sheena, close friends, nothing more, OK?" Brondo shouted back.

"What? A male friend? I know Sheena; she has girlfriends, and what would a younger man like you want with an older married woman? I know what she wants with you—but why on earth would you be wanting anything with her?"

Brondo thought about this. He knew that right now Michelle

was either genuinely asking why, or she was trying to push his buttons. But he reasoned: if a man truly loved a woman, wouldn't he want to be passionate in his stance of defending her? Was this what Michelle really wanted to test? He felt that somewhere in all this she had her own agenda, and that he would not be so easily fooled or sucked in to telling anything, so he chose to answer her in a calm manner, do as Sheena suggested he do. They were just friends.

"Look Michelle, I can understand where you're coming from..."

"No you can't!" she yelled. Brondo felt his anger welling and fired back.

"Look—let me finish. I can understand, as I too am an empath and I am a good person, I am compassionate towards others—and right now Sheena needs a friend; it's quite obvious she needs a friend and a confidante because she can't talk to her own friends about all the stuff her husband has been doing to her. Sometimes, Michelle, it's easier to open up to a stranger because they can't judge you, they don't know you well enough to even be able to pass judgment," Brondo said, and even as he mouthed the words Brondo could feel that he was uttering something deep and painful about his own past, too.

"Well I disagree; you should be able to talk to your *husband* on these things, not a stranger—but then again she's a user and it's obvious the two of you are sleeping together as there's no reason why she would call you two hundred times over the last four months...that's something lovers do, not friends."

Brondo could feel himself slipping now and he knew it, his heart was pounding and the adrenaline rush to his head and extremities made him dizzy. Without Sheena nearby, he knew he would have to deal with this family member alone.

"And what am I supposed to do about this son of hers—my nephew—who's going to have to undergo surgery soon, and my brother, her husband, is shot to pieces about it, he's about to snap under all the pressure, while Miss Floozy runs around town doing whatever."

Brondo couldn't bear it any longer; he couldn't keep up the lie that Sheena had wanted, because, even though she thought things would be better this way, no one was truly going to bat for her. People had more sympathy now for Seedy when the truth was, Sheena was the real victim in all of this. Brondo couldn't listen to another word. All jets were firing now.

"Well, maybe if your *brother* had treated her right, stopped treating her like a possession, hitting her, cheating on her, controlling her and abusing her, then maybe, just maybe I'd have more sympathy for him—but I don't."

"Is *that* what she's been telling you? You know what? I feel sorry for you, then—" Michelle said, the tirade of words dripping off her tongue, "because

all the lies Sheena tells—and there are *so* many—are going to come back to hurt you...oh, and by the way, she will bleed you dry, just as she did my brother—she's a liar but you will find all this out by yourself, the hard way...I'm just

stumped as to what a good looking younger guy would be doing with that trash."

"Well I got to go, as this is not going anywhere, Michelle—good luck with everything." Click.

Brondo took a deep breath and sat down to watch the rest of 8 Mile, but he couldn't focus on anything so he went to Facebook to check his messages. He saw friend requests from both of Sheena's sons and even their cousins, and a message from Max. He opened the message and read it.

"So, you being seeing me mum, hey cunt? Well, you know the saying, every dog has his day and every wog cunt has his day."

Another message filled his inbox; it was from Max's cousin, Paul Borne with lots of spelling mistakes.

"You haV roo-end a gud famely (spelling was off)...cum to Scarborough you cunt, I got a present for ya!"

Brondo shutdown his Facebook page, realising this had become too serious for either Sheena or himself to handle alone. He was going to have to have a serious talk to Sheena when she got to the motel. In the meantime he would wait and watch the movie, try to unwind with a beer. Brondo turned up the volume on the TV just as the scene was heating up—it was right up to the point where Eminem beats his mother's boyfriend up. Brondo could feel his anxiety worsening as the scene played out. This, he thought could be another omen, symbolic of what was to come. His intuition never lied to him. Thoughts and worries flooded his mind, and Brondo took another big gulp of beer when his phone rang again.

"Hello?" he said, and even though he'd never even heard the voice on the other end of line before, he knew it needed no introduction.

"Is this fucking Brondo?"

"Yeah, this is Brondo, who's this?" Brondo replied knowing full well who it was.

"Fucking wog cunt fat cunt, you being seeing me mum—ya cunt."

Brondo didn't waste any time retaliating. He knew this call would one day come.

"Listen here," Brondo fired back with aggression, "you're a selfish little bastard and you treat your mum with no respect—"

Max fired back with threats. "Come to Seymour, cunt, where

are ya friends now, huh? You're gonna need an army, Man—come to Kilmore, we'll show ya something good."

Brondo was surprised Max would suggest Kilmore and not Scarborough his home town, where he had friends and family on his own turf. He thought that maybe Max didn't know he was in Scarborough after all; why would Max have picked these particular towns? Max continued:

"You're gonna need an army, cunt."

Brondo was growing tired of the abuse, this kid was tough; he thought he'd try another tack.

"Look, why don't we try to be friends?"

"Oh, so now you wanna suck up, hey cunt—youse must be some kinda soft cock donkey, ain't cha?—no, I'ma gonna come over there and smash your stupid fucking face in, cunt face."

Brondo could feel himself snapping, but he didn't have the heart to follow through on his aggression; this was Sheena's son, after all, and even though he was being an ass, Brondo knew not to provoke him any further, so he tried to go softly with the kid, for Sheena's sake.

"Nah, kid, I'm not going to meet up anywhere with you," he said steadily. Brondo further argued he wasn't in the mood discussing this anymore; they'd reached a stalemate and he knew there was no point. Max made one final, angry threat before hanging up, leaving Brondo with the very strong impression that Max was just an ass.

Yet he was strangely unnerved by the teenager; he could see that his all his vehement relentless thirst for revenge was only on behalf of his father. And it was hard to take the kid seriously anyway; Brondo had to suppress his own laughter at the high pitched, squeaky younger voice on the other end. No, he'd hold his tongue for the sake of his love for Sheena and his relationship, although at this stage he began to wonder whether Sheena was worth all of it. The damage had been done. Sheena would be left alone, although she would forever be labeled the scarlet woman and face abuse and rejection in the township; Brondo just hoped that whatever they were planning to do to him could be stopped in time.

He put down his phone and went back to the movie. It was now in the final scene where the son beats the mother's boyfriend to a pulp, and it made him squeamish. Was this a sign of things to come? Just then Max sent another message saying that he knew the Hell's Angels Bikies, and that they were not far off finding him and they were coming to get him. By now the time was 16.40pm in the afternoon and Brondo became shaky and fearful; he got off the phone in a panic and his thoughts and anxiety began to consume him. His mind started to wander to crazy thoughts that he would be found shot or stabbed to death in his motel room, his body bloodied and left in a murder crime scene. Only six months earlier he had thought he wanted to die. How ironic that now he wanted to live; he wanted to live, not die, goddam it, and he wanted to find love, real love, and be loved back and have all the wonderful memories of birthdays and Christmases and family gatherings to one day look back upon. He wanted Life. Was that too much to ask?

Instead, Brondo was now falling into a deep panicked state of hysteria; he felt overwhelmed. What would his family and loved ones say and think? How could he explain this mess he had gotten himself into, having an affair with an older married woman? He tried to take a deep breath, hearing the failed attempts his own lungs tried to make as they made grabbing sounds at the air sacs around him; in the distance all he could hear were cars (or, were they motorbikes?) pulling up outside.

Brondo stuck his nose between the striped window curtains and was stunned to see three men walking towards the motel room; they were angry, vicious looking men with badass looks about them and the glint of fury in their eyes.

Fuck. Brondo was shivering now and he wanted to pass out from the sick feelings swirling in his stomach; this was it, he was in his own 8 Mile movie now and they were coming for him. What to do, what to do, he thought. His adrenaline kicked in and Brondo turned and made a run towards the bathroom to jump out the window just as the door opened, and just as he heard the motel manager yell out, "No trouble! No trouble here, or I call police!" and then he saw the three men retreating just as fast as they'd come. He quickly shut the door, locked it and bolted it securely and went back to the bed holding onto his chest. His heart was pounding so hard he thought if he let go it might leap out and bounce all over the floor. Instead, he closed his eyes and pretended he was travelling to a different dimension...Eight miles plus eight miles plus eight miles plus eight...until they all added up to anywhere but here.

The entire day had been a nerve racking ordeal from start to finish. Who were these men, and how did they find him? By now Brondo was ready for anything and he stood up, pacing around the motel room, ready with a steak knife he had found in the little kitchenette drawer. A kitchen steak knife wasn't much of a defence weapon, but it was the best thing he could find at his disposal, so he would keep it out to use just in case he needed something, feeling silly about it all at the same time. The silliness of it all hit him and he decided instead to unlock the door again and put the knife back in the drawer,

Just as he did so, the motel door burst open. Brondo nearly wet himself with fear as Sheena entered the motel room and bounded into his arms. She had the look of reassurance and love which he needed and which turned him to jelly; he hugged her back even though he was shaking cold but he didn't want to be consoled because he was too much of a mixture of fright, anger and humiliation. His mind was still racing and he could barely think straight, but he had to sit down and tell Sheena what had just unfolded. Sheena sat beside him and patted his back sensing he needed to tell her something; she took off her heels, placed her hand on his and lay her foot across his lap. He couldn't free himself from the emotional turmoil he was in to return her affections and so he just sat there, looking at her, blank faced.

Sheena returned his gaze and stroked his hand until she began to see a smile forming at the corners of his lips. Brondo felt himself relax a little and he let his shoulders slump forward as he released the stressful events of the day.

"I knew Max was going to be an angry kid at the discovery of our affair; but you're so decent, beautiful and loving that I just thought they might have a little more of you in them to the point where they wouldn't be so feral," Brondo said sadly.

"I'm so sorry babe, I had no idea—Max even rang me at work and said he was going to cut you up into small pieces and feed you to me." Brondo winced. He couldn't believe she was telling him this; why would she tell him something like this when it would upset him and didn't serve any purpose? Brondo was quickly figuring out that Sheena, for all her good points, could have a pretty thoughtless side to her, too.

"Why would you tell me such a thing—I mean, why tell me that shit, I mean, fuck—do you want me to fire up now? It's almost like you want this whole thing to get worse than it already is. So, how did you respond to your son when he said this?" Sheena just looked at Brondo; she could tell he was ropable by the fierce look in his eyes.

"I just ignored him."

"Well, how does that fix anything, Sheena? So, you just let him win? Why don't you stand up to him and tell him he can't go around making bodily threats on another person's life? You just *ignore him*? Can't you see that he sees your cowardice, takes advantage of your weakness?" Brondo fired back.

Sheena just stood there, and not knowing what else to do, smiled back at him. They were having their first real fight and he wasn't enjoying it one bit, but now she was *smiling* at him. He couldn't make out what she was thinking. It was bizarre and it just infuriated him all the more.

"What the hell are you smiling at, Sheena? You think this is funny? I mean you were so scared of them too, and now look at you, you're laughing, for fuck's sake."

"I'm just smiling because this is our first ever true fight babe, and it's kinda cute, that's all," she said softly, placing her hands on his. She leaned in and gave him a light kiss, a kiss that softened the mood, softened his heart; he was always too easy and gave in to her charms, agreeing to stay the night so long as they could move motel rooms.

"I mean, how did they *find* me here?" Brondo said, scratching his head, trying to shake off the whole thing.

"I think it was an accident; Ally had let it slip what model and car you drove, because she was bragging to one of her girlfriends about how she wanted to ask you if she could borrow it." Sheena shrugged.

"No, I can't believe how stupid and silly I have been—I left it parked out on the main road in Scarborough, what was I thinking," Brondo said apologetically, frustrated more with himself now.

They ordered pizza together and tried to let the dust settle on the day, hoping it would soon become nothing more than a distant memory. The air was still tense between them, and Brondo sensed that Sheena was beginning to feel uneasy again, so he dared ask her what was the matter. Sheena finally cracked.

"I dunno, I guess I was just afraid that this would be the deathblow to our relationship and that you would be scared off enough to want to leave me," she said, pouting. Brondo grabbed Sheena by the shoulders.

"I'll be damned if they or anyone other than me or God dictates the rules to our relationship," he said emphatically. "Only you have the power to end this, Sheena, only you—it's up to you. If you no longer love me, let me know, but please let this be the only reason—not because of anyone else."

Sheena looked up at Brondo, surprised; she couldn't believe how she had misread him, how she thought he was the nervous type who would be easily scared off.

"Well, if you were so sure you thought I was just going to leave you, then why did you come to the motel, Sheena?"

"Because I wanted to make our final night together the best one yet; I wanted to make the most of it before you headed back to Melbourne and left me forever." Tears welled up in her eyes. Real tears, not fake ones.

Brondo was stunned and taken aback by her honesty, yet disappointed that she had so little faith and trust in him.

"It hurts to hear that, babe, I mean, that really hurts. I thought you knew me better than that, but obviously not, hey..."

"Well, what was I supposed to think? My God, Brondo—my son is threatening your life, and now my husband's involved—what was I supposed to think?"

"You were supposed to know that nothing and no one

controls my destiny and after all the intimate moments we've shared together that you would know that I'm not going to just run from you—my God, how much I love you, and you think I'm just going to run?"

"Yes I know, but they're threatening your life."

"Well I'm a big boy too, I can look after myself; I love you and I can easily make threats of my own—what, am I supposed to submit to them like a fucking idiot?"

Sheena looked sad and hurt; she admitted she had failed him. She had a lack of faith and trust in most things in life and blamed herself for being that way.

Brondo softened and told her he was going to bed; he'd had enough action in one day to last a lifetime. Sheena went off to shower, and he thought about her, thought about all the ways Sheena still obviously needed lots of convincing if she was still doubting his love for her. She was a hard nut, a tough shell to crack, he knew that much. He wasn't sure of all that had happened to her in the past, but deep down he could see that Sheena didn't believe she was movable, or worthy of love, and to this, Brondo was out to prove her wrong.

Without realising it, he drifted off into a quiet sleep and never stirred when Sheena came out of the shower dressed in nothing but her skin. He never woke when Sheena stood by the side of the bed and lifted her leg, curled her toes and pushed her foot across his mouth, pressing her foot upon his face, forcing her foot into his mouth as he slept. He didn't even realise when, in his sleep he began to suck and gently bite on her foot, until something aroused him and he awoke, groggy to the sight of Sheena standing over him, laughing down at him; it was then that he pulled her into him, ready to take full advantage of her loins all through the night as willing as she was, and into the early hours of the morn.

The next morning Brondo awoke and Sheena was already up and ready for work; he didn't have to return to work till the next day, though the thought crossed his mind that maybe this thing with Sheena was over, after all. He had lots of anxiety again upon waking but he didn't know how to tell her all that he was feeling. The day before had been a lot to take in, and as she leaned in to kiss him goodbye and wish him a safe trip back to Melbourne he had to wonder if it would be for the last time. This lie was looking like it might be over; and he had to concede that perhaps her boys and husband had won after all, and that all was lost. He would not fight back.

Sheena left and he was left alone in the room to contemplate his life, his journey and his existence; where he had come from and where he was going with her, but most importantly where he was at present, and was the present serving his future? His belly rumbled in the present and reminded him to go eat. So he put on a baseball hat to hide his appearance then went in search of food. He found a little café to eat at, and was ready to say goodbye to Scarborough when all of a sudden his phone rang and he could see—it was Sheena. Brondo hesitantly picked up.

"Hey babe; what's happening?"

"Listen babe, look, I just wanted to say I want you to stay another night...let's make a weekend of it, I don't want you leaving like this."

"What's changed your mind?" Brondo asked, honestly.

"Well, Max has run around town branding me a slut, so I'm now the scarlet woman all over town. It's all been blown way out of proportion, and my younger brother Steve has caught wind of it, plus his mates, and Max's mates are all running me down, all over town."

"But why does that change your mind about us? I thought after last night you wanted to end this to please them, and hurt me," Brondo said, teetering on sarcasm.

"Babe I'm so sorry—but I was really only doing it for you, to protect you, but now stuff them! If they want to behave like that, well stuff 'em, I'm doing what's right for me for a change."

"Well, yeah—it's good that you are doing what is right for you, but the whole thing is that you were ready to call it quits just yesterday for the wrong reasons, ending our relationship to please them—so now I am not sure that I want to stay," Brondo said, getting cold feet.

"Babe please—I love you, I want to be with you, and I want this; please don't fight me on it, please babe...I have already booked the room for another night."

Brondo heard her voice quaver and softened. "Ok," he relented. "I will stay another night with you, but tell me; what happens after that?"

"We will deal with it when we get to it, babe."

So Brondo returned to motel room and tried not to focus on the problems around them; he would try to be more like Sheena and focus only on the now, work on being in the present like she said.

The phone calls had stopped and Facebook things had calmed down, except for the fact that a few girls had sent messages asking who 'Max' was and that he had been contacting them out of the blue, asking if any were seeing Brondo or interested in him. He told them all that Brondo was sleeping with his mum, the whore, who was a married woman, bringing shame upon them both and tainting his good name. Brondo had to reassure many of his friends that things were not what they seemed and that there was a lot more to the story—this troubled kid Max, included.

Most of his friends were understanding, and agreed that there were so many scenarios that could seem hazy at times. He had to tell Sheena what Max had been up to, but when he did, Sheena just laughed and turned around and said, "My, he's got you stumped, hasn't he?" thinking nothing more of it.

Brondo was becoming more and more frustrated by her careless, apathetic attitude and sat alone to ruminate on her unusual responses to it all; he had to wonder if Sheena secretly enjoyed seeing her son and he playing off one another in some perverted way. He knew that Sheena had never had any strong positive male role models growing up, and that she and her sister had been sexually abused by their step father as well. So he wondered whether she needed to fill the void and the hurt of her past with mind games; her anger seemed misdirected at times, and at other times her reactions to things were confusing. But he trusted Sheena and although the relationship was only four months young he knew he loved her and so he had to stand by with the belief that it would all work itself out, in the end, just as she always said. While Brondo waited back at the motel that day, Sheena was still at work and on her lunch break sitting in her car, when she got a surprise visit from Seedy, and he appeared by her opened car door, surprising the hell out of her.

"Hey, gorgeous, how are you—come on, what are you doing with this younger wog cunt? You surely can't be serious about it all..."

"Leave me alone, Seedy," Sheena pushed back at him. He leaned into her, his breath smelled of bourbon.

"Must be so much easier being with a guy who's young, single, not married, no?"

Sheena just looked at him. "Leave him alone, Seedy. And

leave me alone. I love him." Seedy looked startled by this sudden confession but tried to mask his pain with a sadistic laugh.

"Well I'm going to go out and pick up the hottest, youngest girls at the clubs, you're gonna regret the day you were born, Miss Sheena Baxter," he said, smirking.

"Good luck to you, Seedy, do whatever, I don't care," Sheena spat back.

Seedy was furious and backed away from the car cursing and muttering under his breath, and Sheena breathed a sigh of relief, counting the minutes until she could return to Brondo's arms.

She greeted Brondo with the most passionate kiss and within minutes their clothes were on the floor and they were at it, having beastly sex like two lone wolves. Afterwards they lay in each other's arms and Sheena told him about Seedy's surprise visit.

"It was nothing, really—he's just jealous, is all, 'coz he's lost his prize possession, that's all I was to him," she said matter-of-factly. "I'm going to go pick up Ally and bring her here, if it's alright, she's missing her mother, and hanging around Grandma too long is hard on the girl—Varma can be a selfish grumbling old granny sometimes. Can you please make the bed and tidy things up sweety, so Ally doesn't see the mess we have made? I'll be back soon," she said kissing Brondo's temple and flying out the door.

Brondo made the bed, straightening everything in the room and freshening up; he spritzed cologne, washed down the table, the bench tops, the TV cabinet and folded Sheena's clothes into a neat pile that she'd left strewn all over the floor. Within twenty minutes Sheena had returned with Ally and they sat on the end of the bed talking, Ally defending Sheena's actions as she stood by her mother, her anger and frustration towards her father palpable.

"You're so cool, Brondo," Ally said, turning to face him. "You're a genuine person, a beautiful person and a good looking one too; and you make my mum so happy after all the crap my father has put her through!"

"I can see Sheena has raised a lovely young woman in you, Ally; now we just have to work on convincing your brothers!" Brondo smiled. This girl was alright, he thought.

"I just can't believe Max said he would cut Brondo up into small pieces and feed him to you, Mum! He is so demented!"

Brondo laughed along with Ally. "It's ok, Ally, as long as he puts salt, lemon and pepper then I am sure I would taste alright," he joked and all three laughed.

"Mum, can I stay here with you guys? I'll be no trouble, really—I'll be quiet, I'll sleep on the floor, you won't even know I'm here, promise—I just don't want to go back to Dad's; it's a war zone there, everybody exploding and fist fights, and I'm sick of Grandma as well, always bossing me about. Please?" Ally begged, throwing her hair around and pleading like a girl. Brondo shrugged; their alone time, he knew, was over for now, but now at least he felt like he had his own family.

CHAPTER SIX
Meet My Family

I Timothy 5: 8
*But if any provide not for his own,
and especially for his own house, he hath denied the
faith and is worse than an unbeliever.*

That weekend in Scarborough had left Brondo feeling drained and confused; as much as he hated living with his grandmother and was aware of his own familial dysfunction he couldn't wait to get home and decompress from all the Sheena drama. Brondo had never been good with confrontation of any kind; even as a child he had always been the more sensitive one, the one most easily hurt. He turned up the radio on the drive back to Melbourne; it was a cold sunny June day and he often liked taking long drives alone; it was the quiet solitude he sought, where he could sift through things in his mind, take refuge within the confines of his vehicle without having to answer to anybody. He now understood why mothers of young children locked themselves in bathrooms, or checked into hotels overnight—it was to find that sense of personal space that sometimes goes missing.

As he drove, Sheena's voice kept coming to him in his mind; why did she doubt their relationship, why did she think he would disappear?

"I'm losing you and I don't know if you will ever be back after what's happened."

The truth was, Brondo felt there were two different sides to Sheena; there was the bold, flighty independent woman who was a vixen in the bedroom, so sexually fearless and confident she could have anything she wanted—and then there was the insecure Sheena who was kept more well hidden, who lacked the confidence in herself to stand up to anyone or believe she was truly worthy of being loved. In fact, Sheena was one of the biggest people pleasers he'd ever met; she was a pushover when it came to Seedy and the boys, as she'd never had the guts to stand up to the years of their abuses. As much as he thought this past weekend that the relationship was beginning to come to a close, Brondo wasn't ready to give up on Sheena just yet. Sheena admitted she was falling into a massive depression too, and had recently taken to popping some Valiums in an effort to calm herself down when things got really bad. He was surprised to learn this, and, on the last night when she broke down into hysterics, Brondo knew he had to work harder to convince her that he wasn't going anywhere. He knew he had his work cut out for him; he knew it was going to be a long haul, but he still felt somewhat compelled to save Sheena, to be her protector, the one to look out for her at all costs when no one else would, and he would do it with the power of his love.

Brondo walked into his grandmother's kitchen and dropped his bag; he grabbed a beer from the fridge and decided to flop on the couch to watch the footy; he just needed some downtime to process things. His grandmother and uncle were oblivious to the weekend he had just had and kissed him on the forehead and went about things as usual. Brondo grew quickly bored of the telly and thought maybe a long walk would do him good. He checked his phone messages and realised there were a bunch of missed calls from his longtime friend, Juan. He felt guilty because he had been neglecting his friendships of late, probably because all of his time had been consumed by Sheena and her dramas. Juan was up on the whole Sheena saga, so he texted his friend back with apologies for not keeping in touch like he normally did and asked if they could meet up. Juan was a fellow security officer who worked nights for a house in the Maltese community in local St Albans, and Brondo understood well the loneliness of the work, standing for hours on end with nothing to do.

"Hey Bro—why don't you come down tonight, help me out; I gotta private function I gotta do, gonna be boring as all shit—I could use the company, and then we can talk, yeah?"

"Yeah, sounds good, J—I'll swing by at 7, after dinner with Yaya and Uncle," Brondo messaged back. He was only too happy to have a distraction from it all, so at a quarter to seven he headed off up to the hillside area past St Albans to meet Juan. All the way there he was fending off a barrage of incoming messages from Sheena: every second message went back and forth about where she stood in his life, and vice versa; how Varma was an emotional mess about her daughter's life; how the boys had become even more cruel towards her, turning on her and mocking her, ignoring her, especially Max, who had resorted to degrading comments and threats. Brondo felt pained hearing Sheena's situation, and worse, he felt guilty for feeling like he had contributed to her depression; it was as if his being in her life was making matters worse, not better.

"Look, you can't allow your nineteen year old son to treat you like this, Sheena—you've got to pull him up somehow, or its just going to get worse! It's pretty clear that the level of respect Max has for you is zero," he texted back.

"I know, now my brothers are joining in on the act; Steve apparently went to Seedy last night and told him to get his act together, that I was making a fool of him in front of the whole town by running around with you, and that he was only telling Seedy for the kids' sake, that they didn't need a floozy for a mother."

Hearing this incensed Brondo; he was fast realising what kind of relationships Sheena surrounded herself with and subjected herself to; he knew her brothers loved her, but the truth was that they weren't really a loving family that knew how to support and stand by each other in the same way that Brondo's family did—it was more of a conditional based love; their family connection seemed to be based more on things instead of loyalties and the true meaning of family. For all of his family's faults, he knew that Greek families at least knew how to stick together in times of trouble. But not Sheena's family. Whenever things fell apart or disappeared as they usually did, so too did the strength of their unit. *A house divided cannot stand,* Brondo thought to himself. What was that parable again from the Bible coming to him now? He thought he remembered it from the book of Matthew, when Jesus came and warned that those who did not follow Him would build their lives as houses on sand, to be washed away by the elements.

He wished Sheena's family was not such a mess, but Brondo was in too deep now; he was in love with Sheena and was going to fight for her; he wasn't the sort of man to ever take the easy way out.

"Hey Bro, sorry I'm a bit late," Brondo grimaced. "Woman troubles, ya know," he shrugged. Juan patted him on the back, took him inside.

"No worries, Bro, I get it, got girl problems of my own," Juan said and winked.

Brondo worked the shift with Juan and told him the whole weekend horror show; her son Max, the Bikies, the death threats. He confessed he was in love with Sheena and was fierce about committing to her. Juan's eyebrows were raised hearing all this; he knew Sheena was married because Brondo had told him, but all this extra stuff was just too much to handle.

"Look Bro—you're a better man than me, are you sure you're not biting off more than you can chew here? I mean, I'll back you all the way, but you better be careful, 'Coz I don't wanna hear you've been found floating in the Scarborough river, six feet under or out to sea, ya know what I mean?"

That night after Juan's shift was over, Brondo drove home feeling worthless in himself and powerless in his abilities to save Sheena; he needed to help her, she was miserable and cried over the phone telling him how much she needed him, how much she needed to get away. Neither of them had much money, so Brondo decided to swallow his pride and ask his grandmother if Sheena could come to stay. As a strict Greek woman, Brondo had no idea how she would take it, which made him all the more nervous. But he had to try.

"Yaya, it is very important, if you would allow me to introduce this girl to you, and if she could come and stay. I want you to meet her, and I have never asked anything of you like this before, but I am serious now," Brondo impassioned of his grandmother.

"It does sound as though you are ready to take this to the next level, my son—is this true?" Yaya asked, looking directly into his eyes.

"Yes, grandmother Andromachi this is true," Brondo said, seeking her approval. She nodded wisely, giving her blessing, though Brondo could feel her reluctance. She was a very careful woman, his grandmother, far more careful than him.

Brondo was overjoyed to call Sheena the next morning and tell her the good news; she finally had somewhere to escape to, and he knew she desperately needed the break.

"Guess what," Brondo said, grinning through the phone.

"What?" Sheena asked, sounding surprised.

"My grandmother says it's Ok for you to come and stay here, so I am officially inviting you to come on down here, babe, she wants to meet you! I know you're hanging to get away from there, so come down tonight if you can."

Sheena was delighted and couldn't believe her ears, her prayers had been answered; from the minute she met Brondo she wanted him all to herself and now this was coming to fruition. She was ecstatic but also very nervous about finally meeting his grandmother and uncle godfather, and began rummaging through her closet for something appropriate to wear; she thought that her usual getup of mini skirts and leggings would not be quite the desired look she was going for if she wanted to impress his family. The time was now, Sheena thought; she would finally visit the family home of Brondo Violaris and she had to put on her best game face—it was critical that she won them over.

Sheena was disheartened that she had to work first, but she arranged to swap a shift in order to get out early and make the trip to Melbourne. The drive itself was uneventful; twenty minutes before she was to due to arrive Sheena pulled

into a petrol station to fix her hair, apply lip gloss and text Brondo that she wasn't far away.

Brondo came outside to greet Sheena; she looked very ladylike in a straight grey skirt and cream blouse. Ever the gentleman, Brondo walked her in the front door and introduced her to his family, where little old Yaya Andromachi and Uncle Godfather sat in the corner of the outdated 70's living room.

Sheena was pleasantly surprised that Brondo's grandmother was nothing like the strict Greek woman he'd painted her as; on the contrary, Sheena found her nothing but polite and friendly. Still, the vibes were clear that this was an older woman who Brondo had brought home, and there were many questions and stares, raised eyebrows and natural cause for concern. But Yaya did all the right things to make Sheena feel comfortable and to support Brondo, as it was understood that this was the woman he loved and wanted to be with.

Long after Yaya and Uncle went to bed, Brondo and Sheena sat up and watched a double feature, Top Gun and afterwards Nothing to Lose. It felt nice that they could both have a laugh in a place where they could feel relaxed and safe. Sheena commented that she was surprised by how striking Brondo's brother Vito was, and the close resemblance between Vito and her son, Max. They were both tall and well built with chiseled jawlines and soft eyes, though, as Brondo was quick to point out, they were both wildly different in terms of their personalities. Max was angry and high strung, while Vito was relaxed and confident; Sheena found it so easy being around his family; it was nothing like the abusive environment she was used to back home.

When the movie ended, Sheena let go of all her stresses;

she couldn't hold Brondo long enough or tight enough, and she clung to him the way a joey clings to its mother. She kept whispering sweet nothings in his ear, reminding him of how much she truly loved him, and Brondo never felt so much love in all of his life.

Sheena couldn't understand how she had never experienced anything like this before in her life and kept going on and on about how lucky she was, while Brondo couldn't fully understand her attraction; he was broke, barely had a worthy job and was only just scraping by, working in retail and security. Not only that, but he had never had more than two 'serious relationships' which to him meant he had actually dated the same person for more than three months. Brondo had not had much success with relationships in the past; he usually expected to be dumped by the time the fourth month came around as the relationship would run its course then crash and burn. So, Sheena was being all gushy and loving, but Brondo was neither used to it, nor was he really buying it all. Surely this older woman with plenty of experience had to have had more experiences of love than this in her lifetime?

Yet the entire weekend Sheena hung off Brondo's every word like a giddy teen.

They spent the weekend driving around Melbourne, going out for coffee on Lygon Street and window shopping arm in arm, then returning to grandmother Yaya's to watch Greek TV shows together before eating tea. Yaya served up some traditional Greek dishes which she knew were her grandson's favourites; eggplant moussaka for main course, and for dessert semolina cake and baklava sweets Brondo had brought home from Theo's cake shop. Brondo could see that grandmother Yaya seemed to like the lady and was pleasant enough, but he knew his grandmother, and she hid things well.

Sheena left Melbourne feeling invigorated; she had a renewed belief in hers and Brondo's relationship and now it seemed things had taken a turn for the better after their wonderful weekend together. She would return to a divided Scarborough, where some still believed she was the beautiful and loving wife and mother, while the rest had blacklisted her as the scarlet woman.

The couple knew the battle that lay ahead; Max branding Sheena a slut and bitch, running her down to anyone who would listen; Seedy was also getting in on the action, abusing his daughter with threats of violence while still slapping and branding his wife a whore, and Brondo waiting at the other end of it all, feeling depressed and hopeless to Sheena's abuses.

He decided to take it upon messaging Max and Thomas himself on Facebook, but it didn't go so well as the conversation quickly degenerated into smack punk talk, forcing Brondo to go to their level.

"You know what *you* are?" Brondo responded to Max's abuse when he couldn't take it anymore. "You're both a pair of lowlifes—and if you want a war then it's gonna end badly for you."

"Oh yeah, wog cunt? See you on the other side!" Max messaged back threateningly. Brondo knew he shouldn't have responded to Max's baiting taunts, but he couldn't help himself.

"Yeah? Well just watch me hang the both of yers, I'll throw ya to the pigs—better yet, the sharks!" he messaged back, such was the venom in his rage.

"BRONDO!" Sheena called him up angrily. "You're not being the gentleman I know you to be—you're sinking to his level! Stop messaging him right now! Max is going around sharing your messages and bragging about how he's got you all worked up! You're just adding fuel to the fire!"

"Sorry babe—he just got the better of me, I thought I could handle this in my own way. He's just out of control!" Brondo messaged, frustrated.

"I know I know—and Max is also a kid with a brain tumour awaiting surgery—he's just a stressed out kid!"

"That still doesn't excuse his actions in mistreating you at every opportunity, every twist and turn; if anything, he should be supportive of you and realise what a pig his father is. You just don't get it Sheena—you teach people how to treat you, but you're letting him walk all over you."

Sheena sat quiet on the other end of the line, letting Brondo have his say. She was so quiet Brondo had to ask if she was still there.

"I don't get it, Sheena—what's the big deal? You know, I could beat the crap out of your husband—and Thomas—Ok, so perhaps Max might be a different kettle of fish, but I'm not fazed by him either...and if he wants to take this full throttle into a head-to-head battle, then it'll be on, I swear. I am sorry babe, but you need to take control of this, and fast, before it spirals out of control."

It's already spiralled out of control, Sheena thought, but she said nothing. The truth was, she knew he was right. But her personality and her confidence weren't up the the challenge; they were still her babies and she was too soft and submissive with them, and she knew it. She didn't have the spine to stand up to them, or to Seedy, and in part she felt she deserved the life she'd been dealt with. Sheena didn't know which way to turn, and she didn't have the heart to do what was right for herself. It was a hard pill to swallow that she'd finally met someone who was willing to go to battle for her, too; it was a foreign feeling that she wasn't used to.

Brondo and Sheena would continue seeing one another over the coming months; they navigated the vengeful turns Max took as he lashed out at both of them, accusing his mother of choosing Brondo over him.

"It's me—or that wog cunt," Max would threaten Sheena.

Sheena said she wasn't going to choose, that she didn't have to choose anymore; and she started traveling more and more to Brondo's place in Melbourne, spending more time on their relationship.

Yaya went to Cyprus in early July leaving the empty house to Brondo, so Sheena took sick days off work to be with him. She would cook and clean for Brondo while he went to work, and Brondo praised God Almighty for bringing this woman into his life, his faith restored. Brondo had walked away from the church a long time ago; but he had never walked away from God, and he believed His word. The only problem was that now he struggled with the fact that, in the eyes of God he was sinning again with a married woman.

"Do you think you would ever consider getting divorced and remarried?" Brondo asked hesitantly one night when they were in bed.

"No," Sheena replied truthfully. "How can you expect me to believe in the sanctity of marriage after the failed marriage I've had? Come on, Brondo, let's not go there right now, let's just enjoy this night together," she said, snuggling into his chest. "Besides, I had my tubes tied after Ally was born—three kids were enough for me!" She guffawed.

Brondo was silently stunned. He wanted to give up straight away; he was so hurt over the fact Sheena wasn't willing to consider the option of marriage. She hadn't even told him about her tubes being tied. Every time things seemed to be going well for them, something always came crashing down around them.

Maybe this was the final deathblow to the future of this relationship after all, Brondo thought. He blamed himself for not seeing any of it sooner, but this was always the way with him; he'd get his hopes up, then the roller coaster ride would send him careening downhill. This wasn't Sheena's fault he realised, but his; it was his pattern of making bad choices. His mind began to wander now, as he started considering his options; in some ways he felt grateful for Sheena being so upfront and forward with him, because the truth was he was over the relationship. The whole marriage and the kids thing was a big no no to him, and he couldn't fathom what made him pursue it in the first place. Weirdly, Sheena began to feel nervous as she sensed Brondo pulling back.

"What's the matter, babe? You seem distant?" She quizzed him. When Brondo didn't answer because he was about to let her know they were done, Sheena became playful and grabbed him by the chest.

"Well, we *could* still try to have more kids; I mean, I could tell the doctor I want to get my tubes un-tied, and we could get married," she fished.

Brondo felt like a human yo-yo. "What brought this on, why the sudden change of heart, Sheena? A minute ago you were absolute in saying no?"

"Because it's time I stopped worrying about what other people think—and you make me happy, I love you more than anything in this world! We could go Cyprus and get married there, what a trip it will be! Sheena Violaris: has a nice ring to it, doesn't it?" Brondo couldn't believe his ears; marriage and starting a family with Sheena, right when he was going to end it? But again he could feel himself slipping and he agreed to it. He promised her all the things he could promise as a man soon to be wed; he would be the first man to take her overseas, give her a proper wedding, the wedding she had always dreamed of; he would get down on one knee and do it all the right way. And Sheena would have the chance to right the wrongs of her first marriage, he thought; and he could teach her love through the Lord Jesus Christ. Was this God's will, or was it divine intervention? He didn't know. It didn't matter: they were soul mates.

CHAPTER SEVEN
Scarborough

Romans 12: 18
*If it is possible, as far as it depends on you,
live at peace with everyone.*

There were several ways one could get to Scarborough, but by car was usually the easiest as it was just under two hours from Melbourne. There was the country train line, but that was less reliable and consistent, because more often than not the train schedule didn't run as planned, or sometimes it didn't run at all, depending on who was working that day or what day of the week it was. The town was full of lowlifes, too; and by lunchtime the local pub was usually full of bogans, men sporting long beards, tattoos and six inch facial scars.

Sheena told Brondo on the phone one night that she wanted him to move to Scarborough. Given that things between them had grown more serious with talk of marriage and children, Brondo decided to pursue the idea. He couldn't keep living with grandmother Yaya and Uncle forever, so now seemed as good a time as any to move forward in their relationship.

"Yeah, I'm sure I can do it," Brondo said. "I can handle the country; I can live in the countryside." But Sheena wanted to taunt him, tease him for a bit first, make him think that he'd come up with the idea himself.

"Are you sure, babe? There are two angry boys here just waiting to hurt you and beat you up," Sheena laughed, playing with her thighs.

Brondo was unfazed, he was getting used to the situation now, understanding that it would take awhile for him to grow on Max and Thomas; he would leave it to time, believing that time would help things, and that in time the boys would just get used to him being around.

"I'm sure babe—you know, it's kinda exciting to think that we're just starting out in our relationship, and that things are coming together for us now, don't you think?"

"Mmmm, yes, I think—I also think I love the sound of your voice over the phone...it's so husky, so rugged sounding...it turns me on," Sheena groaned as her voice lowered and Brondo heard her breathing become heavier.

"Are you Ok, babe? You sound a bit hoarse," Brondo asked, oblivious to the fact Sheena was now playing with herself.

"Haha—can't you guess what I'm doing now, my big, sexy lover boy?" She said, fondling things. "Don't make me say it, Brondo," she whispered, relieving herself. Brondo blushed. Sheena he knew, was far wilder sexually and far more experienced than him; in the bedroom she was a temptress, a wildcat.

"Are you sure you want to move here, babe?" Sheena asked him, purring like a wet kitten. "I mean, it's such a huge sacrifice you're making." Sheena was covering herself; she was sure to make this Brondo's idea, not hers. And Brondo couldn't see past his own two feet; he was just a lovesick little boy with butterflies in his stomach, chasing down his golden treasure. He was in too deep now, he couldn't turn his back on her.

"I love you so much, Sheena Baxter, and we've come so far and shared so much together in such a short time. I can't wait to marry you and have kids with you—" Brondo said in earnest. He was deeply head over heels now for Sheena; he couldn't get her out of his system, his every thought was of her; they even texted right on cue—they were so in sync it wasn't funny. He would go to send her a text message in the middle of the night and there she was texting him back at the exact same time, 1.56am. It happened all the time too, so he was convinced that either she had mental telepathy, or that they were indeed soul mates.

"Well we can't stay at Varma's much longer—we need to move out, and so I've already been out looking at places to rent; I want us to find a place of our own with Ally. There's a cute little white weatherboard cottage just on the other side of town; it has enough bedrooms and closet space, a verandah and a big back yard! Oh, Brondo, what do you think? Can we do it? You just have to come see it this weekend, you're going to love it!"

Sheena sounded like such an excitable giddy schoolgirl that Brondo found it hard to resist. He made the trip to Scarborough and hadn't been there more than thirty minutes before Sheena was dragging him off to see the cottage.

"We'll just drive by it, see what you think," she said, already packing kitchen items into boxes. "I will need some help from you though, if you know what I mean. I can't do this alone, Brondo—it's because of you I've finally got the strength to leave Seedy for good. And now that he's got some new slutty girlfriend from Queensland, it will be much easier to break away from him."

Brondo helped Sheena; they went out shopping on the weekend and bought some kitchen appliances she needed, including a new $400 microwave. Then she needed Brondo to fix her washing machine, and he bought her a vacuum cleaner and also gave her $400 for the bond. Sheena was all set and ready to move in; now all that was left to do was to decide when Brondo would make the move.

"Well, babe—I was thinking let's give Ally a few weeks to settle in here with me first; I think she needs some bonding time with just me. And the dynamics are going to be different now that I'm not at Varma's anymore, so I think the boys will be coming around more often because they didn't want to go to Varma's—so we are going to have to prepare them as well, ease them into the idea of you and me being together. Plus, you're going to need some time to find a job here too, and then packing and moving and whatnot."

"Oh, um, well ok," Brondo said, trying not to sound too perturbed, "I just thought you meant—"

"I just think it's best this way; Ally is in central Australia for the week with friends—that'll give me plenty of time to get the house set up before she gets back! Ugh, I have such little time to myself these days! Having three kids sure is a workload. You understand, right babe? It won't be for long. Look, I love you—this is all going to be fine," Sheena said as she busied herself moving boxes around.

"Yeah, sure babe—I'm Ok with it all, I just love you, but I have faith in us," Brondo said, though it felt like he was pacifying himself more than he was her.

It was true that Brondo could sometimes be mistaken for being young, innocent and foolish; he was a naturally gullible and easy type of character, easy slather for Sheena, if she wanted to play games with him. She, on the other hand was more buoyant than ever now that things were working out for her, and Brondo was beginning to see that she was awfully good at getting what she wanted.

Brondo got to work job hunting; there wasn't much work in Scarborough and it was slim pickings to try to find permanent work. It was hard being new to the town too, and he wanted to find something low profile where he wouldn't run into anybody the likes of Seedy. He had to be careful who he ran into and what he said; it was a small enough town where chins wagged and goats talked, and he and Sheena didn't need to be attracting any more trouble than they'd had already.

By the middle of August he still hadn't found any work and Sheena messaged and asked Brondo to leave his security job and come help her son Thomas to move some furniture into the cottage.

"It's just his bed, a few pieces of furniture and a few boxes of clothes, I'm sure he'll appreciate you helping out, Brondo, and I thought it would be a nice way for you two to bond a bit," Sheena said.

"Thomas is moving in?" Brondo said, incredulous. "But—what happened? Why the sudden change? How did this play out? What's going on, Sheena?" Brondo felt blindsided because Sheena hadn't mentioned anything about it.

"Look—the kid's had it rough going; he's sick of always getting beat up and clipped around the ears by Seedy, and he knows the rules, babe—he's not like Max, he's different to Max, he's not a hot head—just give him a chance, yeah?"

"Why are you allowing this? I mean, you know how he feels about me and us?"

"I'm one hundred percent sure he's gonna like you, babe. I've gotta get back to work now, but I told him you'll be around soon to help." Click.

Brondo drove from work straight to the cottage, and surprisingly Sheena was right; Thomas was rather glad to see Brondo and they shook hands and Thomas joked that Max had got it completely wrong, because Brondo wasn't a fat, ugly greasy wog at all—he was actually a tall, skinny and handsome Greek-Aussie guy who was friendly and nothing at all like he had presumed from his Facebook profile.

The two hit it off immediately and they fell into an instant, easy friendship. Brondo helped him move his bed and boxes and told him all about his life growing up in Melbourne, and Thomas offered to buy him a burger to thank him for helping out. They took a drive to McDonalds and had a good laugh along the way about how screwed up Max was again, and how he'd gotten it completely wrong about Brondo.

It was awkward for Brondo knowing that he still had yet to meet the feisty, angry one: Max. He had met pretty much everyone else by now; Varma, Ally, Sheena's sister Lisa and two brothers Steve and Nixon, plus a scattering of nephews and nieces. But with Max, Brondo knew he would have to play nice, be the gentleman; he was on Max's turf now, and this was to Max's advantage. It wasn't like being in Melbourne where everything was familiar and he knew his surroundings. Here he felt less safe; and because of Max spreading rumours he knew that there were potential enemies lurking everywhere.

There was a different feel going on now in the new place; he couldn't quite put his finger on it, but whatever it was, was making Brondo feel uncomfortable, despite the fact that he was now so close with Sheena and Thomas. Ally was now getting frustrated with Brondo; he had not been paying as much attention to her as he had in the beginning and she wanted him to move out. She just wanted to just be with her mother after being dislocated from her so long at Varma's house. Brondo was starting to feel the pressure, and the annoying Varma wasn't helping matters, as she began to interfere in their relationship.

"You should be spending less time with Brondo and more time with your kids—they need you right now, and they're my grandchildren too! You aren't doing enough for them! You tell that Brondo 'whatshisname' he needs to get out and get a job and find his own place—why hasn't he got job yet?" Varma prattled.

Brondo could see that the Varma he had met six months ago was not the Varma now; he was surprised to see her true character finally coming to the surface.

"Mother wasn't always so lovely and smiling and friendly—she was responsible for lots of hurts, pain and heartache too," Sheena told Brondo that night after dinner.

"In fact, my stepfather was molesting me and was completely inappropriate towards me and my sister Lisa, I just wasn't comfortable telling you about it before," Sheena said, bowing her head in shame. Brondo was floored with what Sheena had just uttered; he couldn't believe that Varma could be that mother who would subject her two daughters to a man like that.

"I can't believe it," Brondo said, gobsmacked, his eyes wide.

"It's true; there was a court case years ago, it was a really bad time, babe—I kept quiet about it for years because I was so scared and didn't feel that Mother would believe me. Finally when I was fifteen I spoke up and started rebelling against her and him; then I spoke up and told her what he had done. Lisa kept quiet the whole time until after the court case; that's when she kicked him out, but her words to this day still haunt me and hurt me. She said:

"You're the reason your two younger brothers don't have a Dad."

"I don't get it, Brondo—the guy was a creep," Sheena said, her eyes welling up. "He used to make Varma dress like a maid and a nurse, and wait on his every word; he controlled her, used her, abused her—he was just sick and twisted."

"Wow, that was a low comment she made, babe. I'm so sorry this happened to you," Brondo said, wrapping her up in his arms. It was so disturbing for him to think that Varma could make such a cruel and selfish comment—worse still, to expect her daughter to stay quiet and suffer for the sake of giving her younger brothers a father figure? And to think that this man had been violent, had violated Sheena and Lisa like that. Varma had to be a narcissist, he thought. He was furious, livid with Varma for trusting a man like that to be around her daughters in the first place—how foolish, how heartless was she? And yet, she had the audacity just now to criticise Sheena's parenting? He wanted to make them both pay for the pain and heartache they'd inflicted on two innocent young girls.

Knowing he was violent and aggressive towards her daughters started to explain more about Sheena; he thought about her inability to trust him, always thinking he would leave her. He thought about her excessive need for attention and approval, her sexual needs and overdrive. It explained a lot. She was serving a life sentence for all the wrongs done to her as a child. He wanted to kill this man.

"Do you think your mum played favourites with her kids?"

"Oh God, yes—Steve's the clear favourite, we all know that," Sheena said rolling her eyes. Steve was the golden child who could do no wrong in Varma's eyes; he was the baby of the family and she doted on him from morning to night.

"I know it's not my place to say, Sheena, but I don't think your mum has unconditional love for you kids; you don't ever put your kids in harm's way like that," Brondo gently pointed out.

"Well, you'll get the chance to ask her yourself, she'll be over tomorrow to see the kids, I can't get her out of my hair these days," Sheena said, frustrated. "But you'll have to take her on yourself, 'coz thankfully I won't be here, I have to be at work."

The next morning after Sheena went to work, Brondo sat at the kitchen table drinking coffee and eating Vegemite toast when Varma entered unannounced through the back sliding door.

"Ah, Brondo, fancy seeing you here!" Varma smiled, all fake and sweet. But Brondo could now see through the old lady's veiled pleasantries and was more prepared for her. He couldn't understand why she was being so tough with him though, when in the beginning she had seemed more supportive in the fact that her daughter had found someone more decent than Seedy, which wasn't hard to do.

"So tell me, what you doing with yourself these days, besides just sitting around Sheena's new place? I have to know your intentions for my daughter—I cannot let her be with another loser, you know!" Varma said matter-of-factly, boiling the kettle.

Brondo explained that his intentions towards her daughter were honourable and though he hadn't found a full time job yet he was looking hard. He was feeling silently annoyed by Varma's calling it 'Sheena's place' when he had paid for most of it, but for the sake of Sheena and keeping the peace with her mother he kept quiet and held his tongue.

Varma kept on badgering him but Brondo suppressed his frustrations and kept his cool; she had few manners for an older woman and could be very bossy and direct, not unlike Sheena herself. He decided to gently prod and poke her himself, challenging her indirectly; though he was not good at confrontation he had questions of his own, causing Varma to be a little thrown by his questioning.

"So Sheena told me that the father of your children molested her, is that right?" Brondo hinted casually, taking sidelong glances at the old woman.

"Oh nonsense! Fred was just a drunk. I had to throw that fish back into the sea," Varma said in a very blasé way, stirring milk into her tea. Beforehand Sheena's mother had had a hold over them because they had been in her house, under her roof, but now things were different.

"Well, Sheena told me it went to court, so I don't think anyone could call that *nothing*, Varma, and I don't think you should accuse Sheena of lying about such a thing—but, whatever."

Varma didn't stay long after that; she spent some time with Ally in her bedroom and then went on her way, and Brondo was glad to see the backside of her going out the door.

Sheena came home from work in the afternoon to find Brondo taking a nap on the couch after doing stuff around the house all morning.

"My God, Brondo—what did you say to my mother? She called me in tears and said you were rude to her!"

"I wasn't rude—I just put her back in her place at bit, that's all. She was having a go at me for not having a job yet, so I challenged her about what you told me about, the molestation," Brondo said, feeling suddenly on the defensive.

"You had no right to say anything—I shared that with you in *private!*"

Brondo couldn't believe his ears. He felt like he could never do anything right.

"Babe—I was only saying it to *defend* you..."

"Well, I think for now you should look at getting a job, maybe you could find yourself a caravan to stay in for a bit," Sheena said, sifting through the mail.

"I don't think that's such a good idea, me getting a place alone, babe—Seedy could put out some sort of a hit on me...I'd be like a sitting duck," Brondo said nervously. But Sheena as always, was quick to dismiss the idea.

"Oh nonsense, Brondo—he wouldn't do that, as he knows how hurt Ally would be."

But Brondo knew better; he knew that he *would* be a sitting duck, just waiting to be fried. No full blooded man would stand around letting his wife's lover run around town, making a fool of him. But what bothered him even more though, was Sheena: wasn't she the least bit concerned for Brondo's safety? Why only worry about Ally's feelings in all of this? Thankfully, Seedy had taken a holiday to Queensland with his new girlfriend and was out of the picture, but now Ally was on Sheena's back to get Brondo to move out. He was annoyed that Sheena was once again allowing a fifteen year old girl to call the shots over their relationship, dictating what their mother should do.

Brondo felt helpless. He felt ready to pack his stuff and leave. He could feel himself distancing from them. Call it women's intuition or something, but Sheena also sensed he was about to pack it all in and quickly moved to reassure him.

What Brondo didn't know was that Sheena was keeping new secrets from him. As a result of her not paying the house off and Seedy not paying her car off, the banks were about to repossess all the equity they had; she was about to lose the house and their car, and so Brondo had now become very useful to her. What

Sheena didn't know was that Brondo had accidentally overheard the entire conversation between Sheena and Ally the night before.

"Mum, what are we going to do without a car? Can Brondo lend us his car?"

"Ally, be realistic—we can't ask him to move out and then take his car, that's rude," Sheena explained.

"We'll ask him to stay then, Mum, because we need the car! How am I going to get to school without it? Ask him to stay, quick—before he moves out."

Brondo couldn't believe what he'd just heard, but he knew this had to be an act of God; maybe it was a sign that he shouldn't be here after all, shouldn't be getting himself all tangled up in this mess anyway, in their games. He knew Seedy had been asking around town about him, too; where he was living, where he was moving to. Maybe God was at work in his life right now, working to spare him yet again. He was kinda maxed out about it all, to be honest.

Brondo felt that he was knocking on death's door, playing with fire, so he waited until everyone was in bed to broach the subject with Sheena.

"Babe, I think you're right, there's too much going on here at the moment, I think I should find my own place," Brondo said slowly, getting cold feet, applying the brakes.

Sheena just smiled and mocked him sarcastically, stroking his face.

"Naww, my good, little Greek Church boy," she said pityingly. "Don't leave me now, Brondo; we'll figure things out. It'll all be fine. You'll see. And Max is coming tomorrow, so we need to put all our focus into that. Night babe," she said and turned out the light.

CHAPTER EIGHT

Maxed Out

Proverbs 10: 28
*The hope of the righteous brings joy,
but the expectation of the wicked will perish*

Brondo found a permanent position in Scarborough working for SPC as a maintenance man cleaner. The four am early morning starts were brutal, especially on frosty August mornings in the dense fog of country life.

Soon he had developed a throat infection and was suddenly bedridden for days, unable to go to work. His new boss was actually very supportive and gave him the time off, but Sheena looked puzzled and mocked his pain, telling him he had a girly pain threshold. Brondo was livid at her insensitivity towards him, but was determined to prove her wrong, because historically speaking he had often been mocked for being too soft and easy going, always being told to 'toughen up.'

As his condition worsened though, Brondo was in great pain. He finally went to the doctor, and after a scan of his throat they sent him straight into hospital. Brondo had developed a severe case of strep throat.

"Oh my God! Wow—I'm sorry babe, oh my God, no wonder you're in so much pain!" Sheena cried. ewqBrondo couldn't believe Sheena had been making fun of him the whole time. He knew she felt guilty as hell about it, too. She began running around everywhere in his car, getting him medicines and magazines. He was so drained and had such severe fatigue and low energy that he pretty much slept the whole time; he hadn't eaten in days and was barely keeping his fluids up, he didn't think he had ever been so sick in his life. He debated whether to return home to Yaya Andromachi; she would make him a big pot of her traditional Greek Kotosoupa Avgolemono, a big batch of lemon chicken soup and rice to nourish the body and soul. Yaya said that as a child whenever she got a cold she would go to the markets with her mother back in her homeland Greece; they would buy up lots of vegetables—carrots, onion, potato and celery and make a soup out of it all, rich in vitamins and minerals.

'Within twenty-four hours, my cold was already better!' Yaya would exclaim.

Brondo missed Yaya now; he wished she was here. Brondo pulled himself to sit up in bed and as he did he noticed a large blue van pull up outside on the street. Oh my God. Max.

Brondo couldn't believe it. The rotten bloody timing! If there was to be a confrontation of any sort, he was far too sick, fatigued and groggy to fight; he quickly threw himself off the bed and pulled on a pair of pants, trying to look half decent for a sick man.

Brondo also knew that, even if he had been well, he was no match for the bigger guy. He just hoped and prayed that Max would go easy on him. Ally was with her cousin Mitchell in the kitchen when Max came barging through the door. Ally too, was frightened of her big brother now and preferred to stay out of his way.

"Is that fat wog cunt here," Max asked, storming into the kitchen.

"No—what do you want, Max?" Ally protested, trying to stop him, but Max thumped down the hallway towards Sheena and Brondo's bedroom. He flung the door open to see Brondo sitting on the edge of the bed, putting his shoes on. Brondo stood up.

"Max," Brondo said, looking directly at him. Max stared at Brondo for a moment and then walked back into the kitchen. Their first face to face encounter had lasted a whole three seconds, Brondo thought. At least he hadn't punched him out. He could hear Ally's voice now, coming from the kitchen.

"Max, please don't be stupid," but that was all he could hear before things became muffled. Should he go out there, face Max? He wasn't well, but he didn't want to look like a coward, either. He didn't know what to expect, but

he could only hope for the best; he hoped that Max would just give him the same chance that Thomas and Ally had. Even though he was silently sweating bullets about this kid, he decided to be the bigger man, because he was the man in this scenario, after all. Brondo finished putting his shoes on and walked down the hallway to the kitchen. He could see Max standing by the kitchen table, saying something to Ally.

"Max," Brondo addressed him again in a calm voice, and right away Max fired up.

"Don't even talk to me after all the shit you said on Facebook," Max shouted, his fist clenched and in the air. Ally got between Max and Brondo to stop anything before it had even started. Even in his weakened state, Brondo just looked at Max and laughed. Max became even more enraged.

"Don't fucking laugh, cunt, or I will throw you through the bedroom wall."

Brondo laughed and said calmly, "I'm sick, dude—I ain't gonna fight you like this. And I already told ya, I'm not gonna fight ya, Bro. I mean it." Deep down he felt ashamed and humiliated as though he were less of a man for backing down to this kid; but he could see this kid had so much anger in him, and maybe trying to befriend him, build his trust was the way to go. Still, secretly, he wished he could teach Max a lesson, but knew that, for Sheena's sake, he couldn't; it would just spark an all-out family war.

So instead he watched as Max vented, before storming off. This was Max's turf, and he knew it, so the cards fell in his favour. And Brondo would never

inflict harm on Sheena's sons, and Max knew this, too.

Thomas was just coming in the door but Max had already walked out. The brothers said nothing to each other in passing; Max jumped in his van and sped off at high speed. Sheena soon came home from work to see them all just sitting there in the kitchen.

"God, do I have to do everything around here? Couldn't one of you at least have started on making something for dinner? Why do you wait for me to do everything all the time?" Sheena complained, putting down her handbag and clearing the clutter of plates to the sink.

"Mum, you just missed some major drama—Max met Brondo, he was here," Ally said, grimacing.

"Oh God—what happened?" Sheena asked, looking across at Brondo.

"Umm, well he didn't put his fist through any walls—or faces. So that's good, right?" Thomas smirked.

"Yeah, Max came over," Brondo began, noticing the glint Sheena had in her eye, "and I tried to do the right thing, I got dressed to try and have a civil word with him, but he wouldn't have a bar of it, stormed out," Brondo lamented. "He certainly doesn't seem to have inherited your traits of forgiveness, babe, I was wrong to assume he'd be anything like you..." he trailed off. He just couldn't understand how such a pretty, loving woman could birth such an angry, selfish and inconsiderate son.

Sheena looked at Brondo and laughed. She just laughed. He wanted her to say something, anything that would acknowledge Max's poor behaviour, but she didn't; her only comment was that now she'd have to fix the situation and call Max, though he probably wouldn't answer any of her calls. Immediately Brondo sensed he was seeing another side to Sheena, one that deep down he knew had probably always existed, but that he had failed or not wanted to see. Fantasy and reality are surely two different things, and the truth of the matter was that one couldn't be ready to see reality until they were ready to give up on the fantasy. Brondo was painfully aware of this. While he liked the idea of Sheena being dominant and somewhat even nasty from time to time, something sharp bit into his psyche as he realised that, that on some level, he gravitated towards her type because he had been so conditioned to it himself, growing up. It was all he'd ever known. Dominant, possessive, controlling women.

But her laughing like this now made him feel uncomfortable, ridiculed; it was almost as if she were mocking him, taunting him to react—that Max's threatening behaviour had been nothing, and that it was Brondo who was overreacting. But he let her laugh, because he didn't want to rock the boat or lose the woman he'd fallen in love with, so he reminded himself of her wonderful qualities; that, plus the fact that he'd come a long way in beating the miserable depression he'd been battling just six months earlier. And he'd had more compassion and empathy from her than any support he'd received from any of his family, so all in all, it was better to stay put.

"Well, there's more to it than that," Ally began again. "Just before he left, Max told me that his girlfriend Mel is preggers," Ally said, still shocked herself.

"Holy fuck—" Sheena exclaimed. "Well that's just bloody great, that is! I don't want to be a grandmother, I'm too young for all that crap—it makes me feel so old! I'm gonna need to call him, I need to fix this situation, it's all just a fucking mess," she said, breaking plates in the kitchen.

Sheena whined to Brondo from the kitchen. "Oh, are you gonna still wanna be with me now, babe? I'm gonna be an old grandma now, and my little Greek lover boy's gonna leave me... oh God no!" she wailed.

"Mum, wait—it gets better: Max told me he doesn't want the kid, he doesn't want to be a dad: says how does he know it's his, anyway? He told me to tell you that he wants her to have an abortion—and he wants *you* to help him talk her into it," Ally said, eating a banana.

"Oh great—you know, what that boy really needs is a strong male role model," Sheena said, looking across at Brondo and smirking each time she looked at him. Brondo got up and said nothing and just walked out of the kitchen feeling shamed, powerless and humiliated. Why did she have to *be like that to him?* Her tone could go from loving to condescending at the flick of a switch, and he didn't like it.

A few hours later Sheena climbed into bed next to Brondo;

he was still feeling shit from the strep throat and just wanted to sleep it off. They could hear the kids in the living room with the TV blaring; it was the lead up to the AFL grand final between the St Kilda Saints and the Geelong Cats, though Brondo had zero interest in watching it, being so sick.

"Come on, babe, let's have a little snuggle, get it on—the kids are out watching TV, they won't hear us, they can't hear a thing," Sheena said, getting horny and hot under the sheets. She was such the seductive temptress with such an insatiable, never-ending libido that it wore him out.

"I'm really under the weather, babe—do you mind if we don—" Brondo tried to say but she was already climbing atop him in that aggressive, never-take-no for an answer way that she had about her.

"I was right, wasn't I?" Sheena whined, "that you won't love me anymore 'coz you'll make me out to be some old woman, a washed up grandmother, and you'll leave me and not want me anymore."

Brondo was confused; why did she have to resort to questioning him about his love for her again? She seemed to love adding fuel to the fire; subsequently he had to once again adopt the role of the reassuring partner, stroking her hair and telling her that he wasn't going anywhere, even though he was the one who was sick right now and needed caring for.

Mel came to see Sheena the next day; Sheena sat her down in their living room and they talked about the pregnancy. Mel revealed that she might be carrying twins and that she couldn't believe it had happened; she had been on the pill the whole time, and this was an accident.

"You know, when I was your age I had an accident too; you probably don't want to hear this right now, but I was on the pill and sex with Seedy was just a one night stand—the twins were an accident that was never supposed to happen. I couldn't believe it either when I found out I was pregnant. So I know what you're going through," Sheena said, sipping her coffee. "But I wasn't in love with Seedy, and I ended up getting stuck with a man who was all wrong for me. I don't know about you and Max, and things might be different, but, woman to woman advice here: I don't want to see that happen to you. Don't make the same mistake I did."

Sheena was only too happy to see Mel end the pregnancy and hinted that it may be in both of their best interests. Mel opened up to Sheena, telling her that despite the fact that she loved Max, they fought a lot and seemed to bring out the worst in one another.

"All the more reason to call it quits now, then, before its too late," Sheena advised. Christ, this kid was too young to have a baby, she thought. Mel left very emotional, thanking Sheena for her kind words and wisdom.

Sheena came back to Brondo all stressed out while he was still lying sick in the bed. "God Almighty, this girl's not ready to have a baby! She's not ready and Max shouldn't be trapped and stuck with her—she's not good for him he's not good for her. I just hope I talked some sense into her, 'coz I don't want to be anybody's Grandma!" she cried.

"So do you think she'll go through with the pregnancy, babe?" Brondo asked.

"We will just have to wait and see I guess, babe," Sheena said, looking sheepish. Brondo sensed there was more she wasn't telling.

"What?" Brondo said, inviting her to spill it.

"Well...I didn't want to bring it up like this, but I guess since we're on the topic, now's as good a time as any..." Sheena said, circling around whatever it was she wanted to tell him. Brondo grew concerned with the way she was building it up.

"Just say it, Sheena—what is it now?"

"Well, ok—you know how we talked about having kids—us? I went to the doctor the other day, but it seems that's not going to be very likely," she said, playing with Brondo's fingers. "The doc said that reversing the procedure, plus my age, would be a complicated process, and he really just advised against it. But I still do want to marry you, don't think that this changes anything for me."

Brondo looked at her; it was hard to hide his disappointment. Was Sheena not being honest with him? How long had she known this? In his heart he felt this too could be a game changer if things didn't start heading in the right direction again. But now she was pleading with him again not to leave her, as though she were able to read his mind. Once again he felt he had to reassure her that he wasn't going anywhere.

"Well, we always knew that could be a possibility, maybe its just not in the cards for us," he said despondently. Maybe this was all for the best, anyway, he thought: he had to work on his relationship with Max, and that was enough of a hurdle in itself; it made no sense bringing a baby into the mix with all that was going on. Sheena got off the bed and he watched as she tied a pretty pink bowtie in her hair; her green eyes and purple eyeliner were a particular shade of pretty today, and he didn't want to see her make up all smudged from tears.

"We'll be fine babe, everything will work out for the best. Its just like you always say it will," Brondo said, kissing her lightly.

Deep down though, he worried: he wondered whether Max would use this unborn child as a pawn, as a bargaining chip in their relationship to influence his mother into ending things with Brondo. He could see him using the child as leverage, too; that if his mother wanted any part in her grandchild's life, she would have to end things with Brondo. And Max was cunning; he knew how to manipulate his mother, make things work to his advantage. He had already given Sheena plenty of ultimatums—that it would be either him or Brondo. Not that Brondo took any of it seriously. Max was as useless a cigarette in an ashtray; he was nothing more than a big, codependent baby in a diaper, and Sheena babied him constantly, enabling the kid. Max was wet behind the ears; he knew nothing of how to survive in the world and be independent. It was a worry to Brondo that the kid was nineteen already and didn't even know how to pay bills, or shop for himself or manage money—he was spoilt and his mother's favourite, and that was a hard gig to beat.

Over the coming days Brondo got back into work and was feeling better. He decided he would try to repair things with Max, so he called his phone one afternoon while Sheena was still at work.

"Hi Max its Brondo," he said, but he couldn't get anything else out because Max screamed over the top of him.

"What the fuck, cunt—don't you be calling me, Brondo, I'ma warnin' ya," Max said in a threatening tone.

"Look mate—let's talk. Come on, we gotta try make this work, hey."

"Nah fuck you—hang up now…you hang up I tell you, or I'm gonna come over there, you bastard."

But Brondo wouldn't hang up. So Max hung up, even more enraged, and raced on over to his mother's new house to see Brondo. Brondo was oblivious to Max being en route to the house as he was at his place of work, and he didn't think

Max would ever come after him there because there would be witnesses, and Brondo would have cctv footage and be able to claim self-defence.

Sheena told Max that Brondo wasn't home, when Max stormed up to his mother's front door demanding to know where he was; but Sheena just laughed and told him again that Brondo wasn't home. But Max didn't believe her.

"Nah, tell him to come out the front, right now, the coward," Max hissed.

Sheena couldn't understand her son's anger. "Max, calm down—he isn't here, seriously; you can come in and have a look yourself, if you like."

Max was livid. "He better not be here," he warned his mother, and she stepped aside, smiling. Sheena laughed.

"See? He seriously isn't here, Max—let it go."

Just then her phone rang. It was Brondo.

"Who is it?" Max demanded. Sheena didn't answer him so he snatched the phone from her hand.

"Oh, who do you think this is, *loverboy*?" taking Brondo by complete surprise. "I'm coming to get yer, so ya better be ready for me," Max said and hung up.

Sheena made the mistake of telling Max that Brondo worked at SPC in Scarborough, and Max ran out the door to hunt him down. Sheena panicked and quickly tried calling Brondo back to alert him, but he didn't pick up. Shit, she thought, and raced to get her car keys, only to realise that Brondo had already taken the car with him to work.

Max sat outside SPC and waited for Brondo. He'd wait until it was time for him to leave; he'd get him as he was making his way out the door. After twenty minutes had gone by, there was Brondo, exiting the building right on five o'clock, making his way across the parking lot. Max crept up on him from behind; it unfolded so fast Brondo didn't know what was happening. Max threw two punches at Brondo's head then sprinted off into dense foliage, out of sight. Brondo, not seeing his assailant couldn't be sure of who it was, but guessed it to be Max as he went down on one knee. Two security guards came rushing to Brondo's aid, and Brondo muttered that he thought it was his girlfriend's son. The men nodded, they all knew about the troubled kid.

"Ah, so you'll be Brondo, will ya? Yeah, we heard talk about it at the pub, that kid Max was bragging that he had a hit out on yer—word travels fast in this town, and your name is a bit of an unusual one around here."

They helped him to his feet and warned him that this kid was known as trouble around town; he could be dangerous. They cautioned him to be careful, even joked about how they liked him and felt sorry for him.

"Yeah, she's married to that bloke, what's his name, Sean? Seedy? You don't wanna be gettin' in with that mob, they're all screwed up, they are—word has it that he's a bunny, likes to get other people involved to do his dirty work for him, if ya know what I mean. And we don't wanna be comin' into work one day seeing your tomb or hearing your name in the papers, like "there lies Brondo, bludgeoned to death for stealing Seedy's missus," they laughed.

But Brondo couldn't laugh. He drove home with a pounding head and told Sheena what had happened. He couldn't hold it in any longer, and he became emotional with her.

"I called my brother, babe—I needed to tell him what's been going on. He wasn't there, so I talked to Sonia, his wife; they want me to come back home. This thing has gotten bigger than both of us—I've tried reaching out to the kid, but nothing's worked.

I know you don't want me to leave, but things can't go on like this—give me a minute, I've got to go to the bathroom and clean up, splash water on my face and calm down from all of this," Brondo said, pushing by her and heading for the bathroom.

After washing his face he sat on the cold tile floor with his head in his hands. As a million thoughts were swirling in his head, he couldn't understand how he'd gotten to this point in his life. Someone knocked on the bathroom door; Brondo's breath quickened and his neck muscles tightened and he became stressed, thinking it could be Max again. Brondo trembled as the doorknob turned, because he'd forgotten to lock it. He was so shaken because he'd never been jumped like that in his life. It turned out it was Thomas opening the door,

poking his head around the doorjamb, wanting to know if Brondo was alright.

"I'm sorry, Man, my brother can be a real horse's ass," Thomas offered by way of consolation. "Come out, I'll get you a beer, it'll be alright."

Brondo came out and sat down in the living room. Sheena glared at him from the couch.

"Why'd you have to go and taunt him like that?" She said, acting livid.

Brondo sat there, fuming; he couldn't believe the nastiness behind Sheena's accusations, that she was taking Max's side in all of this.

"You know what your son's like and the threatening things he has said—and you've got the guts to say that to me?" he retorted. Brondo was starting to see why Sheena's marriage had been a mess; she had this nasty, cold side that he'd never seen, and she guarded it well.

"Well, you're always saying that 'someone needs to teach

Max a lesson,' so how do I know you didn't provoke it?" She said sarcastically. Things were getting hard now, Brondo could feel it. His phone started buzzing.

"It's my brother—I gotta take it, he's worried about me," Brondo said flatly, going out into the hall.

"I'm gonna kill someone," Vito said angrily on the other end. "Are you Ok, Bro? Sonia told me you got bashed? Things are gonna end bad for her family—no one goes jumping my brother! I'm gonna come to Scarborough and inflict some serious pain, flog him myself." Vito could be as wild and as dangerous as Max; he was as tough as nails had an angry, violent and protective side to him that was very Greek, something Brondo did not have. Brondo could be tough when he had to be, sure, but there was too much softness in him to ever instigate anything. For all their faults, Brondo's family was still a very tight knit traditional family, because Greek families really knew how to stick together and would even kill for one another, if it came down to it. Sheena stayed quiet so she could hear Brondo out in the hall trying to talk his brother down, and she feared for her son's safety. Vito was on speakerphone to Brondo, and she sat and listened to it all.

"I'll teach that little fucking cunt to mess with my brother," Vito said. "I'll pay him a little visit of my own; I'll take him for a little walk around the corner—and only one of us will be coming back."

"C'mon, Bro, I know you're angry right now, I am too, but—"

"Brondo, don't worry about it, she's as good as apples, mate— me 'n me mates, we know all about her 'n her little family, even where they all live—an' we got a bit of experience ourselves in knowing how to lead the lambs to the slaughter. Don't you worry your pretty little head about it, we'll take good care of it." Click.

Brondo returned to the bedroom.

A friend loves, but a brother is for a time of adversity, Brondo thought out loud. Proverbs taught him that in his old church days.

"He really hurt me, Sheena; I don't think you understand how dangerous this is getting, he's really crossed the line this time."

It wasn't often that Brondo ever saw Sheena as truly worried, but she was looking worried now, as worried as she had looked a few months back, back when they were still sneaking around. This was war.

"Vito's coming to Scarborough on Friday to punch Max's head in," Brondo announced.

"I'm so sorry, babe; I don't know how else to apologise. We have to shut this whole thing down. They can't hurt my son," she said, and tears formed at her eyelids. Brondo realised it was rare that he ever saw Sheena cry, and he pulled her into him. She kissed him hard, plied him with her hands and they fell into bed where they had their first make up sex.

Brondo temporarily eased Sheena's fears, but deep down he realised that night that the relationship seemed to be over. He was making up his mind to return to Melbourne, because this had all become just too much to bear.

Thomas turned cocky again on Brondo, texting him a message with all sorts of big talk, like that his brother wouldn't make it out of Scarborough alive if he came onto his turf, and because Max had his friends coming, too. Not to be intimidated, Brondo wrote back telling him he would be bringing an army himself, fully loaded up with guns. Brondo was annoyed at Thomas' foolish responses, and he probably shouldn't have threatened the kid back, but he was sick and tired of lying down and accepting their bullshit while Sheena sat by and did nothing. Besides, he thought, it would do Thomas good to put the fear of God into him, make him scared.

But Sheena just threw her head back and laughed at the text messages between them; she laughed in that god awful way that sent chills down Brondo's spine. It was in that moment he realised that she was, in fact, a nasty woman; only now she was showing her true colours. He didn't know why he hadn't seen the real her before, but this was definitely the *real* Sheena. She was ugly. And he knew it was just going to get uglier, because he was almost maxed out.

CHAPTER NINE
True Colours

Judges 16:15
How canst thou say 'I love thee,'
when thine heart is not with me?

The gold Commodore wasn't running so smooth these days with all the travel back and forth he had been doing and trouble seemed to follow Brondo everywhere he went. He was forty kilometres outside of Scarborough when the engine began to sputter and shake; he looked at the sometimes-working-sometimes-not unreliable fuel gauge and saw that she was on empty.

"I've run out of petrol," he texted Sheena from the side of the highway.

"Oh no, that's no good," came Sheena's only response.

What was wrong with her, he thought? He couldn't believe she could be so cold, so lacking in compassion. If the situation were reversed he would be the first to offer help, lend a hand. But not Sheena. She just wanted to rant about how Thomas and

Max were getting a gang together to challenge Brondo's brother.

"Well I know that my brother's mates aren't to be trifled with, either—some of them have criminal records," Brondo said, hoping she would understand the seriousness of things.

"Same," she texted back. Sheena could be so cocky and bold; she only wanted to outdo him with big talk, and he couldn't believe the level of her stupidity.

"Well the difference is that my brother knows where your entire family is; Vito could end things very quickly, if he wanted to."

"Don't be so sure about that, Brondo," Sheena was good at being a smart alec.

"Sheena, don't be an idiot—these are grown experienced men with weapons that your son and friends won't be able to defend themselves against; they can't even muster enough time to gather an army big enough to protect themselves, these guys will paint the town red with Max's blood if this can't be stopped."

Sheena suddenly realised Brondo was right and quickly went on the defence.

"Well, I will just call the police, then, wont I?"

"Then they'll come for you too, and you'll be involved in all of this—and I won't help you then," he retorted, becoming livid at the stupid games she liked to play. He wanted to show her he could play hard ball too. Sheena's biggest mistake was that she was always taking advantage of Brondo's submissive and soft nature; she thought she had him pegged for being a gullible pushover—but push any man to his limit and he'd eventually snap.

"Max is big enough and old enough to fight his own battles, if you don't like it then perhaps you should have sorted things out earlier—then it wouldn't have escalated to this and reached the limits it has!"

"My brother is not going to let your brat son get away with this—it's high time he learned a lesson—and obviously you haven't got the parenting skills to teach him anything!" Brondo barked back.

Sheena was furious and couldn't handle it any longer. "That's it, we're finished, Brondo—you're a dumb loser!" She screamed.

"You're a loser too!" Brondo screamed back. Sheena hung up.

Brondo had to walk twenty kilometres to the nearest petrol station and buy a jerry can; he filled it up and walked another twenty kilometres back to his car cursing all the way. Bloody Sheena! he thought. He was going to drive back to Melbourne and forget about her. He turned on the radio and Cyndi Lauper was singing *True Colours*. Yet another omen. Omens were everywhere, he thought.

But I see your true colours
Shining through
I see your true colours
And that's why I love you
 So don't be afraid to let them show
Your true colours

When he got home, Brondo was flat and deflated; he kissed Yaya and went to his old room and lay on the bed feeling depressed and defeated. He had tried so hard to make a go of the relationship but nothing was ever good enough for Sheena. It had all been just a waste of time.

He put the radio on and went to raid the fridge; there was leftover Greek salad, Tzatziki and hummus dip and souvlaki. He grabbed the souvlaki and snuck into Yaya's cabinet and stole for himself a shot of ouzo for good measure to calm his nerves. Yaya was taking a nap and Uncle had gone down to the Cyprus Community Club on Lygon Street. He went into the lounge room and put the TV on. He surfed the channels and settled on Inner Space, a good science fiction comedy. He hoped that would put him in a better mood. He sat gathering his thoughts and looking into his own inner space; Sheena challenged him in ways that no one else ever had, yet she seemed to have a hold over him that he couldn't explain. She drove him mad, but deep down he knew he still loved her, that much was sure. Towards the end of the movie (that he could only half concentrate on and half enjoy anyway because his thoughts were all over the shop and only about Sheena), the phone rang and it was Sheena and then there they were, arguing yet again; Sheena pushing Brondo's buttons and being defensive while Brondo played the role of the rational calm man, waiting for his woman to calm the fuck down. Finally she quieted long enough to let him speak.

"Babe, I understand where you're coming from—you only want to protect your son. I get it. But I'm the one who's been wronged here. I don't understand why you can't see that—Max needs to know that there are consequences for his actions, and you're not modeling any of that, you're just wrapping the kid up in cotton wool!"

"You're a fucking judgmental control freak, Brondo! The kid has cancer! And you think it's Ok to send your brother in to beat him up?" she screamed at him.

"If you weren't so psychologically scarred and screwed up from your stepfather's sexual abuse maybe you'd teach him a thing or two about consequences!" Brondo hit back. The final insult, he knew just then, was the last blow. As soon as he'd said it he knew he'd gone too far, and he instantly regretted it.

Sheena hung up, raging with anger. Brondo realised what

he'd said was too harsh and he immediately felt remorseful. He didn't know what to do, but he thought he'd better call her back. Sheena was now avoiding his calls and not answering. He became anxious and kept dialling her number furiously, until she finally picked up.

She answered and was abrupt and rude with him, but Brondo thought he deserved it for the comment he'd made, and copped it on the chin. He told her how worried he was, that Vito was going to pummel Max into the ground and he didn't know how to stop it.

"You have to intervene, Brondo! You have to make this right! Do something!" she wailed on the other end of the line. He told her he loved her and he wanted no harm to come to her son, despite the fact that he still thought Max deserved it; so he would do everything he could and call Vito to try and talk him down. Max was spoilt and a pest, but he was still Sheena's son and deserved another chance. One more chance.

They discussed giving each other one more chance too; Brondo apologised for what he'd said in the heat of the moment, and Sheena forgave him.

Brondo had to do some quick thinking about how to stop his brother—and fast. He didn't know his brother's plans and that Vito and the boys were already on their way to Scarborough. Vito was already at McDonalds waiting for Brondo to show up, but Brondo had already gone back to Melbourne. He called Vito's phone.

"Hey, Bro—where're at? We're here waiting for ya, and we need you to lure Max to McDonald's so we can take care of him there—or, we can go to their house, whatever," Vito said casually.

"Listen, Man—can you please not do anything? I'm jumping in the car and leaving Melbourne now, I'm on my way back to

Scarborough—just don't do anything stupid, Ok? I just got a call from Sheena, and she said that she's resolved things with Max; both her boys are shit scared of you lot—truth is, they've been calling your bluff, but they're just kids and they're way out of their depth and they know it—Sheena said Max is terrified; he's realised that anyone willing to drive two hours out to a country town hell bent on revenge can't be a good thing, so I think we can safely say the lesson has been learned here, boys—so we're all good, yeah?"

Brondo got to Scarborough and Sheena handed her son Max over to Brondo for a good talking to. After a solid hour they were on neutral ground and had lain down their swords, both agreeing to a cease fire. Brondo realised that Max wasn't all bad; he had a good side but was just a very troubled young man with no solid male role models to look up to.

He pulled Sheena aside and told her that he'd told Max his brother was still in Scarborough, and, although he had temporarily agreed to stand down, Brondo could very easily turn the tables and have his brother and his brother's gang at the property within minutes.

"I think when I told Max this just now he woke up to the fact that he would be pulverised and humiliated, so he's backed down now, it's all going to be ok

"I cant believe you've been able to resolve this, Brondo—thanks babe," she said, kissing him. Brondo wasn't completely sure whether he'd done the right thing or not, he only hoped he wouldn't later come to regret his decision to have mercy on the kid. Vito had agreed to back off, but he told Brondo that if there was ever any more trouble he'd be back to finish the job; he'd put Max in the back of his Hilux and drive him the 698 kilometres to the Outback and leave him there to starve.

Brondo moved back in and Sheena was grateful as she now had a car for work and Brondo could take Ally to school most days, so things were looking good. There were no more threats to Brondo's life and it seemed that the anger and hatred was finally over; Brondo and Sheena hoped they could finally get back to a normal life.

Or so Brondo thought.

Now Max and his girlfriend were coming over for dinner most weeknights, as well as Thomas and his new girlfriend Amy Fox. This was awkward because both girls had played a part in exposing Sheena and Brondo's relationship to the boys when things were just new. But for the time being things were good, and it looked like they were all settling in, sharing meals together, playing video games, and on occasion Brondo even driving the boys around town when they wanted McDonald's or KFC. As the year came to a close and rolled around into a new decade, Brondo thought things were looking promising. He could not possibly know of the next set of horrors that awaited him.

In late November, Brondo awoke with a start and he felt like he couldn't breathe. Sheena was concerned and patted his back.

He looked at her solemnly. "I just had the worst nightmare," he said, peeling back the covers and sitting upright. "Please don't laugh at me if I tell you—but, remember how I promised you I would be the first guy to take you overseas? Well, in my dreams I saw a man; he was out there, a dark figure, and he was trying to lure you overseas—I don't know why this came to me, or how or why that's possible, I just see things sometimes, sense things, even though it makes absolutely no *sense*."

Sheena sat staring at Brondo for a moment; she turned tense and her stomach quietly did backflips as her face grew a shade of crimson in the dark bedroom. She didn't know how to tell him, so instead she ushered him out of the bed, telling him he'd better get into work mode or else he'd be late for work. Brondo hopped into the shower, and upon finishing came back into the bedroom to get dressed. Sheena was still sitting upright in the bed where he'd left her and she had a funny look on her face.

Brondo knew something was amiss, his sixth sense was hard at work again; he saw the serious look on her face so he asked Sheena what was wrong. Sheena patted the bed. "Sit down, Brondo; I got a confession to make."

So Brondo sat on the bed beside her, and Sheena reached out for his hand.

"Promise not to get mad at me if I tell you this—" she began.

"Tell me what, Sheena? You're starting to freak me out," he said nervously.

"Well, when I first started talking to you online, you weren't the only one. I was talking to another man as well."

Brondo was shocked, he didn't like where this was going. Had she been lying to him again? He tried to remain calm and not let his thoughts jump ahead and get the better of him. She continued, but she kept looking down, not wanting to make eye contact.

"So there was this guy, he was interested in me too—and I was friendly to him, but that's all it was, Brondo—I flirted with him, but in the end I chose you," she said coyly. "I gave him the brush off, yet he continued to pursue me through private numbers and email. I couldn't get rid of him. Now, don't get mad, but recently he contacted me again—and he said he had paid for a plane ticket for me to visit him, and he even sent it to me, but I haven't accepted."

Brondo couldn't believe his ears; he couldn't believe how

right on the money he was about his fears, about not being able to fully trust Sheena; and now his intuitive thoughts and uncanny sixth sense had led him to the truth again.

"You're a bloody mind reader, and this is frustrating as all hell," she said looking at him.

Brondo was very, very skeptical of Sheena now; he could see the various sides of her at work; there was the charming Sheena, the mousey Sheena, the vixen Sheena, the weak and needy Sheena, and now the predator player Sheena. He looked at his watch; he had to get to work now or else he'd be late. Leave her sitting on the bed with this, he thought. Don't react, just keep your cool. Keep her guessing, when she thinks you're going to be mad, don't be. Let her stew and worry and wonder why you're not more upset, Brondo, he said to himself. He quietly got off the bed, kissed her forehead and said he'd see her later. But later didn't come. Brondo stayed quiet. The next week, however, Brondo got out of the shower and heard Sheena's phone ringing. Sheena was in the bedroom with the hairdryer and hadn't heard it for the noise of the blower.

"Your phone, Sheena—it's ringing," he said, suspicious of who it could be.

Sheena was miffed and turned off her hairdryer and looked at him as though he was a fool. "Brondo you loser, my phone's on silent and down the other end of the house."

But something in him sensed she was acting coy.

"No, it was definitely ringing, Sheena. Who was it?"

"I don't know. Who cares anyway, Brondo—just forget it," she replied sheepishly, wishing it to all go away. But he wouldn't be deterred by her efforts to dodge and weave the issue—he was determined to stand by his beliefs and follow this thing to its ultimate truth.

"Ok, if it's nobody then I won't care—just get me the phone and show it to me, so I can put my mind at rest," Brondo said blankly.

So Sheena walked to the other end of the house and retrieved her phone. She gasped when she looked down, recognising it was the mystery man's number. She handed the phone to him. Sheena was furious at having been caught out in her lie and she threw her phone and keys down angrily in the basin and vented, trying to shift the blame back to Brondo.

"Why can't you work out the fucking Tattslotto numbers with your stupid sixth sense instead of wasting it on knowing these things," she said furiously, punching him in the arm before storming off.

"You think I *want* to have to find out these things?" Brondo shouted, equally furious with her. It was never mentioned again.

In early January while watching the Australian Open tennis final, Brondo was cheering on the Greek Cypriot boy, Marcos Baghdadis, hoping his hometown boy would take the win, when Thomas came in the house all grumpy and moody, because he and his brother hadn't been working much, and both were financially strapped. Thomas snapped at Brondo for cheering at the television set in a loud voice, and suddenly old resentments came to the fore, and both clashed in a heated argument. Sheena came from the bathroom to see what was going on but she couldn't calm them both down. Brondo stood up angrily and faced Thomas, and Thomas challenged Brondo to step outside. Brondo was willing to fight the kid because in his mind there would be no more stepping down, but he didn't want to take it that far over something so minor as a tennis match.

"Jesus Christ, you two—knock it off before I call the cops!" Sheena yelled. Both retreated to opposite ends of the house to cool their jets, Brondo mad as hell that he hadn't done anything wrong to deserve such treatment. These boys just needed to be taught a damn good lesson, he thought.

Over the coming months things started to go downhill again; slowly, ever so slowly, the boys were showing signs of drug use and were becoming violent towards their mother and even Brondo. Sheena didn't want to believe that her boys were doing Ice, though Brondo could believe it: he knew by their violent outbursts and putting fists through walls that they were on something now, but how they could get their hands on it or afford it, he had no idea. It was getting out of control now that they were hitting their sister too; Ally had become fearful of her brothers and she hid from them at every opportunity. That left Sheena to face the barrage of verbal attacks; Brondo told her she had to put her foot down with them, threaten to call the cops, as a way to reign them in. But she wouldn't do it, because she didn't want to get her sons in any more trouble.

Brondo threatened Sheena that he would get Vito involved again, and that she should show some bloody respect to other members of the household by not subjecting them to the boys' violence. Sheena was stubborn and ignorant, though; she listened to Brondo but she didn't heed any of his advice, because she didn't believe the boys would take things as far as they did—instead, she insisted that this was just a phase they were going through, and they'd get past it.

But nothing changed, and things only got worse; the boys were living there now but refusing to pay board or help with paying bills or buying groceries. Sheena begged Brondo to get them a credit card because she had such a bad credit rating from the foreclosure. Brondo could see how everyone was struggling financially, so he set aside $2000 and ordered the cards to help them all get back on the right footing. Thomas decided to move to Melbourne with a mate, which left Brondo at home again with Max; and again they were at odds. It was miserable and relations were strained all around. And yet, through it all, what struck Brondo was that, in a weird way, Sheena was enjoying it along with her twisted sexual fantasies; she loved nothing more than playing her son and boyfriend off against one another, pitting man against man. It was all a game to her, but even Brondo knew that eventually all games had to come to and end.

CHAPTER TEN
Harsh Truths

John 8: 31
So Jesus said to the Jews who had believed him, 'If you abide in my word, you are truly my disciples, and you will know the truth, and the truth will set you free.'

By this stage Sheena and Max were estranged, despite the fact that he was still living there, under her roof. Things were incredibly tense between the four of them. Max had a new girlfriend. Layla Stanton; she was a beautiful tall girl, built like a man, with a wide jaw and strong shoulders. Brondo however, got the instant impression she was not the innocent girl she claimed to be. Sheena never listened to Brondo's warnings, and brushed off his concerns as mere speculation. Things with Mel, Max's ex, had ended abruptly; she had decided she wanted to keep the baby after all, and Max was so enraged that he had become violent with her; and it was no surprise that she had thrown him out.

But what did come as a surprise to Sheena was when, in late May, just after Mother's Day, two police detectives in suits knocked on her door in the middle of the night asking to speak to Max and his brother. Sheena answered the door in nothing but a flimsy nighty, and was both humiliated and embarrassed to be standing there half naked in front of the cops. She told them the boys weren't home; they then asked to come in and speak to Sheena privately. Brondo lay quietly in the bed, straining to hear the conversations being had down the hall, and wondering what the hell the police wanted with them both.

Brondo knew it had to be drug related, it had become a trend; the late nights out, the red, bloodshot eyes in the morning, the daily threats towards Ally and Sheena, the aggressive and shady characters passing through their door.

The police asked Sheena to come into the station the following week to talk with the senior detective in charge. Sheena was scared stiff and asked Brondo to go with her. Their relationship was going well and Brondo felt that by now they had become more of a team, and her efforts towards including him made him feel worthy and more involved in her life. On the last Wednesday in May Brondo and Sheena headed down to Scarborough police station and were taken into an interview room where they met detective Luke Upton. They sat and listened to the detective's report; he had been chasing Max down the last couple of months for drug related charges and home robberies that had taken place around the local area. Sheena got prickly and defensive, and fired back at the detective.

"Where is your proof?" she asked, visibly irritated and upset. The detective smirked sarcastically.

"Max's van has been reported and identified at the scene of multiple crimes already, Mrs Baxter, and when we questioned him over it, he—"

"Wait, wait—" Sheena interrupted, "you've spoken to my son already, but you're looking for him? That doesn't make sense," she retorted.

"We have been looking for him on account of other charges, but we have never been able to catch him in the act; so we have only been able to bring him in for periodic questioning at this time," the detective explained, "but we have had reports that it was indeed his van that had been sighted in regards to the robbery, which may have been used as the getaway car."

"But you have no absolute proof of this, right? I mean this is all just supposition, right?" Sheena counter argued.

"In all my years in the police force and now as a senior detective I have heard some stories—and wild ones at that—but your son's alibi, Mrs. Baxter, takes the cake—it's a beauty."

"Why? What did he say?" Sheena demanded to know.

"Well, he claimed that he was sitting parked out the front with his girlfriend minding his own business, when all of sudden these thugs opened the sliding door and jumped in his van, yelling 'drive ya fuck, drive.'"

At this point even Brondo burst into laughter and the detective looked over at him and smirked.

"It's true right, it's rubbish right," the detective joined in laughing with him.

Brondo was still laughing when his gaze met with Sheena's ice cold stare.

"Excuse me, but this is my son we're talking about," she said sharply, "and *you especially* shouldn't be laughing," she glared, unimpressed, singling Brondo out.

The detective spoke again. "Well Mrs. Baxter, you're his mother, and I don't envy you or any mother in this situation—

but my job is made more difficult when talking to you about this, because I am only presenting facts, informing you of the truth—allegedly, the guy who broke into the house and opened the door to your son's van was none other than your son's girlfriend's brother, a Mr. Luke Stanton. Does this sound like a coincidence to you? Your son *is* going out with Layla Stanton, is he not, Mrs. Baxter?"

Sheena's face went white, making her purple eyeshadow look ghastly in contrast, and Brondo turned and glared at Sheena giving her a look that said 'I told you so.' He had warned Sheena about the girl being trouble from the moment she set foot in the house.

"Yes Detective, he is seeing Layla, but how that involves them, I don't understand," she asked, puzzled. The detective looked at her, surprised by her foolishness.

"Come now, Mrs Baxter, I think we can make a fairly safe and logical assumption as to the connection between Luke Stanton, Layla Stanton and your son's involvement and participation in this," the detective scoffed. Brondo scoffed and folded his arms, shaking his head too. He couldn't believe Sheena's stubbornness and denial in acknowledging clear facts. She would go to any lengths to enable and justify Max's behaviour, even when there was clear criminal intent. She looked ignorant and foolish, he thought, and he just wished that for once she would stop defending Max's stupid behaviour.

The detective continued. "And what would he happen to be doing out the front of a house, sitting in his van at two o'clock in the morning, at that exact same moment his girlfriend's brother is in the act of committing a house robbery? Just a coincidence, or, a most conveniently and well thought out plan? We need to inform you that your son is at this moment looking like the prime suspect, accomplice and accessory to this crime. Open your eyes, Mrs. Baxter," the detective implored her.

Sheena was floored and left speechless by the detective's accusations. Brondo thought she had to be either totally stupid not to see the obvious connections implicating her son, or she was still totally stupid in choosing to continue to defend her son's actions. Either way, to Brondo she just looked totally stupid. The detective had little more to say, and ended the interview and thanked them both for coming down. Sheena was unusually quiet and mellow, humbled by the interrogation. She had to face facts; there was no point to wasting her energies on a rebuttal—her son probably was involved, the evidence was strong enough in support of his involvement. She just couldn't believe Max could be so dumb to get himself involved in anything like this. She got up and picked up her bag feeling more than a little embarrassed, and walked straight past Brondo and out the door. Brondo felt that he could cut the tension in the air with a knife.

They drove home in silence. He understood her heartache; this was her son, and it was hard enough to come to terms with the fact that not one, but now both of her sons were doing drugs. Now she had to swallow the harder pill that they were grown twenty year old men facing the prospect of having criminal records too. There was a lot Brondo wanted to say, but he thought it wiser to stay quiet, give her some time to process things. He didn't need to create any more tension and stress than there already was or make matters worse, so he thought he would make her dinner instead, offer to run a hot bath for her.

They arrived home and Sheena went to lie down, but within minutes she was up again, angry and moving about the house banging things. Surprisingly, she proposed they watch a movie. Brondo was taken aback. Sheena didn't want to discuss it at all, and he could feel her deliberately avoiding and evading the issue. Was this how she always dealt with things, by running away? he wondered? He thought she was acting immature by refusing to even acknowledge that her sons had a problem, which in Brondo's mind only perpetuated the problem.

That night Sheena would go on like nothing happened, so Brondo went along with it and they watched a movie, then went to bed. But the next morning, Sheena got on the phone with her sister Lisa and told her about the saga of Max and his alleged involvement in a robbery with Layla's brother, Luke.

"Maybe my little nephew is not as innocent as we would all like to hope," was all Lisa said, and Sheena bit her head off. Brondo jumped in to comment.

"Not me, I always knew she was rotten," he said, peeling an apple.

Sheena glared at him and rolled her eyes in disgust. Brondo returned her look with a death stare of his own, which only served to frustrate Sheena all the more. Sheena was not paying Brondo the respect he deserved, and he knew it. But to Sheena, it seemed all of her poor behaviours were totally justified. Same for Max. The more he thought about it, it seemed to Brondo as though no one could be held accountable for their actions in the Baxter house...and Brondo was becoming pretty fed up with it.

Max sauntered in the door with Layla, mid afternoon; his eyes were bloodshot and his pants hung low around his waist, gangsta style, it looked like he hadn't showered in days.

"Get your ass in this living room here *now*, Brondo," Sheena barked. Max slumped on the couch, belligerently hanging one leg over the armrest, knowing that it annoyed her.

Sheena was fuming; she laid into Max about the whole visit to the station and his suspected involvement in the robbery.

Brondo was surprised by her sudden firmness with him.

"You are going to get clean, and get off the drugs or whatever you and your brother are doing," she said, laying down the law to him.

Max scoffed, full of attitude. "I'm not on drugs," he said casually, and turned to look at Brondo. He smirked. "You hearing this shit, Man? Mum's gone off her face, she's off her dial!" Brondo had to laugh; just looking at the kid's stoned face, if anyone was off their dial, *he* was. Sheena turned on Brondo.

"This is serious—and this isn't a laughing matter," she glared at Brondo. "The police questioned *us*, Max; do you know how *embarrassing* that was, having to lie for you and stand up for you when I know the truth? And as for you, Layla, well...I expected better."

Layla got riled up. "What are you accusing me for? I didn't rob the place!"

"Maybe not—but your brother did, and that makes you an accomplice. What does that tell you, stupid girl?" Sheena said, becoming even more heated.

"We aren't stupid, Ok?" Layla spat back.

Max got angry then. "Let's go—get the fuck outta here, it's a dump, man. Fuck this shit," he said and dragged Layla by the arm out of the house.

Thomas was next to walk through the door; clearly he was on something, all red eyed and dosed up. Sheena was distressed and overwhelmed to see him in such a state.

"Thomas, my baby Thomas, what have you done?" Sheena said, reaching out to hug her son. Thomas resisted, immediately going on the defensive.

"What are you on about?" he asked, annoyed.

"Your eyes, they are so red and bloodshot, you're on

something." But Thomas was clearly not in the talking mood and stormed off to his room. Sheena looked over at Brondo for help, but he remained quiet. He felt hopeless and helpless.

"What do I do, Brondo?" she said, exasperated, lifting her arms in the air in surrender. She felt so defeated and stumped.

"Get Seedy involved, he is their father too and he needs to take some of the responsibility," was all Brondo could offer. But Sheena just lifted her arms and shook her head.

"He won't give a stuff," she said, "He never cares, never gives a stuff about these kids—it's always just about him and his selfish ego."

Brondo couldn't understand how a father could be so cheap and distant with his own children; not that he didn't understand this in some ways too—his own father had been like that.

"Perhaps they'll listen to their uncles, your brothers, they seem to get along," was all Brondo could think to suggest. She just shook her head.

"No—they can't help, and I don't want them involved knowing all this stuff anyway, Brondo, no way."

"Well we can't do this alone; it's an impossible situation and it's bigger than both of us—you need help, Sheena."

"I'm so sorry, Brondo—you didn't sign up for this and yet here you are, I love you so much," she said, tears in her eyes. Brondo cradled her in his arms, touched and affected by her comments. But deep inside he knew he couldn't get past the situation; he was fast losing himself, losing touch within himself—he was losing his identity, struggling to grasp at reality. Once again he found himself looking back on everything in his life; where he had come from, where he had been, and how on earth he had gotten to this point.

Over the coming weeks things got worse, much worse for

Sheena and Brondo. Max and Brondo were arguing more and things in the house were so tense between them, it was just pure hell. Brondo deliberately took to working more night shifts to avoid Max, with Sheena becoming frustrated at seeing less of Brondo.

One day in late July Brondo walked in the door, and, upon seeing Max in the kitchen, decided to make the offer of his hand, reach out to shake the young man's hand, hoping Max would see the gesture as a peace offering. Max turned, refusing to shake. As Brondo turned his head to walk away, Max king hit Brondo smack in the head. Sheena gasped as Brondo fell to the floor, hitting the tiles, out cold.

"What the fuck did you just do!" Sheena screamed, rushing to Brondo. "He was only offering to shake your hand!" She wailed, rushing to call an ambulance. Brondo woke up in the hospital with a fracture to his cheek bone, drugged up and on painkillers. He was livid and wanted to kill her boys now, and he threatened Sheena to kick her son out or he would involve his family.

Sheena was emotional and hit back. "So now you're asking me to throw my son out, or you will have him beaten up, is that right?"

Brondo was ropable and screamed back at her aggressively from his hospital bed as best he could with a broken face. "He has fucking hit me and cracked my face, Sheena! And I did nothing! How can you defend that cunt and still claim to love me? You've put him first every fucking time, and it's your fault."

Brondo wanted to strangle Sheena right then; the blood boiling in his veins was about to explode. He was a pressure cooker about to combust.

"You're basically asking me to be a punching bag and accept

this level of abuse—while your boys run around on drugs, being criminals and taking cheap shots at me...assaulting me? What if I smash his face in...what then, you fucking hypocrite!" he screamed in full explosion. His jaw pained and ached but it felt great to offload; in that moment he started realising that maybe he had just substituted one crazy family for another. He felt cursed, jinxed; what mysterious force was it out there was it that had been punishing him since birth? Crazy as that sounded, that was how Brondo felt in this moment; he started doubting himself again, feeling that his life wasn't really his own, and he began struggling with reality, unsure whether it was him or the drugs he was on that was doing his head in.

Sheena accused Brondo; she said she thought he loved her for her, and that she couldn't be the bitch he was now making her out to be, because he was in love with the soft, kind Sheena that he had come to know and grown to love. Brondo did love her, but he could feel her manipulative pull at work again, softening him, guilting him into staying.

When they got home, Thomas and Max were both on the couch and down in the dumps, heavily under the influence of the ICE drugs they had taken. They had both lost their jobs, had bought and sold multiple cars and now they were wanting to borrow Brondo's car, forcing him to walk to work. Since the boys began using it, Brondo had been pulled over by the police multiple times for an inspection of the car. The boys had racked up speeding fines and the car was now known as a drug related vehicle to the local police. The boys had been joyriding around in it as far as Phillip Island and Cowes, Seymour and St Kilda, too. They would meet with "chefs" in Melbourne, also known as drug manufacturers, doing deals and taking her out on the freeway at dangerous speeds. The police were now targeting

Brondo, asking him what his involvement was with with Max and Thomas Baxter.

"I'm in a relationship with Sheena Baxter, their mother," was all Brondo could humbly reply. The police officers both looked at one another and let him go, as one of the officers looked back over his shoulder at him, making the comment, "You poor bastard—we feel for you, mate."

Brondo was beyond humiliated now, and he was starting to hate himself. After the police drove off he began talking out loud to himself.

"What the fuck's wrong with me, God? Please, please, forgive me for my sins, forgive me for my stupidity—I am weak, I haven't got the strength or will power to walk away from this relationship. Please, help me," he prayed in sheer desperation. Brondo sat there for an hour in his car and he just cried.

When he returned home, he decided to tell Sheena that the police had pulled him over yet again, suspecting there to be drugs in his car.

"I can't keep doing this, Sheena, I feel like I am at breaking point."

"Oh, grow up, Brondo," Sheena retorted nastily, turning on the vacuum cleaner to drown him out. Brondo became frustrated and started yelling at her over the noise; why did she always do this, why did she never listen to him? Sheena turned around in a moment of pure anger and punched Brondo in the face, flooring him. She hit him side on, causing him to fall to his knees. Brondo got up, the stinging red welt visible across the side of his face. He got to his feet, glared at her, tempted to slap her back. But he had been raised never to raise his hand to a woman, so with no other choice left to him, he walked out. The level of respect, he thought, was atrocious; he wanted to release himself from the grip she now had over him, he wanted out of the relationship. He went down to the lake, not knowing what else to do. It wasn't until he put his hand to his face that he realised he was bleeding and that his fracture had been aggravated. Brondo was hating on Sheena so bad he just wanted to leave. But, he was so trapped, too. He wished he had gone to Cyprus the year earlier and he regretted not going; he wanted so badly to go to sleep and just wake up and have everything be alright again, but this was mere fantasy, pure nonsense. And he had nowhere to go; so eventually, after his jets had cooled, he knew he would have to go back, face Sheena again.

After much soul searching he quietly returned home; as usual Sheena was waiting with open arms, kissing him, apologising for her attack. It was the whole yo-yo affair happening again; and once again Brondo softened, as she lured him to the couch, offering to pour him a Coke, his favourite drink. Brondo, she knew, had a weakness for soda, while Sheena just loved to drink; it had always been a coping mechanism for her, a way to escape her childhood traumas.

Brondo had some Coke and Sheena topped it up again, offering him more. His head began to spin. Within minutes it looked like the floor was moving, the walls were caving in.

"What is this, what's in this?" Brondo asked, suddenly feeling woozy.

Sheena laughed. "Nothing babe, it's just a strong taste with coke," she said, plying him with more.

When Brondo was half passing out on the couch Sheena began unzipping his jeans. Brondo tried to push Sheena off him, muttering that he was angry with what she had done, but he was too weak against her advances. Sheena helped herself to him, determined to get what she wanted. She was the dominatrix, overpowering his submissiveness. Brondo always been submissive and she playfully slapped him twice across the face, but he was so numb he barely felt it. Whatever was in his drink was now in his system, simultaneously taking him over, just as she was. She slapped him again, then placed her foot across his chest and pressed, lifting her foot onto his mouth, taunting him about how she and Max had caused his fracture, mocking him for being unable to handle the alcohol and drugs. After she was done with him he leaned forward off the couch, throwing up all over the floor. She laughed, threatening to rub his face in it later.

Hours later he awoke, groggy and drunk. Sheena had her feet splayed across his lap and he noticed he was down to his boxers.

"Do you know what I just did, Brondo Violaris? I just violated you; I humiliated you, and do you know why? Because you were going to leave me, weren't you?" Brondo could barely make out what Sheena was saying; the earth was spinning—or, was it his head?

"I've been *such* a naughty girl, Brondo," she seethed, "You remember what I did to you?" She just kept asking. "Now that I've been a bad girl, you're going to have to punish me and send me to my room, tie me up on my bed until I learn my lesson," she crooned.

Brondo couldn't believe what was happening to him. He felt like a piece of meat, a broken toy; he was a piece of used furniture, nothing more useful than a footstool. He felt broken and violated, like his soul had been raped a thousand times until it shattered into a million pieces, until there was nothing left of him. He was her slave now; he had been broken down bit by bit, until he had become fully submissive to her, nothing more than a plaything to be controlled, abused. That was how Sheena liked it. And she knew he'd keep quiet now, too; he'd play along with her fantasy, protect her boys, submit to her will...because his life was on the line and he knew it. He was slowly connecting the dots and coming to the realisation that all along he had been fearing Seedy, fearing Max; but now he knew that he had been a complete fool, because all along he had been fearing the wrong person.

And the truth shall set you free...

CHAPTER ELEVEN
Connect The Dots

2 Corinthians 4: 17
For our light and momentary troubles are achieving for us an eternal glory that far outweighs them all.

August was fast approaching and Yaya Andromachi and Uncle had just returned from three glorious European summer months in Cyprus. Brondo had big regrets that he'd decided against going on account of his relationship with Sheena, and imagined how much more fun he would have had, if things had been different. He had been terrible at keeping up with his family, too; he hadn't even spoken to Vito in probably seven months or more, so sapped as he was by Sheena and all her family dramas.

Brondo had been estranged from his immediate family for years; his mother and father, brother and sister in law all lived on the outskirts of Melbourne, but since he'd moved in with Yaya their communications had slowly died off. Vito's 30th birthday was fast approaching and he knew he needed to push himself in an effort to make contact, because he knew there would be a big traditional Greek pannychis, an all night feast and party in his honour, to celebrate the occasion and as was typical of large Greek families, he knew they would all be there.

The problem was that Brondo hadn't been speaking up to his family; he had sworn to himself not to involve a single person in his difficult life, for fear that they could ever be hurt. And so, over the weeks and months that passed, Brondo had slowly retreated into himself, feeling very alone with no friends or family in Scarborough to speak of. And Brondo was no fool either, to the role Sheena had been playing in separating him from his family. She never spoke about his family or asked him about them, and if ever he did say he was going to reach out to Yaya or Vito, Sheena would be quick to discourage it, or distract him temporarily, until it slipped his mind. But as the situation became more dire between Brondo and Sheena, the more she tried to keep him from his family, and the more she tried to drive a wedge between Brondo and his brother. He was starting to realise what was happening here. Sheena had isolated him beautifully and oh so gradually over time, and he wasn't liking it one little bit. No. Sheena had just played her last ace.

Brondo told Sheena that he was going to Melbourne with or without her, despite her efforts to stop him. He told her that he wanted to visit his grandmother alone, but Sheena was only too happy to go, despite the fact that Yaya no longer held any good opinion of the woman. Yaya was too much of a lady to tell her to her face, and she would never say anything in front of Brondo to embarrass him; but Yaya had her own subtle ways of sending disapproving messages in Sheena's general direction, but only when they were alone together. Yaya called Brondo up one day and told him that Vito was having his 30th birthday party in Port Melbourne and that she hoped to see him there. She never mentioned anything relating to the inclusion of Sheena, and Brondo became well aware of the silent non-invitation he could read, in between the lines. But Brondo was super excited about seeing his brother for the first time in over a year; he couldn't believe all that had happened or how much time had passed, and they had a lot of catching up to do.

The date was set for the big party: August 7, 2010. Despite Brondo's concerted efforts to dissuade Sheena from coming Sheena was hell bent on attending, with or without an invitation. She was apprehensive, too, for the first time in their relationship; through Brondo's stories of his mother, Sheena knew how strong willed and aggressive his mother could be—and if she was anything like Yaya, who herself was as tough as any Greek woman around, then Sheena had every reason to be scared. Brondo reassured her that she would be fine, but Sheena wasn't sure, because Brondo had foolishly, previously told his mother about Sheena, unwittingly twisting the knife in her back; he knew too, what his mother was like, especially when provoked, and that they were both two strong willed women to be reckoned with. Sheena tried to deflect her fears.

"Brondo, your mother's short like your grandmother, I'm not going to be afraid of her!" she said, laughing off creeping feelings of intimidation.

"My mother's not as short as you think, " Brondo retorted, wondering what height had to do with anything, anyway. "In fact, she is the tall one in the family and she is almost tall as you, how do you think she managed to have a tall son like me?"

But Sheena only laughed condescendingly at him, unbelieving of his claims, and Brondo sat, quietly frustrated by her blatant show of arrogance and lack of respect for his word.

"Fine—don't believe me or listen to me, then," he said,

infuriated by her. Brondo could get so easily annoyed now by Sheena; she was always making out that she knew more than him, and more often than not it would be about something she knew nothing about. She had never met Brondo's mother, Maria; yet she claimed to know his mother better than he knew her, himself. It was ridiculous. There was just no point in arguing back.

Max and Thomas were still doing drugs and barely home; in fact they had been coming in at all hours of the night, and Sheena still let them borrow the car while Brondo was at work. He had been juggling several jobs just to survive; washing cars, maintenance work, the odd security job. He had recently lost his job at McDonald's because the stress of home life was now affecting his employment.

The day of Vito's birthday they left Scarborough and drove down to melbourne in the old Commodore; Sheena had booked the motel in Coburg they had frequented when they first met. The drive itself was uneventful, although Sheena had been awfully quiet the whole way down. Brondo was worried that, despite all that he had been through with Sheena, that he was still being lead like a lamb to the slaughter. He hoped that with the passing of time his family had forgotten about the bad things and would be able to view their relationship in a renewed light.

How wrong he would be.

They arrived at the motel; it was a lowly, cheap room, and Brondo cringed when he saw the disgusting filthy surfaces covered in grime; on top of that there was no hot water or amenities, no heating and the carpets were dirty and looked like they hadn't been vacuumed in years. Brondo spied several huntsmen spiders running around, making their homes in the corners of the room and Sheena screamed and ran out the door in her bathrobe, to Brondo's brief amusement. Sheena was incensed by his laughing at her in such a moment and his lack of display of empathy. She cursed him for it, whacking him around the head for not being more sensitive to her feelings.

But it was hard for Brondo to show Sheena any respect these days; Sheena certainly wasn't showing him much respect and was quick to jump on him, criticise him for the tiniest thing.

At Sheena's insistence, Brondo went to complain to the motel staff; he was very upfront and matter-of-fact, handling the issue with just the right amount of aplomb. The manager apologised and admitted their hot water system was slow, but Brondo shouldn't have been so surprised, for the motel was on Sydney Road in Fawkner next to Coburg, and in one of the most undesirable areas, near the airport.

Soon they were headed down to Beaconsfield Parade in Port Melbourne for the party; the venue was in a lovely beachside location and Brondo was excited to see his brother and catch up with his family. Sheena was unusually nervous, nervous like hell, and she started drinking in the motel room. Then, as Brondo drove, Sheena pulled out a second bottle of liquor and kept drinking in the car. Upon their arrival, Brondo was immediately greeted by a sea of familiar faces, many people from his former church congregation and life house church; there had to be a good two hundred people there, possibly more. He raced over to hug his brother and then introduce Sheena, before going off in search of his mother, grandmother and sister in law. For the first time in many months Brondo felt excited, uplifted and peaceful in being surrounded by so many of his family. Maybe the time had come, he thought, to heal the wounds of the past. He saw his mother and father and hugged them more than was necessary; his mother Maria clung to her son, overjoyed. He shook his father's hand, and although relations were still cold and awkward between them, they managed a civil meeting. Brondo was happy to see him, but in true, emotionless fashion, his father callously asked, "What's wrong with you?" which surprised Brondo.

"What's wrong with *you*?" Brondo's mother Maria bit back at her ex husband, furious, in defence of her son. "I haven't seen my son in over a year—what's your excuse?"

Brondo's father, Bill, was a real piece of work; he had memories and flashbacks of the man who had been violent and abusive towards his mother, growing up, and he didn't blame his mother one bit for her ongoing resentment towards him. Sure, they had been divorced now for many years, and although it should by now have been water under the bridge, old pains and bitterness died hard there.

Brondo left them to be, and after introducing Sheena to his parents he wandered off into the crowd to meet new people, but not before having one last dig about his mother's height.

"See—what did I tell you about my mother? She's not short, she's almost the same height as you." Sheena was surprised and caught off guard and just made a face at Brondo, to which Brondo replied, "Well, why didn't you just believe me in the first place?"

Brondo hated that Sheena didn't listen to him—but enough of that, tonight was about celebrating his brother's birthday party, and he wasn't about to let a little spat with Sheena ruin it. Within moments Brondo saw his sister in law, Sonia and they hugged, happy to see one another. Brondo immediately noticed the prominent stomach bulge under her lovely black dress.

"Yes, Brondo—I have some amazing news to share; we're pregnant!" She said, glowing.

"My God—this is the most wonderful news! You're going

to be a mother! I can't believe it, Sonia—you are going to be a mum, an amazing mum, oh God! I can't wait, this is beautiful!" Brondo exclaimed, genuinely thrilled for them.

"Yes—and *you're* going to be an amazing uncle," Sonia replied, equally joyous.

"Do you know what the sex of the baby is, or do you not want to know?"

"No we want to keep it a secret, a surprise."

"Good—well, what an exciting time you have ahead of you! Couldn't have happened to a better couple," Brondo said, kissing her cheek. Brondo was ecstatic; he knew how long Veto and Sonia had tried for kids and finally they were living their dream.

The night was a great affair; Brondo was enjoying himself for the first time in ages; he was having such a good time that he had completely forgotten to take care of Sheena, stay by her side as she'd asked him to do. He looked around at the party and the sea of faces, but Sheena had disappeared. When he realised she was nowhere to be seen he became anxious and walked out of the bar to call her phone. Still unable to locate her, he walked out into the parking lot. Sheena had made herself scarce alright; Brondo walked up to his car and found her lying across the back seat, fast asleep and rotten drunk. He opened the car door and tried to wake her, but the stench of vomit made him dry reach. He was so angry with her, he started to cry. Sheena had embarrassed him, let him down at his own family reunion, and he had let her down as well. To make matters worse, his father had been lurking nearby, and upon seeing Brondo, walked over to the vehicle. He saw the woman passed out cold on the back seat.

"What's wrong with this woman? Look at her—she's drunk and making a fool of herself, and *you*," his father said, angry.

Brondo couldn't find much to say, because he could only find himself agreeing with his father for once on something. Brondo felt so disappointed. His father didn't liked Sheena, in fact not many did; Bill had met her once before too, the year earlier when Brondo decided to make a go of things again with his dad. But his father was a cold, harsh and judgmental man who, for all his faults couldn't be fooled. And things between father and son hadn't improved much in a year, either; Bill was so critical, and Brondo could never do anything right in his eyes. Brondo had decided that, after all the efforts he had made, he had no energy left to give his father any more chances. And now Bill had even more ammunition to be disapproving of his son, enjoying the moment to shame him.

"Just what are you going to do with her?" Bill continued, "She's too old for you, she'll never have kids with you, just look at her, she's a mess!" The ouch Brondo felt wasn't anything he didn't already know, and despite his father's frankness, he knew he was right for once.

"Brondo, a woman letting herself get that way is just a disgrace—your brother's having kids now; don't you want that too one day?"

Brondo was hurting, he was shattered; he felt that he had been trying to make a life for himself away from the judgment of his family, only to fail miserably. Now they judged him even more. He loved Sheena, but he needed to get away; and the strong feelings he'd had in his need to protect her were now coming undone as he realised he needed to start protecting himself. He was disheartened upon hearing his father's words. The truth stung.

"Come over here, look at this," his father continued, walking around to the rear passenger side of the car. "Just who hit the car?"

Brondo was miffed. "What do you mean?" he asked, genuinely surprised. His father was furious. He had bought the Commodore for Brondo years ago; it had been the one thing Brondo felt his father had ever done for him over the years. Brondo walked to the passenger side and looked at the back end, where his father was standing. He looked at the crumpled damage to her body. Someone had definitely hit the car, but Brondo could only think it hadn't been him; he had barely had a chance to drive it these days anyway, and if it had been him, then surely he would have noticed it before now.

"She got drunk and drove it and hit it, didn't she? His father said, and Brondo sensed that this was more of a statement than a question. It must have been one of the boys, Brondo thought to himself. It was only logical explanation, because Sheena was always ensuring the car was washed and cleaned and that the insurance and registration was all sorted; Brondo knew she was always on top of these things. It didn't make sense that she would hit the car and not inform him of it, either; no, this had to he Max's handiwork. Max had been suffering seizures as a result of his tumour lately. Perhaps that was it. Max had probably been under the influence of drugs and seizures, and this would have caused him to lose focus and crash the car. Brondo could see it all happen in his mind's eye. But, where and when did this happen? Did Sheena know about it? Was she covering *again* for the boys? It was bad enough that the car was known as a drug car to the Scarborough police; and now this.

"By your reaction just now, I'm gonna guess you had no idea, did you? She is playing you, Son," his father said, looking at the drunken body in the back seat.

Brondo felt his face grow red and he couldn't decide whether the burning sensation was coming more from humiliation or a deep internal rage. He couldn't deal with her—with them—anymore, and he told his father nothing more than that he would sort it all out. He congratulated his father for the good news that he would soon become a Papou, Greek for grandfather, and his father just nodded, forced a smile and walked off without another word.

Brondo made the rounds without Sheena in saying goodbye to his family; he kissed Yaya and hugged Uncle, he promised his mother and father he would make more of an effort to stay in contact, see them more often; he kissed Sonia and congratulated his brother who was now a soon to be father, thanking him for always having his back; and he briefly said his goodbyes to old church friends who he hadn't seen in forever. He formed fake smiles for everyone to let them know he was doing ok—but inside he wasn't ok—he was dying and crying, because this night, his life—and everything in it—was moving around him in circular motions and he felt as though he was on a merry go round that he just wanted to get off.

The night ended and Brondo drove back to the motel through the dark midnight streets of Melbourne; he was in complete silence with the exception of a disoriented Sheena snoring in the back seat. He felt a quiet blanket of anxiety and depression envelop him as he drove; something had to change, he thought...something had to give. That night he slept fitfully in the filthy room next to her; it repulsed him. She smelled of alcohol and vomit. In the early hours of dawn a still drunken Sheena would wake him, trying to act out her stupid dominant fetishes, grabbing at him, jerking him, relieving him. Brondo lay there feeling disgusted with himself, then, briefly, sexually relieved, then disgusted all over again. Was real love meant to feel like this? he wondered.

The next morning they awoke; Brondo got up and showered while Sheena lay there half naked, looking like shit on a plate. He got a call from his mother asking him meet her and her partner Joe one last time, just for a quick lunch before heading back to the country. Brondo thought about waking Sheena, then thought better of it; let her sleep it off, he thought—he'd rather go by himself, anyway; save himself from the risk of any further embarrassment. He left her a note saying to sober up, that he'd be back to collect her by two o'clock.

He met up with his mother and Joe, lying that Sheena was under the weather, though secretly relieved she wasn't there. He needed time to work on his relationship with his mother; Brondo decided he needed to give his mother more of a chance—maybe he had been wrong about her, perhaps she had changed for the better. It seemed a year away from each other had done them both the world of good. And Joe was proving to be good for his mother, too; Maria glowered with a newfound radiance as she sat there with her love by her side. Brondo wanted that; selfishly he wanted that happy glow of love more than anything in the world; he wanted the happy, expectant smiles of his brother and sister-in-law; and he wanted the merriment again of family gatherings that, while he could be the first to admit came with their own set of problems and had their own elements of dysfunction—while not perfect, could still be good. But most of all, he wanted his mother's glow, he wanted to find his own glow again; not the drunken glowing haze that he woke up next to and that smelled like chuck.

The party was well and truly over.

CHAPTER TWELVE
Rock Bottom

Genesis 13: 14
*When I was down to nothing,
God stepped in and gave me everything.*

There lingered a quiet and newfound peace in his heart, for Brondo was happy to have finally made amends with his family. But the drive back home to Scarborough with Sheena was a nightmare and they were barely speaking because of Sheena and her hangover; she was a pressure cooker just waiting to blow up at any mention of his suffering at her hand.

"You completely ruined my weekend with my family—and you have just embarrassed the hell out of me in front of my entire family and friends, Sheena!" Brondo said, rightly fuming, and Sheena watched his face twitch in profile as he drove. They were the same facial twitches she'd seen in his mother, too.

"You know, you're still as cute as all hell when you're angry," Sheena said, trying to smooth corners while sporting the world's biggest hangover.

"Stop trying to change the subject," Brondo grumbled. He was well aware of her manipulations now, and they just did not work anymore.

"I don't see what the big deal is, Brondo—it's not like I'm the first person to have ever gotten drunk at a party, you know. You're a lot more like your mother than you think," she said plaintively, holding onto her thumping temple. "*And* she has the same facial twitches as you, too."

This stung Brondo; he had had a lifelong battle with his mother's dominance and control, and prided himself on the fact that he was *nothing* like her at all. Where she was dismissive, he engaged and listened; where she controlled and railroaded, he wanted to be a model of support and understanding. No, he was nothing like his mother. Except for the facial twitch. But that was a generic trait that he couldn't help. What did Sheena know, anyway? He was annoyed by anything Sheena said on the way back that day; if she had pointed out the sky was blue, he would have been annoyed by that, too. "The twitch, yes, my mum's had a hard life; she was battered in the past by my lowlife dad, and that *affects* a person, Sheena—*you* of all people should know *that*," he said sternly. "You and my mother also have more in common than you realise," he pointed out.

"Ok, don't get so defensive, grumpy pants."

Brondo was frustrated by Sheena's inability to have even a simple discussion; he had told Sheena many times before what his father was like growing up, yet Sheena never even heard him, or never listened, or both.

"Look, it might be better if we just ride in silence," Brondo said, thinking he would actually prefer it that way. The silence was looking more and more beautiful to him these days.

Sheena knew she had some makeup work to do on Brondo;

he was still majorly pissed at her weekend antics, getting drunk and embarrassing him.

"Look—I shouldn't have drunk so much—but you left me on my own, what was I supposed to do?"

"Ok, I admit: I should have stayed by you more, but I was excited to see my family, Sheena! We see your family, your mother all the time, and I haven't seen mine *in over a year!* Plus, you're a big girl, you always seem to be tough and can take care of yourself," he bit back. Funny how she could play the dominating bitch one day and femme fatale the next, he thought to himself. He noticed how easily she could manipulate the situation right now to make *him* feel guilty, when he'd done no wrong. As though it had been his fault that she felt so isolated, that she'd needed to get drunk. He shook his head; he knew the reality was, it had nothing to do with him. He was so soft, weak and gullible. She could get away with anything, he thought. He snuck a sidelong glance at her now as she was busy applying lip gloss in the car's little visor mirror. Something felt off in his gut and he didn't know what; it was just that his instincts were speaking to him again, and he knew he just couldn't fully trust her.

"So, you also didn't have to have the sulks and walk off, you could have stayed with me. You're the one who chose to leave—and you're the one who decided to get shit faced! Also: who hit the car?" He shot back, glaring at her.

"Max had a seizure and hit the car—God, this is why I didn't tell you—because you're unreasonable," Sheena said sarcastically.

"I'm unreasonable—I'm unreasonable? Your son crashes my car, you don't have the decency to even tell me about it—but *I'm unreasonable?* Come on, Sheena—even you can do better than that," Brondo said, fuming. "Well if I'm so unreasonable, why did you fall in love with me? You're the one being unreasonable:

I can't even ask about my car—you keep it a secret about who hit the car, and you can't even tell me the truth? Even my dad noticed it; and I had to cover, tell him it wasn't you, while you we passed out on the back seat!" He yelled back at her.

Now she was crying. Now she turned on the tear taps. She always knew how to make him feel bad, as though she were the one worse off.

"Ah, whatever," Brondo muttered, disgusted. "It just needs to be fixed, Ok."

They drove home in silence. If Brondo were any less of a man he would shake her until she came to her senses, could see reason; that was how far she had pushed him, as a man. But he couldn't be that person, he couldn't be violent like he had seen his father be towards his mother growing up; it just wasn't him. He kept quiet, kept his thoughts personal and private, because he was fast becoming restless with Sheena, and he no longer wanted to share his whole self with her. He had to learn to protect himself, he had to stop being so vulnerable and gullible with her. They walked in the door two different people, Sheena announcing she was going to go visit her sister, leaving Brondo home alone with Ally and her daughter's friends.

"What's wrong?" Ally asked Brondo, sensing the tension between them.

"Nothing to worry your pretty head about—your mother and I just had a little blue, that's all," Brondo replied, playing it down.

Ally's school friend Maddie wanted to hang with Brondo; she always told Ally that she liked Brondo and thought he was cool. She threw popcorn at him now across the kitchen table, being playful. It lightened the mood and Brondo let go of things and they laughed. Ally got up and asked if he was hungry, she was going to make some nachos and watch TV, if he wanted to hang with them. Brondo nodded but deep down he was depressed, thinking about what he wanted and truly needed from his life.

When Sheena returned a few hours later, she had seemed calmer; although when she saw Maddie throwing tennis balls at Brondo and laughing and whacking his leg in a playful manner, Sheena became furious again. Brondo thought nothing of it, he just saw it as the girls mucking around.

"Leave him be!" Sheena barked at them and they instantly stopped playing around. She asked where the boys had gotten to, but Ally just shrugged and said she had no idea.

Eventually the girls headed out the door, saying they were going for a walk.

"Make sure you're back before dark," Sheena sang out to them. She looked across at Brondo, tried to think of something to say to break the ice between them.

"Looks like little Maddie there has a crush on you—she likes you, can't you tell?" Sheena commented sarcastically. Brondo, sensing a spike of jealousy in her tone, retorted, "No, not really—I think she just likes me 'coz I'm a cool guy, that's all."

"Look—I've had some time to think about it, and I want to apologise for blaming you for my drunkenness—I spoke to Max just before on the phone and I've told him he has to fix the car, too." Brondo's ears pricked up.

"Oh yeah? What was his response?"

"He claims he didn't do it, and that he would remember if he did," she said, shrugging. Brondo rolled his eyes.

"Typical," Brondo said, over it.

"God, you deserve better than this—" Sheena began, tears welling. "I'm so sorry my son did this to your car, babe—you deserve better than this. I am so sorry; I can be a bitch sometimes too, can you forgive me?"

Brondo felt her sincerity and once again he forgave her; this was the soft, honest side of Sheena that he loved; he just wished he could see more of it. He didn't care that she had her wild sexual side; he didn't care that she could sometimes have outbursts, it was Ok to be human. What he couldn't deal with was her using her power over him and abusing it. Because she did abuse it. She sought out his weaknesses and abused him.

"Ok, well things are going to be different from now on," Brondo said calmly. "I want to see more of my family—it's my mum's birthday in September, and I want to go to Melbourne and see her," he asserted.

Sheena nodded; and so, come September they travelled to Melbourne again for Maria's birthday. Brondo would take his mother to her favourite little Greek restaurant in Carlton; through the course of the dinner something was said about Brondo's not being able to pay for the whole dinner because his job didn't pay well enough and that he wasn't good at saving his money. He and his mother had their first argument since things had made a turn for the better; they started to fight at the table, Brondo telling her that he was sick of her putting him down, telling him that his job wasn't good enough, that nothing was ever good enough in her eyes, that she always made him feel like a failure. Sheena sat back and watched the whole thing unfold; Brondo was seething, he had had a gut full and asked Sheena to get up, they were going to leave. But Sheena just sat there, not moving.

He couldn't believe it.

Why was she like everyone else in his life? No one respected him, everyone ignored him. Sheena took him outside and asked him to calm down, and he reminded himself that he had come down to make the effort at a new relationship with his mother. It was hard, but he had to try. He went back inside and resolved things with Maria, but Brondo was still angry that Sheena had deliberately ignored him when he had asked her to leave. He was disappointed too, that his mother still knew how to push his buttons, that they still had the ability to bring out the worst in one another. More than that, she had the ability to make him feel so low about himself, and so guilty; he was angry that he got no respect at all from his family. He was just seen as a failure, because he still wasn't saving money, still wasn't being the successful son that Vito had turned out to be. And he was just sick of feeling crap about himself. They had no idea how hard he worked, or how generous he was, all the money he spent on Sheena's kids, helping Sheena. They knew nothing. And he didn't tell them.

They stayed for the whole weekend because it was the first week of the AFL finals and Brondo's team, the Sydney swans, was playing. Sheena agreed to stay and they decided to forgo the dumpy old motel for The Quest hotel in Preston; it cost a little more, but it was far more decent than the filthy room they'd had to endure on their last trip. Brondo payed for it all. The hotel. The shopping trips, the meals out. Ally and her new boyfriend had come to Melbourne too, and Brondo got lumped with paying for their dinners, too. Ally was now nearly eighteen, and had found herself a boyfriend; a promising young AFL prospect with a big attitude, Jarrod Jones.

Sheena's boys were by now full blown ice addicts, their heads screwed up beyond comprehension by all the drugs. They were violent and abusive and Brondo worried, his head was all over the place in terms of how to deal with them. Sheena typically didn't want to talk about it, preferring to keep her head well and truly stuck in the sand. On the drive home with Sheena snapping at Brondo over little things, he pulled over in Nagambie, just forty minutes out of Scarborough. Frustrated with her nastiness, he told her that he struggled with the fact that Sheena could produce such a vile human being for a son.

"He's a drug dealer, a drug user—he's full on Seedy's son, he's just an arsehole like him, following in his footsteps, Sheena—it's time to facts."

Sheena slapped Brondo across the face.

"Get used to it, Brondo!" She screamed. "He's not perfect—but he's *my* son, he is MY son, get it?" she repeated. "My son, my son, my son, drug user, my son!" She said, screaming in his face.

"Shut uuuup!" Brondo screamed back, and grabbed Sheena by the hair, screaming shut up over and over, serving up his own style of madness back upon her. Sheena cried out in fear and punched him in the face and Brondo let go his grip, realising what he had just done. He whacked Sheena in the arm till she cried and she screamed a blood curdling scream again at him and hit him in the back of the head. Brondo then sat back in his seat, and, frustrated, put his hands on his head. He felt tired. He felt defeated. He slumped back into his seat and looked out the window and broke down. He cried and cried until Sheena put her arms around him and told him she forgave him.

"It's ok, it's ok—" she said, stroking his hair, trying to soothe him. "I punched you in the face first and made you bleed—let it go, honey, let all of your emotions out now; we'll calm down, then we'll drive home," she said.

Brondo waited a minute then turned the car's engine back on and drove home. After a short while he looked across at Sheena; she had fallen asleep. He lost control of his emotions and began crying again, thinking about their physical altercation. He was hating upon himself, for he had done the one thing he'd sworn he'd never do: he raised his hand to a woman. Sure, Sheena had been hysterical and out of her mind, screaming—but he had no right to do that.

Sheena awoke and sat there staring at him; she gave him a look that said, 'hey, well, you brought that upon yourself.' He felt like he was the scum of the earth, and right then he wanted to kill himself.

"Pull over here," Sheena said, spotting the Nagambie pub. "Let's go there for a nice meal—come on, let's go." So Brondo stopped the car and got out and they went into the pub for pies and pasties, a salad and some drinks. The footy was on the big TV screen, and Sheena suggested they stay and watch a bit of the game, Carlton versus Sydney. Brondo's team lost by five points, but he was happy that he'd seen such a close game. Sheena was disappointed, too, and they drove home discussing the finer points of the game.

Back in Scarborough Brondo returned to work, but he was so riddled with guilt, anxiety, heartache and depression. He could not get the altercation out of his mind. He could not believe that he'd lost control like that, or that she had driven him to that point.

His mindset at work was terrible, so much so that he walked off the job site where he had been working as a casual truck detailer. He went off to the bathroom and he cried so hard and for so long that his anxiety levels went through the roof and he ended up making himself sick. It was a hot December day and the sun beating down on him had made Brondo dizzy; at one point he became so disoriented that his body spun around and he lost balance and fell down, almost to the point of nearly blacking out. Brondo was hoping for death, because he just felt like he couldn't cope anymore. He loved Sheena and hated himself for hurting her; but he couldn't control his frustrations anymore, they were bubbling over now, and he felt like a failure, a loser who couldn't get his life together. He had hit rock bottom and just wanted to die.

In desperation, he reached out and called his mother; he hated the idea of calling her, for she had her own set of health problems and was popping Xanax tablets for some kind of bipolar and psychosis she now suffered with. His mother could be the most loving and gentlest soul with a heart of gold, but other times she was hot and cold, even violent when provoked. Her moods were wildly inconsistent, much like Sheena's. He didn't care; he was now desperate, and he needed to talk to someone that he felt he could trust.

"Mama, I need some help—things are not going so well here with Sheena," he said nervously, praying she would be good and kind to him, not judge him this time. But she was no help, in fact she brushed off his concerns with nary a care.

"I can't help you Brondo, I have my own problems," she said, sounding cold and distant. Brondo realised that perhaps his mother truly didn't as care much for him as she made out; maybe she revelled in always seeing him fail. The truth was, Brondo had always been a punching bag for her, since she took out everything Brondo's father did to her on him, and Brondo always found himself on the receiving end of things, the one to cop the brunt of her frustrations. He hung up the phone and took a deep breath, returned to the factory floor and got back to work.

The day ended and Brondo waited for Sheena to pick him up; they said very little and returned to the house where Brondo went straight to shower. Sheena had started making dinner when he came out to join her.

"I love you," she said, "but what happened yesterday can never happen again, or else we will be over," she said, looking hard at him. Brondo felt ashamed.

"Well I don't know what to do anymore; I feel that I can never please you—you always ask me to be more assertive and aggressive as though I'm not manly enough for you—but when I do try to take the lead, you squash me. I want to be more forceful with you, but I don't know how."

"Well not in that manner, not by manhandling me," Sheena replied.

"I'm so sorry," he said again. "I don't know what else I can say. All day I was depressed, I made myself sick. I don't know how to get past this, the pressure's really getting to me. I feel that you don't respect me, and you push me until I crack; I, I don't know what to say—" he said, looking at her sadly.

"Remember me punching you, Brondo? I could inflict that kind of punishment on you again, you know. Don't push me, either," she said, kicking her shoes off to the floor. "You can start by making it up to me right now with a foot massage."

As usual Brondo gave in to her demands, disgusted with himself for being so weak. His self esteem had flown out the window, and his dignity along with it. Sheena continued to control him with her sexual manipulations and Brondo was too weak to resist her; now he had the additional guilt hanging over his head for his actions, which she lorded over him. Depression hung over him like a heavy cloud full of rain; were they God's tears, he wondered? Was He crying for him, too? Brondo submitted to her fully, knowing he was indebted to her, he owed her, and she owned him. At a more personal level, he needed to prove to himself that he wasn't his father's son, either; he was no wife beater like Bill or Seedy—because he was better than that.

Brondo focused on getting himself together by working harder and saving money. He was working hard juggling three jobs and paying bills, and Sheena would take his bank card while he was at work and spend most of it on shopping. Brondo felt frustrated but tried to keep calm about it.

"Babe, how are we ever going to save money and go on a holiday if you are spending my entire weekly wage on shopping?"

Sheena automatically flew on the defensive. "You do realise there are five mouths to feed under this roof, right?"

"Well babe, come on—I hate to say it, but your two sons are nearly twenty-one; surely they can find work and make money too? They make more than us both doing what they're doing now anyway, and we can't keep supporting them—it's not fair."

Sheena sighed. "Here we go again," was all she said. Brondo could not get through to her: this woman was a brick wall. He left well enough alone and gave up. Brondo got up to walk out the room, thinking it was better not to fight and Sheena turned on him. "Where are you going? Ok, fine, then go on, walk away," she baited him.

Brondo was sick to his stomach. Something had to give. He decided he wasn't going to give Sheena any more money; his credit card had grown and the card was now maxed out to its limit. He owed the bank $1600 and interest rates had gone up too; and now his car was damaged, and she was spending all his money on unnecessary shopping. Brondo started to secretly plan to walk away from Sheena once and for all; he started looking for full time work in Melbourne, applying for various positions. He looked at a job for a repair technician, and another one in trades telecommunication work; all sorts of jobs were out there, and some even offered the training necessary for him to enter into a traineeship.

In the middle of September, Thomas and Max burst through the door looking terrified. Brondo had never seen their faces so white. They just stood there in the hallway pleading with their mother.

"Please, Mum! Help us! John Holm is coming, and he wants his money!" they both cried, looking scared shitless.

Sheena didn't seem fazed, however; the boys had smoked shit, done ice and God knows what else—and she knew they'd been dealing too, selling for the underworld, mainly bikies and outlaws, so she didn't take the boys seriously. But they pleaded with her; they owed Holm several thousands of dollars and had no way of coming up with the money. Now though, he was threatening to come chase them down for it. Brondo was secretly pleased for the first time; he didn't want harm to come to Sheena's sons, but he knew it was high time they paid a price for their actions; they had to learn a lesson somehow, they had to learn that people couldn't keep saving them.

He also felt he could walk away now and be free of Sheena, wash his hands of her and her motley crew. He had served his sentence and he needed to move on with his life, and he knew the only way to do that was to start afresh. Brondo had secretly been fielding several phone calls for possible job leads; it was keeping him sane.

Sheena came into the bedroom and pushed her hands onto Brondo's chest, pushing him backwards onto the bed. Then she straddled atop him so he could go nowhere.

"What are you doing, what was going on?" was all he said.

"The boys are in trouble, they're scared—John Holm is out to get them," she said. Brondo tried to not to look gleeful; he tried not to feel anything, because she could read him so well.

He did feel sorry for the both of them, but he also felt overjoyed that finally God had seen to it that they were getting a taste of their own medicine.

"Who's John Holm?" Brondo asked.

"Oh, some weird boy they knew growing up; actually, he's a really obnoxious prick, a show-off, they never liked him, " she said, laughing. "I told them he's only one person, what's there to be afraid of? But they were both crapping their little panties! My God—you boys can be such worrywarts sometimes, such drama queens!"

It did strike Brondo as odd that they could be afraid of one guy when there were two of them; they'd never been too scared to shoot their mouths off to Brondo and his brother, way back when. Like Sheena, Brondo found it mildly amusing, but kept his thoughts to himself. He wasn't going to be around here for much longer anyway, and he didn't care anymore. Well, he did care, but he'd always cared too much. And he was finally figuring out how to care less, like Sheena did. He would give them as much respect as they showed him. No more, no less.

A week later there was a knock at the door; it was a Saturday afternoon and Brondo was home alone; he got up and answered the door and was met with a tall, 6'3 young man of athletic build. He looked fit, but lean, and his face was menacing.

"Where's Max and Thomas?" he asked. Brondo guessed this to be Holm, whom they'd been running from.

"They aren't here," Brondo spoke boldly and plainly, guarding the door. Brondo showed no fear, and Holm just stood there, sizing him up.

At the first hint of trouble, Brondo was ready to start swinging; he didn't give a shit who this man was, he'd take him down all by himself.

Eventually Holm stood down. "Tell them Holmy is looking for them," he said then walked off.

Brondo closed the door on the man and took a deep breath; in his imagination he had seen it all; Holm would beat Brondo until he was left for dead in the hallway, lying in his own bloodbath. He saw a new war on the horizon that he wanted no part of, and he didn't want to get caught up in any of it.

That night Max and Thomas were near breaking point; Sheena sat in the kitchen with them and they showed her the threatening messages Holm had been sending. Brondo told them that Holm had paid a visit, and that they'd better pay up, or he'd be sending his army around.

Sheena tried to downplay it. "John's just a kid you guys went to high school with—he's no threat, this is just all hot air and big talk."

"Mum—you don't know John Holm, he's changed: he'll come to the house, he'll hurt us all—Brondo too. " Sheena was still unfazed though and couldn't be convinced otherwise. There were shadier characters in town than John Holm. She even knew the kid's mother from their school years; he was nothing but a big Mama's boy.

The next day Brondo had to walk the seven kilometres home from work, from one end of Scarborough to the other because Sheena had the car. When he got to the house he was surprised to see Sheena already there and his car in the driveway. The entire front of the house had been smashed in and vandalised with baseball bats.

"Jesus Christ!" Brondo said, shocked. He hated using the Lord's name in vain, although sometimes there was a time and a place for it.

"Fucking bastards!" Sheena swore. "Because they couldn't

find the boys, so they trashed the house. Thomas was hiding in the bushes, he saw them and he told me John didn't come alone, there were several cars. I've got their father, Greg Holm's number somewhere inside, I'll go call him," she said and ran inside to get her phone.

What's wrong with these *people?* Brondo thought, incredulous.

Sheena came back outside, madly inputting Greg's number into her phone.

"Well, the boys did warn you that this guy was serious and he meant business—but you never listen, do you?" Brondo said, furious. He was so sick and tired of Sheena's excuses. She looked back at him in shock.

"What happened to the man I fell in love with?" she asked. But Brondo didn't care.

"He got sick of not being listened to, too—" Brondo shot back sarcastically and walked off, leaving her standing there all alone, in front of the house.

Brondo went back inside; he thought it was laughable that Max should be so afraid of this guy and running from him after all the pain and heartache he'd inflicted upon Brondo. *What goes around, comes around,* he thought to himself. He walked into the kitchen, grabbed a glass and filled it with water.

Whatcha gonna do now, Sheena? he thought to himself. *You've let your son abuse me, and I've let you use me and abuse me—and you've never shown me the respect I deserve, you've just treated me like shit—and now you want my help? Oh, the irony of it!* He laughed to himself. It was the kind of deriding laugh that came out of him now; the kind of laugh meant only for criminals, or the insane.

That night they gang bashed another one of Max and Thomas'

friends, Lester Holt as he sat in line in his car at the McDonalds drive thru. They opened his door, pulling the unsuspecting Lester out of the car and beating him to a pulp on the sidewalk. Lester would be hospitalised and later diagnosed with serious brain injuries, and word spread around town of the horrible acts of violence committed upon an innocent young man. Max and Thomas took it as a clear message from Holm that they would be next, because the money deadline had already well and truly passed and they hadn't shown up with the goods. These guys were out for blood, and they weren't going to stop till they got their hands on Max and Thomas. By this stage any girlfriends the two boys had, had long disappeared, though Max still had a thing for Layla Stanton.

The boys were running scared now and they played hide and seek about town, hiding out in the back yard of friends' homes, ducking in and out of Sheena and Brondo's place for bread and basic food supplies. Brondo felt himself second guessing his decision to walk away from Sheena as he felt compelled again to save her from this mess; he, better than anyone, knew the horribleness of what it felt like to feel rejected and abandoned at the hands of family turning their backs on him. It was such a deep and gut-wrenching pain that he never wanted to inflict on anyone. So Brondo chose to stay, hoping he wouldn't pay dearly for decisions he'd made.

Two weeks passed; it was a calm night in early October and the winds were still; Brondo awoke to the sound of noises coming from down the hallway. He poked his head out of the bedroom door to see Sheena's boys running down the hallway in the middle of the night. They ran down the hall, out the back sliding doors into the yard, leaping and clearing the fence into the laneway. Puzzled, he checked that the front door was locked and returned to bed. Sheena awoke, asking what was going on. She grabbed him then and hugged him tight.

"Oh God, Brondo—I don't want to lose you, I can't lose you—please, God, not now, please God," she begged. Brondo had never heard her say the word God so many times in one sentence. But before he could answer, the heavy pounding sound of a fist came at the front door. Then a voice.

"Police—open up, we have a warrant to obtain entry. Police! Open up—"

Brondo grabbed his jeans hanging over the chair, pulled them on and raced to the door to meet with two police officers in blue.

"Do you know of any drugs on the property?" they commanded, flashing their badges. Brondo stood there, horrified, his heart pounding as he shook his head. Sheena was silently relieved to see that it was the police, and not John Holm. Brondo was confused, because now they were not running from Holm, but from the police, too.

Sheena came running to the door in her night gown, yelling out, "There are no drugs here, no drugs."

"This is Constable Fisher, and I am Sergeant Collins—we'll be brief here; we are now pursuing your sons for drug related crimes—and we have warrants for their arrests; we know about the war going on in the streets of Scarborough, and your sons' involvement in a drug trafficking operation. Now, do you know of their whereabouts?"

"No—God no!" She exclaimed, frightened.

"You do understand that you are required by law to disclose their location, should you come into this information? Or you will be seen as assisting, aiding and abetting a crime?"

"No Officer? What is that?"

"It means that, even if you are not the principal offender, if you help or assist another person in the commission of a crime, you can be found guilty of a secondary offence, by association," the second officer explained.

"Oh," was all Sheena could say. Brondo thought she could be pretty dumb, sometimes. But, then so could he, he thought, for staying with her.

The following Tuesday was Melbourne Cup Day, 2010; the first Tuesday in November, it was a day Brondo always looked forward to, because it was a national holiday, and he liked taking the day off to relax and place a bet, maybe get lucky with a win or a place.

But this Tuesday he was sick—real sick—he had low blood pressure and gastro and was running with a high fever. Layla, Max's on again, off again girlfriend had come back to the house and was now staying there permanently; she felt she had to save Max from his enemies. Layla walked past the bedroom and saw Brondo.

"Hey, Sheena just left and mentioned you were feeling sick? I hope you get better—I can make you some chicken soup, if you like?" Brondo nodded, it hurt too much to speak.

While Layla was in the kitchen, Brondo could hear the key turn in the front door; he knew it couldn't be Sheena, because she wasn't due to finish work for at least another six hours, and as for Max and Thomas, they were in hiding. In his weakened state, Brondo got up to see who was at the door. He stood in the hallway in his boxers, and there he saw the shadow of a tall man coming in. He was stunned and horrified, frozen to the spot in a dreamlike state. John Holm and a few Bikies walked right in the house behind him; Holm came up to Brondo's face, taunting him with the key.

Holm waved the key in Brondo's face in a threatening manner. The other two bikie guys cornered Brondo as John got right in his face; in a panic, Brondo raised his fist, but John simply told him, "You're an Ok guy—we got no beef with you; but where the fuck are Max and Thomas?"

"I —I don't know," Brondo stammered, petrified. He felt so weak he could barely speak. Layla cane around the corner into the hallway and screamed.

"Get out! Who are you? I'm calling the police!" she cried. Brondo didn't know what to do, he was unprepared and unarmed in the face of two thugs. Max and Thomas had done this; they had jeopardised Brondo and Sheena's safety, thrown him and their own mother under a bus. Brondo heard Holm threaten to trash Layla's car as he walked back outside, but just then Layla's uncle drove past and she ran outside to alert him, crying, "Uncle! Uncle! Help! Help! and Holm and the thugs jumped in their car and sped off.

Brondo was speechless; he felt his life was in danger now. Layla rang Sheena for Brondo, and relayed what had just happened. Sheena came home early from work to face a shivering Brondo sick in bed, still with a fever.

"We're in too deep now, Sheena," a sick Brondo whispered, his voice so hoarse and sore. "I'm going to have to go buy a sawn off shotgun from somewhere, the underground," he said reluctantly. "We can't keep being sitting ducks like this; Max and Thomas have endangered our lives. We have to take matters into our own hands now, 'coz we're fools if we don't."

Brondo told them to keep quiet about it; he sent Greg Holm a message on Facebook saying he would take whatever precautions were necessary to and protect Sheena and her daughter. He knew that he should just walk away from this toxic poisonous relationship but he didn't want to be branded a coward, didn't want to take the easy way out, right when things had gotten worse than ever. He wanted revenge.

Holm sent a threatening message back, warning that Brondo shouldn't sleep, 'coz the thugs would come again like prowlers in the night. Brondo was speechless. He felt defeated and defenceless. He hid the shotgun under the bed and hoped like hell they wouldn't be back.

Sheena got word that the boys had fled to Melbourne and Queensland in hiding. But, as usual her boys couldn't leave well enough alone, and they returned to Scarborough to cause more trouble. Holm got the tip off that they were back; an ex-friend told him their exact location—a run down, boarded up old house in the middle of a field out in the countryside. It was in the middle of nowhere; Holm and the Bikies jumped in the car and sped out there. They started kicking the door in, and Thomas and Max attempted to make their getaway, with one friend staying back as a cover, a decoy. That friend got a pummelling from Holm too, and ended up hospitalised for the severe beating, all for ensuring that Max and Thomas got away.

But that night Brondo and Sheena got a phone call and were told that Thomas had been caught and bashed rather badly. Brondo's heart was in his mouth; he may have resented her boys for all the bad things they did, but he never wished evil on anyone. He leapt out of bed in the middle of the night, sick as a dog, and drove around town asking anyone and everyone whether they had seen Thomas Baxter, even calling out his name.

Sheena was eternally grateful, swearing that Holm's blood should be bottled.

In the morning they called around to all the hospitals, asked if Thomas had been admitted anywhere; Sheena was hysterical and beside herself with worry until they received the news that it hadn't been Thomas at all, but another kid bashed in a case of mistaken identity. Brondo and Sheena went home relieved, but when they went to bed, Brondo found it impossible to sleep. The stress was just too much; he was sure that these thugs would get to him soon, yet at the same time he didn't care anymore. He no longer had the energy to fight. He lay there in the darkness of the room looking at the patterns the shadows made on the ceiling— Sheena and her boys would be the death of him, he thought, and he had no one to blame but himself.

To make matters worse, he and Sheena were drifting apart; their relationship was unravelling and falling apart at the seams, and his heart just wasn't in it anymore. He had done his best to try to protect her and do the right thing all along, but it had all just come to nothing.

Brondo began to feel the end was near and he was prepared to meet his Maker. He dared not involve his family; he wanted no danger or harm to come to them, nor did he want to be seen as a failure. But the truth was, he *did* feel like a failure. All his life he had been a people pleaser, making terrible decisions that served others and never himself; and all of these mistakes, all of these poor decisions would bring about his own undoing. More than that, his life now lacked meaning, it lacked purpose; and so Brondo started to prepare for the end—he was ready to meet God, his faith in the Lord Almighty growing in his veins. Yes, this was his destiny, he had failed at life on earth.

He must have drifted off to sleep, because Brondo awoke in a daze. *Why am I still alive?* He wondered, surprised. *Why didn't the thugs come to get me, or why didn't God come to get me? What are they waiting for?*

He dragged himself out of bed and showered and went to work, dragging a heavy cloud of grief behind him. He got into an altercation with two other workers, and threatened to pound their faces in. The supervisor had to intervene, and told Brondo to take the day off, go home. He had too much on his plate and couldn't focus on anything, he just lived in a permanent state of fear, wondering when the thugs were going to come back.

But miracles do indeed happen. And when the police called to say they had arrested Holm and his thugs on the Great Victorian highway in a kidnapping attempt, Brondo fell to his knees and thanked God for this one small miracle.

The Judge would sentence Holm and his mates to fourteen months prison time, with no chance for parole. Sheena texted her sons telling them they could come home now, start over, get off the drugs and get back to a normal life, as Holm was in jail. She had also taken out an IVO intervention order on Holm, just to be sure.

Brondo was amazed and stunned at how God had come through for him. Wow. God delivers. But he kept this thoughts private as he usually did, though he could feel this chapter of his life was coming to a close. They went to bed, and Sheena took Brondo's face in her hands, and facing each other, she looked at him gently through the darkness.

"Wow, it's over, isn't it," Sheena said, rhetorically, in reference to the arrest.

"Yes. Yes, it's over," Brondo replied, referring to something else entirely.

CHAPTER THIRTEEN
A Fraudulent Life

Matthew 24:4
And then Jesus answered and said unto them:
take heed that no man deceive you.

"Karma finally got you, didn't it, Holm?" Sheena posted on Facebook.

She loved moments like this, revelled in the fact that she could gloat and rub it in. She loved the sweetness of victory and revenge and could slay any man with her nasty tongue.

Brondo, however, didn't like her rubbing it in. While Sheena was always the one lecturing to Brondo about the fact that he need to ignore things and let things go, she could never take heed of her own advice. Brondo often picked up on just how hypocritical she could be; and while he knew she had the upper hand and Holm was now done for and locked behind bars, he thought she was foolish to antagonise him further, because that was just asking for trouble. Yes, they were finished etc., but they were behind bars now and there was just no need for anything else. Why not just be happy and have peace, let sleeping dogs lie? Brondo thought.

Max and Thomas came home and for a few weeks at Sheena's insistence they tried to kick their drug habits, but sadly after a few attempts they relapsed and fell back into the drugs and things got nastier then they had ever been before.

Max was smoking ice freely in front of everyone now, and it got to the point where police raids on the house became the norm. Brondo wondered how he had gotten himself so tangled up in such a bad drug scene; he had been clean all his life, had never once committed a crime. He felt embarrassed and ashamed; it was demoralising to be living in such an environment, associating with such serious crack heads—but he had zero control over it and there seemed to be no quick solution to him getting out of it, either.

Sheena broke down and begged her boys to please stop the drugs. After the police left Sheena started on Thomas, begging him to see the light, to change his ways.

"Mind your own fucking business, whore," Thomas screamed at her with bloodshot eyes, violently pushing Sheena up against the wall. Brondo charged down the hallway and got between them both, and Thomas turned on Brondo, throwing his fist out wildly, just missing his broken jaw that had only just healed from the last assault.

"Leave Brondo alone!" Sheena screamed wildly, lunging over Brondo's head with an attempted swing at Thomas' face. But Sheena, for all her roughness still fought like a girl, and Thomas side stepped, returning with another swing. Brondo, desperate to shield Sheena from her son, stepped in between them, taking a punch to his rib cage. They were all hysterical and Ally and Thomas' sometime girlfriend, Amy Fox came running down the hall screaming at them all to stop, or they'd call the police again.

Thomas was out of control; with all the ice still in his system he had turned into a sad excuse of a young man who was down and out with a drug addiction that was ruining his life.

"What happened to that little boy I raised, where did he go?" Sheena wailed in true desperation. "Max, your bloody brother, is the one to blame for all this—if he'd never started drugs you wouldn't have been introduced to it, either," she said, tears in her eyes. She marched in the bedroom and began screaming at Max that this was all his fault, as Thomas stormed out the front door.

"Shut the fuck up, bitch—or I'll fucking kill ya, I swear!" Max blew up, threatening his mother. Brondo had never felt more helpless; he didn't have the energy to put himself in the firing line again and fight Max, and Max knew they were both afraid of him now. He faced off against her, pushing himself up into her face, the drugs in his system making him feel powerful, invincible.

"I can't just stand back let you bash your own mother," Brondo said, only he knew he couldn't fight Max, either. So he tried to talk sense into him instead. "I won't let you hit your mother—" Brondo repeated slowly, hoping that the words would be enough to de-escalate things. Max glared at Brondo, raising his bare fists at him as he wobbled from the drugs, trying to maintain a stance that looked like he was ready to fight.

"I could smash you so easy—" Max gurgled.

"I would like to see you try," Brondo thought, but said nothing, knowing it would only inflame matters.

That night Sheena and Ally got into an argument, too; Ally was getting older and also showing her mother less respect these days. Brondo had no idea what it was over, but he witnessed them out in the back yard as their yelling at each other quickly degenerated into a near fist fight; in frustration, Sheena shoved Ally, then her daughter in turn pushed her mother back. They were about to get into it when Brondo raced out and intervened. He stepped between the both of them, and both women started crying hysterically. He put his hands on his head and walked back into the kitchen, completely fed up. He went to reach for a soda, and seeing Sheena's bottle of Jack Daniels, grabbed that instead. Brondo was not normally a drinker, but all of this was taking its toll. He walked down the hallway to the bedroom, skulling the whiskey straight from the bottle. It was so powerful it almost made him gag. He wondered how she could possibly drink the stuff; it was toxic, like pouring gasoline down his throat. But he didn't care anymore; it was Friday night, and he didn't have to go to work the next day anyway, so why not get shit faced like everyone else in the house already was, he thought.

Brondo fell asleep on the bed; things between Sheena and Ally had settled and the house was now quiet except from the sounds of the movie they were watching. Brondo was by now pretty drunk, but he stirred upon hearing his name being called.

"Brondo," Max called out. "You awake? Hey—you wanna make an easy twenty grand?"

"What do you want, Max?" Brondo mumbled back, half pissed.

"Look, Man—sorry about today, but hey, we can make easy $20,000. Are you interested?" Brondo sat up and listened to the scam Max now presented.

"All you gotta do is tell the Australian taxation office, the ATO, that you got ten primary school kids and ten high school kids—and they'll give you a grand for each kid." Brondo had never heard such nonsense, and he looked up at Max in his drunken state.

"Max—that's stupid, man," he slurred, "they've got my information on a database—and they *know* I don't have twenty kids…I'm not even old enough to have that many kids!" Brondo laughed, threw his head back on the pillow. "It's criminal mate. Just criminal."

Max laughed though; he told Brondo how him and his mate, Shawn Horton, had pulled it off, plus a couple of other mates. Nonetheless, Brondo shook his head.

"Yeah, Ok, whatever, Max—nah. Not interested." Sheena had now heard the conversation and walked down the hallway to tell her son off.

"Max that's so brain dead stupid—my God, what do you want, to wind up in jail for real this time, and take Brondo with you? Jesus, is that what you want?" She said, skulling her Jack Daniels.

"That's enough to land you in federal prison, which is nothing like a normal prison, mate; that would be a federal crime if you went through with it. Don't do it." Brondo warned.

Sheena grabbed Brondo's paperwork with his tax return details and lodged pay slips and receipts and took them out of the room and Brondo went back to sleep. The next day Max and Thomas had been out and came home in the afternoon, gloating about how they had $5000 in cash.

"My God—when are you boys ever going to fucking learn? I don't want drug money in this house!" But the boys boasted that it wasn't drug money; the Commonwealth Bank had made an error, a glitch in the system, to which large sums of money had been mistakenly deposited into customers' accounts.

"You will still have to pay it back, don't think you'll get away with it," Sheena warned. But the boys didn't care, though; all they cared about was the here and now, and the fact that they were rolling in it.

In the coming days, the bank's computer glitch had made national headlines. It was just a week before Christmas, too, so even though the boys knew they would eventually have to pay it back, this did not register with them—and they went around town on a spending spree, buying themselves Christmas presents.

Right before Christmas, Brondo's mother announced that she and her partner Joe were coming to make a visit. Brondo knew that Joe was as tough as nails, and if the boys played up in front of him he would surely belt them both. Brondo knew Joe to be lethal; he may have been small in stature but he was well-built and as strong as an ox. Brondo just prayed that the visit would be uneventful and that nothing would happen; the last thing he needed was his mother knowing about the boys' drug problems.

Maria and Joe arrived for lunch; Sheena was at work, so Brondo showed them around town, taking them for a pleasant walk by the riverfront before stopping by the pub for a hearty chicken parmigiana for lunch. He sent on Sheena's best regards and they left in the afternoon. Sheena came home from work, mentioning she had gotten her tax return in the mail. Brondo wondered why she should be getting hers before him, when he had submitted his a month before her. Another two weeks passed and strangely he still hadn't received it; why it was taking so long, he wondered? But he waited it out, reasoning that it was probably due to the holidays and the end of year rollover. In January Brondo finally got the envelope in the mail; it was post-dated, but he recognised its stamp coming from the ATO. He expected he would probably receive a cheque for $3000, given what his year had been like. He opened the envelope, instead seeing it was a letter addressed to him. It informed him that he had acquired a large debt from the taxation office, one debt in particular incurred for a $9000 penalty. He stood there and began shaking, the letter trembling in his hands. He was so stressed out he couldn't see; the piece of paper became blurry before him. This couldn't be right; he couldn't understand what had happened, and thought he had better make a call to them first thing Monday morning when they re-opened.

"I got my tax return," he said to Sheena that night at the dinner table. "It doesn't make any sense—it says that I owe them to the tune of $9,000 —but I know this can't be right, I know what my yearly earnings have been," he said, baffled by it all. Maybe it was another mistake, just like the recent mistakes the banks had made. Sheena was no help, she just shrugged and went about cleaning up the kitchen.

On Monday Brondo also received a phone call about a stolen ATM card having been reported in Coburg; the CCTV footage they said, showed images of a short and stocky man, his face half covered in tattoos, trying to access Brondo's debit master card at a hole-in-the-wall. To add insult to injury, Brondo received another phone call, recorded for security purposes, stating that he was now under investigation for tax fraud with the federal government, having compromised himself. Brondo sat down on the sofa; he was crushed by the news and broke down, putting his head in his hands. This could not be happening, he thought. He cried out to God in frustration, asking for help; then he went to Sheena to ask her how this could have happened. Sheena's face turned ghostly pale.

"Oh God no—" she began.

Brondo's heart felt like it was going to stop.

"Babe. I am so sorry."

"What?" Brondo said, his mouth so dry he could barely speak. Sheena said nothing and began entering numbers into her phone.

"What??" Brondo said with increasing urgency. He listened to her as she spoke into the receiver.

"Max," she bellowed, "DID YOU USE BRONDO'S TAX FILE NUMBER FOR YOUR SCAM?"

Sheena was furious, her face burning red as she turned back to look at Brondo. Max laughed on the other end of the line, joking about whether the cheque had come through yet. Brondo felt sick. In the days that followed, he could not eat, sleep or speak; he had reached breaking point, could feel himself turning into fragments of himself, shattering all over the floor. He had to think: he was going to be under investigation, possibly indicted for tax fraud. He sat quietly with the realisation as it loomed before him. Jesus! What was he going to do? He would throw Max under the bus, that was for starters; he was done with the kid this time, it was the final straw.

It was New Year's Eve and Brondo wept and went to bed early; he was in no mood to welcome in a new year, especially not now, and especially not with Sheena. She was pissed at Brondo, telling him he needed to make more of an effort with their relationship; in desperation, she had suggested that maybe they could go back to where it all began two years ago at the Coburg Motor Inn, recapture the spark they once had by reigniting exciting memories. Things would surely get better again, she said. But Brondo was fast realising that this was what she always said; yet the sad realisation was that things never got better, they never turned corners, they never found a sense of normal and he had never found the peace and love he had so long hoped to find with her. How much more could he take?

Sheena was especially attentive that night, and the next night and the next. She pulled out all the stops; nice home made meals, ice cream and a romantic movie. She suggested they watch The Notebook, one of the first movies they ever saw together. The next couple of days were nice and enjoyable and peaceful enough, but it was while driving to Brondo's grandmother's place that the final nail was driven into the coffin. Sheena confessed to Brondo that she missed the good old days, where they used to sneak around, where he put his life on the line for her. She loved the element of danger. The thrill. Brondo went quiet; he just sat there and listened as she went on and on about all their dramas, all of the exploits that had consumed his life for the better part of two years.

"Plus, your family don't like me, only your Uncle Chris has ever shown me any respect," she prattled on. That wasn't the case, he knew that; but Brondo felt defeated, he wanted to argue with her, but there was no point—because they always arrived back at the same old dead end street.

True; his family had made life difficult at every turn, especially so when Brondo wasn't around. Their nasty looks and cold attitude towards her had not helped; and their cruel judgment of his life and Sheena's family had not been right, either. But, he realised: this was not his biggest problem. It was the manipulations, the sneaky attempts to get Brondo to go out to the shops or get Brondo to pay for new furniture or have Brondo give over his car, work three jobs, pay all the bills, stand on his head, break his back, doing everything for them—only to be abused by her entire family and bled dry financially, until he had nothing left but his sanity—and, not even that, he realised, because even his sanity was hanging by a thread these days, and barely had that intact. No. He was losing his mind. It had all been just a ruse. He had to get out.

The drive home was the same old, same old; his family would show Sheena enough pleasantries on the surface, then they would say things behind their backs. Brondo would suffer the long drive home, where Sheena would complain about them, that she didn't want to go anymore. Brondo would argue how little they saw his family, compared to hers, and it always ended up in a bitch fight, with days afterwards spent not talking.

"And, just look what your family has done to me," he said when they got home. "They've ruined me, but do you see me complaining about your family, the way you complain about mine?"

For once, Sheena admitted that he was right, but that she had no control over it—to which Brondo replied, "Well, I got no control either."

Coming home, Sheena complained of having some pains in her back; she later had heart palpitations, so Brondo, stressed out, called immediately for an ambulance.

"This is what killed Nan and most of my dad's side of the family," Sheena uttered, panicked and teary eyed. She feared she had inherited her father's bad genes, which had a family history of heart conditions. Brondo was wary and accompanied Sheena to the hospital; he spent the night by her bedside and called Varma to come in. Varma was at the hospital within twenty minutes.

"My daughter! My daughter! What happened!" Varma cried. Brondo tried to calm Varma, who herself was now in her eighties. He calmly explained that Sheena had complained of chest pains; that, combined with the back pain raised the alarm of a possible heart attack. He explained they were running tests now, and would know more in a day or two. They both sat in silence next to Sheena for hours like that, neither one speaking, quiet and only with their thoughts.

Sheena would be discharged two days later; the results showed nothing, although they commented that her blood pressure was unusually high for her age, and to take it easy.

But as soon as they got home Sheena was upset to see the boys still on drugs and coming and going in the night; they had lost a lot of weight and Sheena tried booking them into a drug and alcohol rehabilitation centre. She reached out to the boys' girlfriends, asking them to help, but nothing could be done; the boys were both twenty-one now and of legal age, and the rehab centre said it would be up to them to make the adult decision. Sheena went to bed and cried and cried, and Brondo tried to console her, reminding her that it was in her own best interests not to get upset, for the sake of her own health.

March rolled around, and Brondo's date with the ATO crept up on him; he had to appear at their head office in Spring Street, Melbourne. He was expected to appear in front of a panel to discuss the allegations and the investigation he was under.

They drove down on the Sunday afternoon prior, planning to stay overnight in a hotel close by, and would discuss the particulars of his appearance.

"I want you to play dumb—make it appear you know nothing about the fraud, protect the boys, whatever you do. Don't slip up or implicate them in any way—it would be the death of them, Brondo; my boys would go to jail!" Sheena pleaded with him in earnest.

Sheena dropped Brondo off outside the tall grey building on Spring Street early Monday morning; she kissed him and said she would be back in the afternoon to collect him when it was over.

"Good luck!" Sheena called out as he left her behind by the sidewalk, engine idling. Brondo took the elevator to the thirtieth floor, nervous and not knowing what to expect. He walked apprehensively through the large double doors and into the office suite; there he was instructed by the receptionist to sit and wait. Wait he did; the time felt like forever as he watched the hands of the clock go around and around on the wall until his nerves were frayed beyond measure. Brondo had no legal representation; he wasn't even aware of what his options were. He basically had to just give his side of the story as to what happened, and hope for the best. He had been sitting there like that for so long and was so nervous that he didn't even hear the teller call out his name and number.

"Brondo Violaris," she called out twice to a numb and frazzled Brondo. He stood up and a sick feeling swirled in his stomach; his bad anxiety was kicking in.

Moment of truth he thought, this is the moment of truth. One more round, one more round. 'I can do this, I can do this,' he said to himself, though the truth was he didn't think he could. He pictured himself telling all. He pictured himself coming undone, throwing Max under the bus and pleading for mercy. Serve his fucking right, he thought. After all Max had put Brondo through, this was the final straw. He took a deep breath and walked into a large room where two men were waiting for him.

"Please take a seat," one said, while the other retrieved the file. The seated one explained that the interview would be recorded and he was required to answer all questions.

"It seems that a fraudulent claim was made in the last six months under your ATO—were you at any time aware of, or involved in, this activity?" The first suit asked.

"Nnnn—no, no, it wasn't me, but go on," Brondo stammered nervously, honestly. He didn't want to stutter; he thought it made him look guilty.

"Well, then someone got a hold of your tax file number and made the claim that you have twenty children—ten high school and ten primary," they said.

"That's fucking ridiculous—it's absurd," Brondo said angrily.

"Well, only a fucking idiot would dare make that kind of claim—and you clearly don't look like a fucking idiot to us," they said.

Brondo replied that he had nothing to gain by committing such a gross and blatantly fraudulent act—and why on earth would he risk doing such a thing, when he considered himself a law abiding citizen with a clean record who had never broken the law in his life?

The two men asked him once more, "So, do you know who did this to you? Because they would need to have had access to your taxation information, or banking details or similar. Someone you know, perhaps? An ex, a disgruntled work colleague?" They hinted, fishing for information.

Brondo pondered that, if ever there was a chance to bury Max once and for all, it was now. He thought about the damage he could inflict on the kid. He'd be put away for awhile, at the very least. He thought about seeing Max's face behind bars. He could hear Sheena's voice pleading with him when he was back in the car with her. This was it.

"No," he replied softly, "I don't know who it was—I got no idea who would be stupid enough to do this, because I don't associate with fucking idiots," he said, point blank at the two men. He sighed. He couldn't do it. He'd failed again.

The men looked upon Brondo trying to ascertain whether he

was telling the truth; they knew that they would have to let him go, as they had nothing left to go on for the time being, though they tried to press him again and again with the questions until Brondo got so annoyed that he told them he wasn't a criminal, and didn't appreciate being treated like one.

The meeting over, Brondo left; he decided on his way out the door that he would involve the tax ombudsman and old resentments resurfaced with regards to Max. The stress poured out of his body as he left the building; as far as things stood for now, the investigations would continue and Brondo would have to just wait and see how it all unfolded.

Sonia was just days away from giving birth and Brondo thought about how he wished he was in a more normal relationship; a healthy relationship like his brother's, where the biggest dramas didn't involve criminal plots, but babies and marriage and all the good things in life.

Instead, they drove home to Scarborough, returned to the same old dramas and nightmares they'd left behind a day earlier. Thomas had taken off again; according to Amy Fox the police were pursuing him for new drug related criminal activities and he had gone on the lam. Brondo just rolled his eyes at her and excused himself to go lie down. His life had turned into a daytime soap opera, like Days of Our Lives—or worse, some crappy reality TV show like Desperate Housewives, or Big Brother. It was all he could do to laugh—he had to laugh now; laugh as maniacally as Sheena always did; it was either that, or go completely mad.

Brondo got up again an hour later and went into Max's room. He wasn't going to get off that easy, Brondo thought.

"You fucking did it, didn't ya?" Brondo said, enraged at a drugged up Max who was sitting cross legged on the floor.

Max, in a drug induced state, emerged from the bedroom with a golf stick; he raised it to Brondo's face and told him he was going fracture his jaw again. Brondo just stood there waiting for it, daring him on, and Ally raced down the hallway and stood between her brother and Brondo, desperate to calm the situation down. Ally too, was at her wit's end; she knew all about her brothers and their criminal ideas and she was similarly fed up. She threatened to call her boyfriend Jarrod, who was at that moment at the hospital attending to his sick father who was battling cancer—or she'd call the cops. Jarrod was a smart ass, though he and Brondo actually got along, because like Brondo, Jarrod couldn't believe how crazy Ally's family was; he even told Brondo to call him by his footy nickname, 'Spider,' as a sign of friendship.

"Back off, Max, or I'll stick the cops to you so fast—" Ally threatened, trying to defend Brondo. Max continued to wave the golf stick around erratically.

Brondo stepped away from Max and went into the kitchen, trying to ignore him while messaging Sheena as to what was happening. Sheena messaged she was on her way home and to chill the fuck out and stay away from Max.

When Sheena got back, dopey Max was still in his room, smoking Ice. Brondo stayed in the kitchen and Sheena went out the back, drinking. Moments later, Max appeared in the lounge room, his pupil's as wide as golf balls. He came at Brondo aggressively, taunting him, his demeanour wild and threatening.

"Come on, let's end it right now, you fucking Greek wog cunt—you don't deserve my mum, cunt."

Brondo stood up and Max had one hand around the golf club, while with the other he made clenched fist; Brondo, in a panic, grabbed a butter knife.

"You come near me and I'll put this knife in your fucking brain tumour," he yelled, sick to death of the brain dead lowlife. "And *you* don't deserve a mother like Sheena!" Brondo screamed back, murderous with rage. Max lunged forward to attack Brondo but Sheena intervened and called the police. Brondo was hysterical; the police arrived in minutes and sided with Max's story. They took Brondo out the front door, instructing him not to resist or they would have to arrest him.

"Arrest me? What the fuck for? I didn't do anything! Take a good fucking look inside at that doped up, bloodshot, Ice addict! That's who you need to fucking arrest!" He was hating the police right now; he needed someone to listen to him but the butch police officer was abrupt and rude, looking at Brondo like he was the perpetrator, as though *he* was the menace. Sheena came out to the sidewalk; Brondo looked to her for help but she barely spoke, her emotions were frayed. Brondo hurt; in the moment when he needed her, she was never there. The police ordered Max to vacate the property and go to Seedy's house; after a few minutes they let Brondo go with a warning.

Max went to Facebook and the threats started up again.

"I'm gonna get you, stupid wog," Max messaged, threatening him.

"You think you're gonna steal my tax number and commit fraud and get away with it? I'm gonna kill you, Max," Brondo shot back.

Both quickly came to their senses and deleted all evidence of the posts, fearful of retribution. But the threats were out there. The threats were real. And the police returned again to raid the house after receiving further reports of drugs from neighbours. Then Sheena got a letter in the mail that was an eviction notice on behalf of the realtor, based on the number of complaints about them.

From the threats, to the police raid, to the tax fraud: and now this. Eviction. Brondo couldn't believe it all.

Brondo couldn't help himself; he had to send Max one final message. It read,

"Karma's gonna get you, bitch."

CHAPTER FOURTEEN
Abort Mission

Genesis 2: 7
And the Lord God formed a man from the dust of the ground and breathed into his nostrils the breath of life, and the man became a living soul.

Once upon a heartache, Brondo had wanted to kill himself. For a short time he thought he had found life again, thought his purpose here on earth was to love and find love. Now he was back to wanting to kill himself again. Life and death, death and life. Life was hard. Life was suffering. Just breathe in, breathe out; that's what Brondo kept reminding himself he had to do. *This too shall pass,* the scriptures reminded him. What was life anyway, if not suffering? He was coming to understand that, although his suffering had seemed to be greater than anybody else's, he also understood now that it was necessary, too. For, how could one know joy without pain? Hate without love? No, life was precious, and in the understanding of it, one couldn't have the yin without the yang, he thought.

They had three months to find a place, and Sheena needed Brondo more than ever by mid-April. Brondo had started a new job working with Sheena at her aged care facility where she worked, the Ava Maria Southern Cross Care. He took on the job of a domestic service assistant and carpet cleaner and started training and studying for a Certificate in Aged Care. One positive step lead to another, and Brondo and Sheena found a nice place on the north side of Scarborough, better than the last one they had. Brondo had contemplated leaving her, but neither could go anywhere in the poor and rocky boat in which they now floated, thanks to Max's fraud scheme which sent Brondo financially down the river. Ironically Max was now rolling in moolah and off somewhere living it up with his drug dough, while they struggled to make ends meet. Brondo was hoping for something cheaper so they could save; but Sheena was wanting the high lifestyle again, the nice house, the jewellery, the clothes and shoes, the dinners out. It was never ending.

Brondo had to agree though; it was a cute little house with a sweet back yard, and temporarily it raised his hopes with the promise of good things to come, the peaceful happy life he so desperately wished for. Maybe things could turn around with Sheena after all, maybe he shouldn't have been so hasty to pack it all in. They moved in in late April, and Thomas and Ally came with them. That month was a beautiful month; not only was he studying and working a good job, but Brondo felt more positive overall than he had in a long time. They spent the whole weekend cleaning up the property until she was looking spick and span, her lawns manicured, her white walls washed. They had lost the bond on the last place, what with the holes and marks left in the walls, a sad and violent reminder of Max and Thomas' drug chapter. Sheena had cut her losses and walked around their new home, chanting positive affirmations in the act of blessing it, even though she was hardly what you'd consider a religious person.

"It's a safe house; it's a beautiful, peaceful new home—this is a new start, this will be a house of peace and no dramas...ok, you two?" she lectured, directly addressing Ally and Thomas. Ally looked at her mum in amazement.

"What are you telling me for? I'm not the trouble maker!"

Thomas overheard Ally's comment and already wanted to have go at his sister before Brondo and Sheena had to step in again and remind them that things had to change if they were ever going to get better.

"Thomas—there will be no more explosions in this house, and that kind of behaviour is exactly what we were just talking about," Sheena warned. "I will have no problem at all now kicking out anyone who disturbs the peace of this house," she said, enforcing the new rules. Brondo was surprised.

"Fine—I'll leave then," Thomas challenged her in his bratty way.

"I really don't want it to get to that, Thomas; you're my son and I love you, but we have to try harder at this," she said, unpacking boxes.

Over the next week things were looking good; apart from a few disgruntled women he worked with (and who were a bit rough around the edges themselves, giving Brondo a bit of grief) he put his head down at work and worked hard, cleaning the facility and putting all his energy into his job. The women frowned on Brondo and Sheena, disapproving of their age difference, judgmental of the boys' past drug problems as well, but Brondo ignored them all. They were entitled to their opinions, he thought, but they knew nothing, had no idea where the real truth lay. He just shut up, stayed quiet and worked hard, because he needed the money and couldn't afford to lose another job.

April 27 was a wonderful day to remember; Brondo and Sheena jumped in the Commodore and zoomed down to Melbourne to celebrate the arrival of Vito and Sonia's beautiful daughter, Alicia Rain Violaris.

Brondo looked at her ten perfect fingers and toes, held the bundle of life in his arms. He could feel her precious little heart beating, working away at this new thing called Life. It was a miracle. What a beautiful little baby girl; her eyes were so alert and she had both Vito's and Sonia's striking features. Brondo held her close to him and was proud that he was now an Uncle; this was his niece. He had just missed his father, who had come and gone and already paid his first visit to his new granddaughter. Brondo and his father were again at odds over Bill's derogatory comments towards Sheena's drinking. At one point Brondo had ashamedly lost control of the conversation and told his own father that he would smash his face in should he ever talk about Sheena like that again. He instantly regretted it.

But today was about Alicia, and Brondo wanted to celebrate this gift from God he now held in his arms. What he wouldn't give, to have a child of his own one day; sadly it did not seem to be in the cards for him.

Brondo's mother Maria was getting back to her nastiness and inconsistent personality; she couldn't seem to help herself and made digs about Brondo at his expense and at every opportunity—he just couldn't understand why she insisted on doing it.

"Oh you are looking more and more like your father every day," she said, knowing full well how much this bothered him.

He turned away from her with Alicia in his arms and rolled his eyes at Sheena. She tried to suppress a giggle.

After spending most of the afternoon at the hospital holding and cuddling Alicia, Brondo and Sheena left to go back to his grandmother's place. They sat down to eat a big Greek meal of spanakopita and lamb, and toasted to the birth of Alicia with ouzo.

"Ya mas! Yassou! Opa!" They all clinked glasses, to the health of the next generation baby. And just like that the weekend was over, and Brondo and Sheena started on the drive back to Scarborough.

The following week they went back to Melbourne to visit Alicia in her home; Sonia was settling into motherhood and glad to finally be home from the hospital. Brondo and Sheena showered baby Alicia with toys and gifts. But an ever present Maria was having reservations about Sheena and started making life difficult for her; she was the next matriarch in line after Yaya and she was enjoying her new superior role in the family as the new grandmother. She had even gone to calling Brondo on his phone to voice her opinions.

"I am only saying this as your mother, and only out of concern; you must watch yourself, she is not the sort of woman I would trust if I were you—only a blind fool would not see her true colours," his mother warned. "I must also tell you that I have discussed this with Joe, and he similarly has expressed the same reservations about her character."

Brondo had still hoped for a better relationship with his family; he felt terrible, as he knew they wanted the best for him, but they had pushed him away, and they kept pushing him away by involving themselves in his life. He felt they had no right to dare interfere; he was his own person and a grown man, and it was his life, and his choice. What further annoyed Brondo was that he had hoped he could start anew with his mother, but she had already betrayed his trust by reverting to the same old habits. She knew trouble was brewing between them, and she began making her own waves, gossiping slander about Sheena behind her back.

"I told you that my mum would be like this," he reluctantly told Sheena.

"So how did you survive your mum growing up, if she was always this bad?"

Brondo laughed. "So: you finally believe me? Have you finally realised that what I've told you all along is true?

Sheena nodded. "I feel so sorry for you—I mean, my mother's no saint either, and she put me and my sister through hell…but your mother's something else. I mean…she's crazy, she's controlling and possessive—she has no boundaries and she doesn't respect other people's boundaries, either."

Brondo smirked. He hoped that the few home truths in this statement were also hitting home to Sheena. "Well, you haven't made it easy, either—I mean, I tell you things, and you don't listen. I tried to warn you about Layla and you didn't listen…I warned you about your boys and their drugs, your ex-husband and his antics…and I tried to warn you with my family, too. But you never listened; you never respected me enough to listen—and now you're paying the price."

"Ah, who cares anyway," Sheena said, blowing him off with her hand. I don't care—people are going to do what they're going to do anyway…"

"That's just the problem, Sheena. You don't care. Maybe you need to start caring a bit more, then bad things won't happen, things won't turn into such a train wreck."

"What do you know, Brondo? You care too much, then you get hurt!"

Brondo was connecting more with his family again and more regular trips to Melbourne were fast becoming a trend. Brondo dearly loved his niece and couldn't express his joy enough, wanting to spend more time at home.

Back in Scarborough the drug problem with Thomas had reignited despite Sheena's pleas, and he had moved out yet again. Max, on the other hand, was making inroads and cleaning up his act. He had been living in Echuca and was hoping to move back to Scarborough with his new girlfriend, the beautiful Chloe.

Max and Chloe came back to Scarborough for the weekend; Brondo half expected to see Max still looking like a red eyed punk druggie with some cheap girl with glitter in her hair. He was surprised instead to see a clean shaven Max in trendy jeans, crisp polo shirt and loafers with a tall, leggy beauty by his side. He wondered what rubbish he'd spun to get a woman like her, and figured he had also filled Chloe's head with all sorts of hate against Brondo.

Nothing could be further from the truth, however; Max shook Brondo's hand and introduced him to Chloe, who took an immediate liking to Brondo.

"Hello, I'm Chloe—nice to meet you," she said with doe eyes and perky breasts. It was clear she was quite taken by Brondo, and he found her charming and polite as well.

Was this the same Max, who, just six months earlier had been involved in the drug scene and a fraud scheme, Brondo wondered? He did a double take, so confused and taken aback was he by the grand entrance of a new and improved Max. With all the others Brondo had known where he stood; Mel had been a dumb, young puppy, while Layla had been a flirt and a manipulator (who had now gone off to have a baby with someone else), but Max now had this beautiful girl, and Brondo instantly liked her. He gave Max an approving nod and a thumbs up to his new choice in a girlfriend.

Max returned the nod but grew quickly uncomfortable by the fact that Chloe had taken such a liking to Brondo. He marked his territory fast, putting his arm around Chloe, giving Brondo the clear signal that she was his.

"We just came by so I could introduce Chloe to Mum, but we're heading down to Melbourne for a party," Max said confidently, trying to impress Chloe, while she stood in the kitchen, making small talk with Sheena.

"It's been a pleasure to meet you both," Chloe said before leaving, throwing an extra smile Brondo's way.

Who was this fine creature, and what did she see in Max? Brondo wondered. If only she knew.

The footy season had started back and work was getting busy again for Brondo; he had joined a local gym and started training and running again. By now it was just himself, Sheena and Ally at home, although Ally was now spending her days unemployed, looking for work or not looking for work and sleeping around the house for lengthy periods of the day. Sheena confided in Brondo that she feared it was now Ally's turn to backslide, and that the girl had fallen into a slump and into a deep funk. Things seemed to be rocky between her and Jarrod, and she was constantly moody, biting everyone's head off if they dared come within six feet of her.

"She may be pregnant," Sheena whispered, but Brondo couldn't understand why her being tired necessarily meant she had to be pregnant. But Sheena only sighed and pulled Brondo into a mighty big hug.

"Oh God, you're so adorably gullible, but I don't want to lose you baby—I love you more than anything in the world."

Brondo couldn't figure where that came from either, it was so out of the blue, unexpected. Still, he was deeply touched and moved by her words.

"Why would you think you would lose me, though?" Brondo asked, puzzled. It was the same old story. Sheena remained quiet and did not answer him; she seemed in a world of her own.

"I'll seek out Ally in her own private time, and take her to the doctors if necessary to get scanned and checked for a possible pregnancy."

The next day Brondo went to work and then afterwards to the gym. When he got home he found Ally and Sheena walking into the kitchen; Ally quickly disappeared off into her bedroom as Brondo met with Sheena's expectant gaze. It was that 'I told you so' look again he knew so well now. She dragged him off to their bedroom and pushed him on the bed.

"I need some fun and distraction," Sheena said forcefully.

"Not now," Brondo resisted, "it's five in the afternoon, Ally's in the house…it's…it's not right," he said, pushing her off him for once.

"Ally is four months pregnant—at least four and a half months," Sheena said plainly.

Brondo looked back at her, stunned.

"How can that be?" he asked, shocked. "I mean, how can she be that far along and not show, or not be nauseous, or anything?"

"She *is* pregnant, Brondo; the doctor said it's what's known as a cryptic pregnancy; you don't show any symptoms, most women aren't even aware they're carrying until the third trimester or even until they go into labour—but the signs are there, though, the nausea, the abdominal swelling, the fatigue... sleeping a lot, always tired—that's definitely her right now. The doctor also said it tends to occur in younger females with a history of drug abuse—but I don't think she's done any drugs, do you?"

"Wow," was all Brondo could say. He shook his head; no, he didn't think Ally would be the type to do drugs, and especially not after seeing what her brothers had done. But they were just so young, too—too young—to bear the burden and responsibility of parenting a baby, especially when they could barely provide for themselves.

Sheena whispered. "The doctor also said she could slide into denial, as many women do not believe they are pregnant because they haven't travelled the normal developmental route of a pregnancy—he said she could fall into depression, or worse, *mental illness.*"

"What about the baby? Is the baby safe? And does Jarrod know?" Brondo's brain was awhirl.

"Shh—don't get excited, I don't want to wake her," Sheena said, closing the door. "I don't think Jarrod knows—and yes, the doctor said that the baby is fine—but we are going to need help in this...I'm going to have to tell Seedy, even though I can't stand the thought of contacting him. But this is about Ally now, and how to help her through it...God, her debutante is right around the corner, Brondo! She'll be devastated! Poor kid, she'll be showing by then...

Sheena called Seedy. "Seedy," Sheena said firmly. "We have to talk. It's about Ally."

"Yeah, what," Seedy said, slurring his words. He sounded half tanked. Brondo could hear him through the speaker too, he sounded a mess.

"Seedy I need to talk to you about Ally—she's, she's... pregnant."

Seedy scoffed. "I knew something like this was bound to happen—what did she expect, with sleeping around like her mother and no protection."

Sheena was mortified at how cold and callous Seedy could be; she had to bite her lip though, let his digs wash over her, tell herself he wasn't worth fighting against. He was just a stupid drunk. Sheena asked him what they were supposed to do, to which Seedy had no answer; all she knew was that they were going to have to put their differences aside for this, help their daughter as best they could to get her through this crisis.

"Well, we have to involve Jarrod and his father in the decision—I know his dad, he's a prick but I'll give him a call in the morning. I gotta go." Click.

Sheena felt her life was spinning out of control and karma was now coming back to bite her in the most vicious of ways; she started questioning her own mothering skills, as she saw snippets and flashbacks in her mind of the three babies she had raised. There were her boys, dealing with anger issues even from when they were young, with a drunken, abusive father who had beaten her up over the years; she could now see the patterns of their downfall, how they fell so easily into the on again, off again drug scene; then there were the endless stream of police raids over the years, the Bikies, the evictions. It had been endless. And now her daughter was facing a teenage pregnancy. She felt like a failure for the first time in her life.

Seedy called Sheena back the next day.

"I spoke with the boy's father; he said Jarrod doesn't want the baby, and if Ally is up for it, his father will foot the bill for the abortion—Jarrod has a big future in AFL football, and he can't have a baby messing up this dream; it would be a huge setback."

"I—I don't have the money, I can't possibly afford it," Sheena said blankly.

"Don't worry about it—Jarrod's dad is good for it, I told ya I've already spoken to him—ya stupid wench!" Seedy blasted and hung up on her.

Over the coming days Brondo sat back as he watched more drama unfold. Sheena felt she may have to allow Ally to follow through with the pregnancy, even though she secretly didn't want her daughter to go through with it.

"I can't do it, Mum; I'm so scared…I'm not ready to be a mother—but how do I tell Spider? I just can't—I'm afraid he won't love me anymore! But I *love* him, Mum, I truly love him and I don't want to lose him!" Ally said, and cried into her pillow.

Sheena looked down at her daughter and saw a younger version of herself; she had to admit, it was painful to think she had been in this exact same position some twenty odd years ago. How her life could have turned out differently, she thought. Life was just like that. It was just about choices. Not good or bad. Just different. Make one choice, turn right. Make another choice, turn left.

They saw doctors and specialists, and Sheena realised that it may in fact be too far into the pregnancy for Ally to have the abortion anyway; things were getting extremely complicated the more time wore on, and the dangers to Ally and the unborn child only grew. They found an abortion clinic in Croydon, an hour and a half east of Melbourne. The $5000 was a steep cost, but Jarrod's father was only too happy to pay it; in his mind he wasn't aborting his grandchild but protecting his only son, saving him from a life choice that would have changed the trajectory of his fate.

So they decided to pay for it and get it over with. It was mid-June and the procedure would not be an easy one as Ally was by now five months into her pregnancy. They would have two days of counselling before the procedure and another post-operative session to ensure Ally had all the medical care and support she needed. Sheena was by her daughter's side for support; Brondo however, stayed back, blaming work reasons. But silently he struggled with the whole idea; he was not on board with it. He knew it was not his place to say anything either, as it was Ally's body, therefore Ally's choice. But he wondered what choice the unborn baby had had. For, just as Vito and Sonia had given birth, now another life was being terminated. No matter how hard he tried to support Ally, Brondo just couldn't agree with it. And it drove yet another wedge between him and Sheena.

As Ally cried out for her mother in the next room, her blood curdling screams seeping through the clinic's walls, Brondo was left to wonder whether this unborn child wasn't doing the same thing as its own mission towards life was aborted, its ancient internal screams falling upon deaf ears.

CHAPTER FIFTEEN
Brutal

Psalm 23:4
Yea, though I walk through the valley of the shadow of death, I will fear no evil: for thou art with me; thy rod and thy staff they comfort me.

It was late July and winter's storms were rolling in from the west; Brondo's heart was clouded over after everything Ally had been through, and life had turned a darker shade since the abortion. Plus, his casual job wasn't working out, either, and there was mean gossip being spread in the town about Sheena's being a whore and a bad mother. But Brondo couldn't afford to lose his job; he was working plenty of shifts and studying for another certificate and trying to keep up his gym membership all wt the sane time, and all in an effort to take better care of himself, despite living in an unhealthy home environment.

To make matters worse, Thomas had come back home again, trying to get clean, then relapsing and using again. He stole Brondo's one treasured item of clothing and used it for drug money, and Brondo was devastated: it was an expensive black jacket that had been gifted to him by his grandmother, Yaya.

Thomas hadn't been living at home for months, and since Max and Chloe had been at Seedy's, Brondo had to admit that things had been easier without the boys around those past few months. But the jacket had gone and Brondo wasn't going to take any of it lying down anymore.

"You owe me a grand now, Thomas," Brondo demanded. He didn't want to be at odds with either of Sheena's sons, but he had felt that in the past things had been better at least with Thomas; with Max you couldn't reason, but Brondo and Thomas' relationship had at least sometimes shown glimpses of civility. But here was Sheena once again not reprimanding Thomas over what he had done, and worse, selfishly letting him come back into the house like he had done nothing wrong.

Thomas walked in the house and said hello, distracted by something else he was up to. He heard Brondo but deflected the situation, asking instead what he could make himself to eat.

Brondo had reached his limits and could feel his hatred was boiling over; Sheena had done little to help resolve the issue of the stolen jacket beyond sending Thomas a few text messages, saying that he should return it.

Thomas continued to ignore Brondo and Sheena could feel the situation between them becoming more and more tense.

"Thomas, come and sit down for a minute, we need to talk," Sheena commanded, foolishly thinking that she could fix this thing before it escalated.

"Tell the fucking wog to shut up and get over it!" Thomas yelled back at his mother.

For the first real time in their relationship, Brondo exploded and let loose a gigantic roar.

"No you stupid, Anglo convict motherfucker—I'll fucking smash *you*, you cunt, you thief, you drug using cunt!"

Ally called out in disbelief. "Brondo! No!"

But it was too late; at that precise moment Thomas walked in the living room and threw a punch at the back of Brondo's head. Brondo grabbed Thomas by the throat as the two men threw each other into the walls.

Sheena, horrified, started screaming out to Brondo.

"Watch out for the walls…and the glass table!" but Brondo in his fury could not hear her; he only continued to throw Thomas around the lounge room, hell bent on making him pay for his crimes. They scrambled, knocking the glass table over as things went flying. Now he was on top of Thomas, his hands around his neck, choking him until his face started turning a bright shade of firetruck red. Sheena and Ally both jumped on top of Brondo and Ally grabbed a book, striking him by the side of his face.

Brondo yelled out furiously at Ally. "Ally, stop fucking hitting me!"

Ally served a second blow to Brondo's head; blood was now streaming down the right side of his face. He almost blacked out after the second strike; with Ally straddled over his back he couldn't move his right arm to free it, and this limited him from being able to defend himself. He had no idea that with Ally and Sheena sitting on his back he couldn't move his right arm—and this freed up Thomas to swing from the side and he clocked Brondo twice more to the head.

Brondo could now feel himself fighting for his life; it was a three against one game, and he tightened his grip around Thomas' neck, as Thomas tried to gouge Brondo's eyes out. The pain was excruciating, enough to drive Brondo to bite Thomas's hand with his bare, bloody teeth. Thomas screamed and let go, and Ally grabbed the phone to call police while her mother screamed frantically.

The two men were released from each others' grip, though the pulse of their rage encircled them all. Brondo felt terribly disgusted upon seeing Thomas' face all purplish and blue, his eyes bulging. He couldn't believe that in his blinded moment he had almost strangled him to death. But Thomas wasn't finished; he scrambled to his feet and ran into the kitchen, grabbing cutlery throwing it at Brondo, picking up vases and smashing them against the countertops then cutting the top of Brondo's foot as well as throwing apples and other fruits from the fruit bowl. It was utter war.

Brondo stood up and grabbed a butter knife and ran towards Thomas, who backed into the wall and then soccer punched Brondo, dropping him to the floor again. Brondo grappled to get up; then he picked up Thomas' protein powder tub and aimed it at him, only just missing, as it flew by his head, putting another massive hole in the wall. By this stage Ally had called the police for backup, and within minutes the sight of blue and red glaring lights were coming through their living room window. Thomas walked out the front door towards the cops and Brondo pulled Sheena aside, threatening her that if he was to get locked up he would kill Thomas and leave her.

Sheena just had this stupid look on her face as he left her for the bathroom, spitting blood from his jaw into the sink, his foot bleeding with a wide gash from the glass.

His thoughts were interrupted when he heard Sheena call out to him.

"Brondo—the police want to talk to you, you need to come outside and talk to them."

He felt drained but emerged from the bathroom where he was startled to be met by two police officers who immediately yelled at him.

"Where's the knife? Drop the knife!" The policemen ordered. Out of the corner of his eye, he could see they were holding pepper sprays and immediately raised both his arms in a panic, assuring them that he was unarmed and repeatedly stating that it was only a butter knife. But the police grabbed Brondo, throwing him to the ground, and then they struck him to the head as he lay there, helpless. He could faintly hear Sheena telling them not to hit him again, but his mind was in a fog; the last thing he heard was the police instructing her to close the door.

Brondo was nearly broken; he couldn't believe the police brutality, nor the injustices that ensued. He could see now oh-so-clearly how people abused their positions of power, and it sickened him.

He tried to reason with the police, plead his innocence, but they were an unreasonable lot and they handcuffed him, telling him that he wasn't on the lease and therefore needed to find somewhere else to stay. Brondo wanted to kill Sheena right then and there for her betrayal; he also wanted revenge on the shifty police officers. If ever there was a time in history where he felt he had nothing to lose, this was it. The police transported him in the divvy van to the lockup station and he was placed in a holding cell for several hours without any contact with the outside world. Brondo sat in the corner of the concrete cell hating upon himself, his mind racing between thoughts of murder and suicide. It seemed there were the only two options left in this dumpy little town. After two and a half years of abuse and exploitation here Brondo sat, ready for the final showdown.

As soon as the police released him, he thought, as soon as he was set free, he would pack up his life and leave for Melbourne first thing in the morning. There was no more looking back.

It was over and the end of this chapter of his life had finally come to a close.

"That fucking bitch—what a lowlife dog she is; fuck her, this isn't over yet...I'll teach her for doing this to me, fucking leaving me to get arrested and not even defending me in my own home, and my name not even on the fucking lease even though I pay for everything...how *dare she*."

Brondo was muttering out loud to himself; he did not care who heard him anymore, he did not care who knew—he just had to speak the truth out loud and clear for all to hear. He was done.

It was now in the early hours and Brondo figured it had to be after or around four in the morning when the police finally released him. As he walked out he was planning all of his movements in his mind, visualising the brief confrontation with Sheena as he quietly went about collecting his things. However, as he exited the cell block he was shocked to see both Sheena and Ally just sitting there, up against the wall in the waiting room.

They had both been in tears and were so emotional that Ally rushed towards Brondo to hug him first. Suddenly Brondo felt the anger drain from his face, realizing he had gotten it all wrong again. Sheena had been worried sick and had explained to the police that they had gotten their wires crossed; she insisted that Brondo was on the lease and had taken documents to the station to confirm his residency. Ally also gave conclusive statements pertaining to Brondo's living at the same address and providing testimony that he was in a relationship with her mother. Brondo said nothing; he was too exhausted to care. He just wanted to get home to his own bed, get some sleep and forget the nightmare of the last twenty-four hours.

He had felt lost and disoriented when he fell asleep; so it wasn't much of a shock when Brondo woke to find himself strapped down, hands tied to the bed post as Sheena forced tequila down his throat. Angrily she pulled his pants down and helped herself to him, taunting him the whole time about what her son had done to him.

"Oh, you think you're so smart, hey? Well, not this time—Thomas showed you well and good, didn't he? Oh my good boy, Thomas..." she said as she violated Brondo again. Brondo gave in to Sheena's crazed acts, succumbing to her will as she continued to get him drunk. Each time he drifted off to sleep she would wake him up again, shaking his head with both hands, rotating his face and chin through the use of her foot and treating him like nothing more than a piece of meat.

As dawn broke through the venetian blinds, Brondo found his wrists had been untied and he quickly got up, desperate for the shower to wash away his sins. Sheena was groggy when she woke, laughing in a crazed, tequila kind of way about their night of fun. Brondo hated himself more than he had ever thought possible in that moment; he detested Sheena for all of her crimes against his person, but he despised himself more for not being strong enough to break free of her games.

Nothing more was said of the night; Sheena told Brondo that Thomas had been ordered to leave, and she was advised by police to get an intervention order because, as they had warned, kids like that with drug problems always felt there was a debt to settle and would return in vengeance to settle the score.

Max was now completely clean and off drugs and working as a tiler; he and Chloe continued living with Seedy but they would come around on occasion to have dinner. One night Max was secretly fuming at one end of the dinner table about Brondo's having gotten his brother evicted from the property and taking out the AVO order on him, and he continued to bad mouth Brondo to Sheena, telling his mother how much he hated her boyfriend. At the other end of the table Chloe was opening up to Brondo, telling him of her own hard past, her mother who had been a drug addict and had been molested as a child. Brondo could feel that he and Chloe had a connection and were growing closer as a nice and easy friendship developed between them.

"It's incredible that you've overcome the darkness of your past and that you remain so positive about life, considering what you and your mother have been through," Brondo commented sincerely. "I'm also surprised that after what Max has probably said about me, that you continue to be so nice to me."

"First of all," Chloe said, "Max has a temper; he gets angry at things and he vents, but deep down he cares—he's just misunderstood, that's all. And, between you and me, a lot of that repressed anger is towards his mother—he's never felt that Sheena has ever truly seen or heard him. Just don't tell him I said that."

Brondo nodded, deep in thought. He could understand this, given that, growing up, his own mother had made him feel the same way. And he could certainly understand how Max had never felt heard by Sheena, because she had pretty much done the same thing to him. Funny how he'd never looked at things this way before; he'd never seen it from Max's perspective.

"Hmmm...yes, I think I can see that," Brondo agreed, looking at Max now talking to Sheena at the other end of the table.

"And Max can say whatever he wants about you—I'm a big girl and I can make up my own mind on these things. I told Max it's my choice to decide; and I said I wanted to see what kind of person you were for myself."

"And what's your final decision?" Brondo asked honestly.

"You're an amazing guy—and nothing like he said you were, which makes me think that sometimes Max is full of shit," she said, and genuinely laughed. Brondo was surprised that Chloe would want to be with a guy like Max; he was clearly out of her league.

In late November Brondo bought a Tattslotto ticket, and he and Sheena won $1400. He called Sheena excitedly to tell her.

"Wow, babe! We just got a nice little windfall from the government," Brondo joked. Sheena was ecstatic and told him not to tell the kids as ehe wanted to spend it on them. He quickly regretted telling Sheena; he thought it would have been nicer to put the money aside and live off their wages for awhile, perhaps use it for a little holiday for themselves.

But Sheena wanted to go out and spend it on new couch and a dining set; then she wanted a new bed and a TV in the bedroom. Within days the windfall had vanished. He kicked himself for ever saying anything; he still had the credit card debt and the damage to his car was still not fixed and now Sheena had blown it all again, completely disregarding their other financial woes. On top of it all there was still the tax debacle hanging over his head too, and Brondo sat waiting in hope that the ombudsman would clear it, though it had been nine months and so far and hadn't heard a word from the ATO. He also discovered that the mobile phone he had gotten in his name for Max made him the responsible party for it; and Max had acquired a $5000 mobile bill in Brondo's name. It was all piling up and Brondo felt slowly more and more defeated by it all. His credit score was now shit and he was bearing the brunt of all their mistakes.

Ironically, both boys now had two nice girls in their lives; Max had Chloe and Thomas had Lauren, a good clean girl who had set him on the straight and narrow. They really seemed to finally be getting on top of things, what with new relationships and solid jobs; life was getting better for the both of them, while Brondo sat sidelined in his own life, drowning in their debts.

Sheena spent all her time trying to sort out her boys' lives, but had completely forgotten about her wayward promise to divorce Seedy and marry Brondo; she never seemed to follow through on anything, Brondo thought, and he knew he'd foolishly built for himself a life on sand with her. Where had all the promises gone? The trip to Cyprus? Moving to Melbourne? Marriage?

This wasn't going to end well, this Brondo already knew; but each time he tried to disengage and distance himself from Sheena, the more she pursued the relationship again, coming back stronger than ever before. Sheena had a weapon, and it was sex, and she knew how to use it, how to hold Brondo sway; once again she confessed that she was into voyeurism and even suggested that she loved the idea of Brondo being in a kinky sexual encounter with another woman—she wanted to be able to watch; she said she needed to be turned on. Sex, Brondo thought, was like a drug to her; and she didn't care how she got it, as long as she got it.

But for now he was still a sitting duck; Sheena had bailed him out of jail, and because of this she lorded so much power over him...and because of his crippling finances he felt had nowhere left to turn.

Leave her to her sick and twisted fantasies, he thought; let her think he would be a willing participant, because he needed it to buy himself some time. Brondo had always been monogamous; as far as he was concerned he was a one woman man, and he wasn't about to cheat with another woman no matter how much she pushed him to. Still, she tried.

"But babe, I trust you—and I know that you're coming home to me so it doesn't bother me, in fact it turns me on..." she said seductively.

Brondo was a far more tender-hearted man, though; he wrote some beautiful poems for Sheena, would surprise her and present her with something he had worked on and written, straight from the heart. Sheena would thank him for his poem, tell him he had a way with words, then put it away in a drawer somewhere like she did with everything else, to be forgotten under a pile of other stuff.

Brondo and Chloe were getting really close now as friends; she would come to him and confide more and more about the problems she was having with Max in their relationship. Brondo was flattered that this young and beautiful girl was now looking to him as a role model to open up and talk to, though he had to be careful not to let Max catch wind of it, lest it upset the apple cart. Brondo had to just trust his intuition, he knew that this girl was headstrong; she had a good, solid head on her shoulders snd she wasn't about to allow Max to dictate to her or control her in any way, shape or form.

Over the next few weeks Max and Chloe would fight and clash in the kitchen after coming over for an evening meal; and Max would inevitably be the first to back down, which shocked Brondo to no end. Max, he saw, had finally met his match in a woman who was unafraid and ready to stand up to him.

Thomas had now made amends with Brondo and had even come to apologise for his actions; being a God fearing man, Brondo had forgiven him again, although in the back of his mind he harboured the memories of the jacket theft, the sins that had been committed against him. He knew he had to forgive; it was just the forgetting he had trouble with. The forgetting, that was the hard part.

One day in February of 2012 Brondo was at home, sitting on the edge of the bed in his bedroom having just showered and dressed, when all of a sudden he heard yelling and screaming coming from Max and Chloe in the other room. He was about to go out and break up the commotion when Chloe came running into his room, crying. Brondo felt nervous getting involved in any of it, but tried to comfort her as best he could.

"What's wrong?" he asked, genuinely concerned.

"Max cheated on me and has given me chlamydia," Chloe sobbed, falling into his arms. He took her into his arms, putting his arms around her as she cried uncontrollably. He couldn't find the words; his heart just sank for her.

He told her it would all be Ok and not to worry; Chloe looked up at Brondo with such hopeful eyes in that moment that it made his heart melt. She moved Brondo's face towards her, and he panicked. Ally stood in the doorway the whole time watching them embrace, then a mad Max appeared at the doorway, too.

Chloe closed the bedroom door on Max, but he wasn't having any of it; he forcefully kicked the door in with his foot and raced for her, grabbing her by the wrist.

"What do you want, what are you doing, let go of me!" Chloe demanded.

"Come with me," Max said, pulling her away from Brondo out of the room. Chloe gave in to his demands, looking over apologetically at Brondo as she left.

The whole experience left Brondo feeling emotionally drained yet also funny and rather uncomfortable inside. It was clear that this girl was drawn to Brondo as he was to her, and it was obvious that she trusted him far more than any of the others. Dangerously though, he had to wonder how far things might have gone, if the others had not been home.

Integrity however, was deeply rooted in his Greek makeup, and as tempted as Brondo might have been in the moment, he felt his body clam up in response and he became very tense over her advances; it was an awkward and unexpected situation he had suddenly found himself in, to be sure.

A week and a half later Max was called in for his pre-surgical preparations. He had been on a waiting list for nearly three or so years to have the surgery to remove his benign tumour. The date was set for early June 2012, and Sheena and Thomas would make the trip to Melbourne with Max to support him, while Chloe and Ally stayed behind with Brondo to keep the house going.

The whole family were at the hospital for Max's first appointment as well as to attend an informational seminar on what he would have to expect, both pre and post surgery. They had scheduled the operation for the second week of June and everyone was understandably nervous; they had come to understand the serious risks involved in such an operation and tensions were high, with even Max coming to express a few of his own choice words before his God.

While everyone was in Melbourne supporting Max through his pre surgery preparations, Chloe needed help getting to the clinic for her appointment. So Brondo jumped in the car and took her down to her appointment on Corio Street. She had by now come to depend on Brondo quite a lot and cane to confide in him over a great many things; she divulged how she and Max had practiced safe sex until recently, when she said he had forced her, pushing her down on the bed and refusing to use protection. He came inside of her and she was horrified, never expecting that he would ever do such a thing.

Brondo didn't know what to say to that; he was empathetic to Chloe for the position she now found herself in, worried she may well be pregnant.

"Things aren't always what they seem with Max," Brondo said, lacing his comment with a warning.

"What does that mean?" Chloe asked, genuinely curious.

"Well, he's done some bad things in the past, and done some bad things to me, but I'm not going to go into it, this isn't the time or place—just be careful of who you trust," he said, wanting Chloe to heed his warning. He wished he'd had someone warn him the same way, way back when.

Brondo sat in the car while Chloe went into the clinic; he waited and prayed for the poor girl, as he thought of how selfish the Baxters could be. An hour later Chloe walked out; she got in the car and lay her head on Brondo's shoulder and broke down in tears. She began to howl, really howl.

"I'm pregnant," she said through her crying. Brondo didn't know what else to do; he held her in his arms, trying to comfort her, trying to remind her that this was not the end of the world, and that it could be a good thing, a blessing.

"How do you feel about it?" he asked, when she had sufficiently gathered herself from the initial shock. Chloe wiped away her tears.

"I guess I am going to have to consider what I really want," she said, sniffling into her sleeve. "I haven't told anyone this, not even Max—but I have a medical condition, so I only have a certain number of years to have kids. Maybe it's best this happens now..." she said, though not sounding certain.

Brondo felt real concern for this girl; here was Max reaping the rewards off the drug money he'd pocketed, not telling Chloe anything of his past or his criminal record, while leading her astray and violating her body. It was basically rape in his eyes; consensual rape, date rape, relationship rape—put whatever label you wanted to put on it, dress it up any way you like: it was still rape. And now there was another baby on the way. Brondo couldn't speak, it was all too overwhelming. He drove Chloe home after comforting her as best he could, then he withdrew and went to his room, needing space.

In the next week Brondo would receive some good news for once: the tax penalty had been wiped and he was no longer under investigation with the ATO. He felt like he could breathe again. Also, the Telstra phone bill company had worked out a payment plan with him and he had less stress on making the monthly payments as he would engage Max to assist in paying down the debt which was rightfully his, not Brondo's, responsibility.

Brondo was certain of one thing: this time around, things would be different. He would make Max face up to his responsibilities no matter what. He would follow through on everything when it came to Thomas and Max, because it seemed as though this was something that had been missing their entire life. Was he still frustrated about the debts, the bills and the damage to his car? Yes. But, for now, it seemed, the only way to recovery was to take things step by step, little by little. He wasn't going to get overwhelmed anymore, and he wasn't going to let his anxiety overrule; he just had to be firm, be brutal, stay focused and stay disciplined towards the end goal. It was time to get brutal.

CHAPTER SIXTEEN
Bianca Brady

Judges 16: 19
She made him sleep on her knees...and had him shave off the seven locks of his hair. Then she began to afflict him, and his strength left him.

Max had returned from Melbourne feeling fragile from all the surgery talk and was not his usual self; he seemed withdrawn and shaky, petrified of what could go wrong after learning about all the associated risks. The doctors had explained that they would not know what they were dealing with until the operation was underway; though the tumour was benign, if it was too close to the brain cavity and they tried to remove it through a partial resection it could result in causing blindness or partial paralysis. The surgeon said he would know more in a few days after examining the MRI results through brain mapping. Sheena wept openly upon hearing this; she couldn't bear the thought of her son going blind.

The surgery was scheduled a week from Tuesday if it was to

go ahead, and tensions in the house were through the roof.

Max and Thomas started in on one another to the point where Brondo had to step in to break it up; Max became infuriated, feeling that Brondo was taking sides with Thomas.

"Back off, Brondo—I'm *warning* you," a very sick Max threatened.

"I'm breaking you two twits up before things get any more heated," Brondo returned, unfazed by Max's idle threats.

"I SAID back off—or I'll take you both outside and drop you myself!" Max shouted angrily. Max was explosive; he was out of control and rageful, just looking for any opportunity to vent his frustrations.

"I hope you fucken' die under this surgery!" Thomas yelled. Then he turned to Chloe. "And as for you, bitch—you're with the wrong brother!"

Max stood toe to toe now with Brondo and Thomas, daring them to take him on. Ally and Chloe started screaming to stop it and that they'd had enough. But Max was now focused only on Brondo as old resentments resurfaced, and they stood there like that, eyeball to eyeball, challenging each other.

Brondo blew up and lifted the lamp stand, telling Max to back off, or he was going to smash his face in and cut his throat.

The police were called and they told Sheena to break up the party; someone had to be asked to leave and it was up to her to decide. She looked across at the four faces staring back at her. It was either ask Thomas to leave, or cut Brondo out of her life, or ask Max and Chloe to move out; any way you sliced it, it was a lose lose situation.

That day Sheena told Max and Chloe they would need to go back and stay with Seedy, but Sheena was devastated, heartbroken by the fact that Max was facing surgery and Chloe was pregnant; she cried for them both and became fearful they would turn on her again and deny her access to her first grandchild.

"God Jesus, I am so over all of this fighting and hatred—I'm so sick of missing out on what could be a happy family life, it's too much to bear," she bemoaned.

"There's not much I can do—I wish I could fix it, but I can't stop the shit that keeps going on…I mean, the real problem is that your sons have been on and off drugs for years; they're angry, they're unreasonable and they're inconsistent with their anger… it's just an out of control situation, and there seems to be no end to it. All we can do is let the dust settle and focus on getting Max through this surgery and Chloe through her pregnancy; they have a lot in front of them to deal with right now, for their age," Brondo remarked honestly.

Sheena nodded; she knew Brondo was right—there was a lot going on, too much for one person to deal with. They just had to take things step by step, day by day and get Max through this perilous time in his life.

On June 16th Max was called into surgery at St Vincent's hospital in Melbourne. Sheena and Brondo opted to stay at Claire Fielding's house in South Melbourne on the beach; she had been an old friend of Thomas' and had opened her doors, inviting them to use her spare bedroom in an effort to help out. Over the next five days Chloe, Brondo, Ally and Sheena all stayed there, darting in and out and sharing shifts to be with Max while he underwent the surgery.

Brondo's family were concerned for Sheena as well; on the day of the surgery they sent their prayers and best wishes, although Sheena was a wreck, her worrying and anxiety had gotten the better of her and she needed the help of Valium to calm her nerves. Max had lots of support and eventually came to after the surgery with the doctors deeming the procedure a complete success. They had been able to remove over ninety percent of the tumour and told them that within several months Max would be back to normal.

"I don't know if that's a good thing or a bad thing," Ally said only half jokingly, and everyone laughed in relief.

"Maybe we can decide to make this an end to all the bloodshed and hatred in this family, finally make peace with each other," Sheena announced. Max had a constant stream of visitors to the hospital, and Brondo took some time out to go visit his brother and sister-in-law. Sonia was by now pregnant again with their second child, and glowing at five months along. Brondo was so excited to think that in a few short months he would be an uncle again to a little niece or nephew.

By November everyone it seemed was having babies, with the exception of Brondo and Sheena; despite a few minor complications, Vito and Sonia had welcomed a beautiful baby girl, Jane Maddison Violaris into the family; and just two days after that Chloe and Max had announced the arrival of their precious baby, another girl, Charlotte Jade Baxter. Sheena's brother Steve and his partner had their fourth child, Ryder, too. It was a time of hospitals and presents and baby showers and celebrations all around. Life was such a funny and fragile thing, Brondo thought; it could arrive or be taken on the flip of a dime. And now two new angels graced the world with their presence.

But, even amidst all the celebrations, things were not without their problems; in the hospital where Brondo and Sheena visited Chloe and Max, things had become tense between Seedy's new girlfriend and Sheena, as an exchange of dirty looks were catapulted back and forth between the two women, plus a few cold comments thrown in, for good measure. Ally only came to the hospital to visit one time; the birth had been a difficult thing for her to grapple with and she just wasn't herself; it stirred up too many old and lost emotions about her abortion and triggered painful memories. She and Jarrod had broken it off not long afterwards, and Ally had gotten her license and signed up with the Australian Navy and was due to ship out any day now, much to Sheena's protest. Brondo saw the pained look in her eyes as Ally saw her brother's new baby girl.

"I got robbed of all of this joy," Ally said quietly, hugging Brondo and burying herself into his shoulder. "Mum doesn't say anything about it; she doesn't even seem to care...she's *glad* I had the abortion! How can she be so coldhearted? How can she not even care? It was her grandchild too?" She sobbed. "My baby girl lies in a casket somewhere, and it's all my fault."

Brondo held Ally then; he felt helpless, as he didn't know what more he could do. He couldn't justify what Ally and Sheena were responsible for any more than they could; what they had done was done, and now Ally bore the heavy burden of guilt that it seemed she would carry with her, for the rest of her life.

But Ally was right, too; Sheena had moved on from the abortion without even an ounce of guilt, and had left Ally to deal with all the reverberations of it, alone.

The last month and a half of 2012 saw Brondo pursuing a new profession; he had grown tired of the aged care facility and though he had now obtained his certificates he decided to undertake a six week training course as a prison guard, with the promise of full time employment to follow at Dhurringhile Prison. The sixty-eight room homestead had been an internment camp that had housed alien civilians in World War II; it would later be used to house prisoners of war before becoming an orphanage. By 1965 it was turned into a minimum security prison, though to Brondo it looked more like a sprawling farmstead based around the historic Dhurringile Estate. His job as a prison guard was to ensure the smooth running of the inmates; he would supervise their lunchtimes around the main mess hall, supervise their working hours in woodwork and metals, and take care of the largest fifty-four block unit of prisoners known as Kyabram.

Working at the prison was at first a daunting experience and nothing like Brondo had expected; but he so dearly wanted the chance to make something of his life and felt proud of his graduation into the role that January. Sheena had attended the ceremony and was proud of Brondo for accomplishing this new title; he was now a Senior Prison Guard and was qualified to work for Corrections Victoria, under the Department of Justice and Community Safety.

Community safety, Brondo quietly thought to himself; now that was an oxymoron, if ever there was one.

But things had cooled down with Sheena's boys and Brondo was feeling safer, glad he was finally getting along with them in small doses; Ally and Brondo had formed a tight union as well, as she messaged him often from her new position as a Navy recruit. Ally had become more protective of Brondo since the night of his arrest; she had seen the many injustices that had been done to him and had sided with him on all of it.

The remainder of the year was a strange one for Brondo; he spent lots of hours working mostly overnight shifts, and in that time Sheena started up her antics yet again. *When the cat's away, the mice do play,* Brondo thought. He knew she was up to something, because she'd had far too much free time on her hands; he just couldn't figure out what.

Brondo had spent lots of hours on an online AFL page called 'The Big Four' and Sheena had taken it upon herself to create a fake account under the alias of Bianca Brady. Bianca Brady had begun chatting to the boys on the page, flirting with its members and generally stirring up trouble. Unbeknownst to Brondo, Sheena flirted with him as well. He had no idea who Bianca Brady really was, though he had suspected she was a fake and a phoney on account of her fake address; but the rest of the boys were only too eager to flirt and meet up, and Sheena would string them along with her messages and promising taunts.

Brondo had formed a friendship with the lovely but fiery and tough Tanya Smith, too; but both had agreed they did not trust this Bianca character by a long shot, as some things she'd said seemed amiss and simply didn't add up. Brondo tried not to think too much about it, choosing instead to focus his energies on his new job, even though the footy boys were messaging him, asking who he thought this Bianca Brady person was. But Brondo was no fool—for all he knew, Bianca could in fact be a 'Bianco', some weird dude hiding behind the screen and he wasn't about to take his chances.

Brondo went to work that night in early March, but he could not have known that that night while he was gone, Sheena would use his password to access his account on Facebook and talk to many of his friends, posing as him. She would sometimes even make wild posts, pretending to be him, just to stir up trouble. But Brondo knew nothing; he would come home from work in the early hours of dawn and fall asleep, too tired to check into his account and oblivious to her escapades. Sheena would carefully cover her own tracks too, by deleting posts and conversations and removing any evidence so that Brondo had no idea what she was up to.

It was that one night in March, early in the footy season, when Brondo was jumping around in front of the television excitedly, watching Carlton play Collingwood when things would begin to unravel for Bianca Brady. Brondo was a loose cannon, jumping and screaming at the TV screen. "Come on, Blues! Come on, smash those bastards!" he yelled, and Sheena just laughed at him. Brondo came over to see her and saw that his account was open on the laptop.

"Who's been checking my account?" Brondo asked, surprised. Sheena just shrugged and got up to use the bathroom. Brondo then noticed there were messages from this Bianca Brady, asking him to send some pictures of himself. But Brondo was already spoken for and messaged this Bianca person back, telling her as much. Sheena came back from the bathroom and began to laugh even harder.

"What's so funny?" He asked her, puzzled. "Was it me just now, making a fool of myself, screaming at the TV?"

"No," Sheena replied, almost doubling over with laughter. She couldn't even speak, so instead she gestured with her finger, pointing at the laptop screen. Brondo got up off the couch where he had been sitting and came over to where Sheena was sitting, in the recliner. She showed him the screen, pointing to the name on it, revealing the secret that she was Bianca Brady. Brondo was shattered. *She* was Bianca Brady? What on earth was wrong with her?

"Why, why are you doing this? God, I thought it might have been Tanya or some other random idiot and now I find this? That it was you all along? Why, why would you do this? Don't you know you're headed for trouble?"

Sheena laughed. She just laughed.

"Oh shut up, Brondo! It's just funny, lighten up! God, you can be so *boring*."

Brondo felt so disappointed, though; he felt ashamed that a forty-seven year old woman, a grandmother no less with three grown kids, was behaving this way. Sheena continued on with both accounts, hers and the fake one, for another week, gloating about her double profiles, trying to get a reaction out of Brondo. She deliberately turned on the location settings and sent a message to the chubby overweight Mitchell Ipsalintos, who saw the location listed as Scarborough on his phone. Mitchell immediately took screenshots of Sheena's message and put it on The Big Four noticeboard online, exposing Sheena's location as coming from Brondo's computer. Tensions quickly rose, because by now the guys on the footy page were feeling insulted by the games Sheena had played and sent her threatening messages telling her to stop what she was doing; they knew Brondo was her partner, too, and in a vicious attack they turned on him as well. Brondo was furious with the messages and came to Sheena's defence.

"You can blame me for it, but don't you dare blame Sheena," he fired back.

But most, if not all of the people believed it was Sheena was behind it all, because it just didn't make sense why Brondo would do such a thing. They argued with Brondo, explaining that IP addresses and location settings couldn't be faked, and that if it wasn't him then it had to have been Sheena posing as him from his account. He argued that that wasn't possible; only a high tech person would be able to hack his account, and Sheena didn't have that capability.

Eventually Brondo left the football page and deactivated his account, but he felt depressed because he liked the footy guys;

even though they were online and even though he'd never met any of them, they had come to be his virtual friends. He just couldn't figure out who would go to such lengths as to hack his computer, pretend to be him and then frame him like this.

In his depressed state, Brondo began to drink. One beer, two beers, six beers, eight. He fell into bed drunk, until Sheena awoke him in her usual manner, slapping him with her foot and pressing it into his face until he came to.

"God, you could sleep through an earthquake when you're drunk like this," she said, and struck him hard again, twice across the face.

Brondo, dazed and groggy, was still hurting over the Facebook events in his mind as Sheena taunted him now.

"Haha, I gotta say, it was my own perfect mastermind; I logged on as you when you were at work, turned on my location services and sent messages to Mitchell, so that they'd believe it was really you—and it worked! It was brilliant! I got everyone to turn against you, just like that," she said with a click of her fingers.

"But why? Why do it? Why hurt me like this—I'll admit, you've played me well, but you've totally screwed me, I mean—"

"Try fucked babe: I totally *fucked* you again," she confessed with an evil grin, twirling her hair in her fingers.

Brondo was thunder struck; he was so surprised by her level of deviousness and wondered how he could ever break free of her devilish nature; he could clearly see her evil designs now: to isolate him, make others turn against him and hate him, just so she could have him all to herself. But he could not get over the fact that she had hurt him deliberately and intentionally; that she could be so manipulative and sneaky to do such a thing. He had well and truly lost all respect for her.

And now he was moreso angry with himself; it was a flaw in his own character that he always wanted to see the best in everyone, and that, because of this weakness he would fail to see Sheena's demonic ways. How could he be so delusional, so gullible? Things were hanging by a thread between them, and he wondered how much longer they would last; it was his own wishful thinking to hope that she'd eventually change or that things would get better, because it was clear now that nothing would change and things weren't getting any better. In fact, they were getting worse. He could see it now; his family acting all smug, gloating that they had been right about Sheena all along, and he so wished he could have just this one victory against them, prove them wrong. But it was a waste of time, it had proven to just be all a waste of time, because Sheena wasn't about to change—Sheena was never going to change; and he had to wonder what on earth had ever made him think that she would.

CHAPTER SEVENTEEN
Drifting

Proverbs 21: 9
It is better to live in the corner of a roof than with a contentious, vexatious woman.

Drifting along and drifting apart and drifting through life was how Brondo felt these days; he felt directionless again, the way he had years ago when he thought his life meant nothing and he was ready to end it all. Now, here he was again, going through the motions; get up, go to work, hit the gym, eat, sleep, repeat. He did make a concerted effort towards spending more and more time at the gym, but only because it made him feel good, raised his self confidence and self esteem, which he needed because all Sheena ever did was put him down. He continued to train hard, and even got into training with Max at the gym; since his surgery Max had gotten on a health kick too, and they often trained together, growing closer as a result. Max told Brondo that he was on steroids for a short time and he told him how his focus had changed since becoming a father; his whole world now was about Chloe and Charlotte Jade, and he told Brondo how having a child had given his life a new purpose, a new meaning. Brondo told Max too, how much he adored his two nieces, who adored him back, and he still connected on a deep level with Chloe who was now a proud mother herself. Charlotte adored Brondo too, and they all agreed he was a natural with kids.

"You should think of a career working with kids," Sheena said off-handedly one day to Brondo. To be honest, he had never thought about it before, but maybe she had something; he loved kids and they loved him. Brondo had a softness and an easiness about him that was endearing and that drew kids to him.

Sheena began showing more signs of jealousy as Brondo grew closer to her granddaughter, Charlotte, and she accused him of not learning to say no more often.

"You know, you're very hypocritical, Sheena; one moment you're saying I should pursue a career with kids and that I have a gift and am good at connecting with them and looking after them—and then the next minute you're saying that Charlotte only loves me because I'm sweet and soft—so, which one is it? Because it can't be both."

Brondo was annoyed with Sheena and he was becoming more and more annoyed with her, with every passing day. Sheena tried to dismiss him then, downplaying it all as a joke and accusing him of taking things too seriously.

Lighten up, Brondo! Can't you take a joke, Brondo? You're way too serious, Brondo! Or, you're so boring, or needy, or too weak, or too tough. Her criticisms never ended, he thought.

But Brondo knew better, and he could sense a changing of the guard was coming. He was actually having a tougher time in his job than he thought, too—it was no joke being a prison guard, and he was subject to daily taunts from the prisoners who wanted to bully him, test him, make him crack. Maybe he had been too quick to want this kind of work. Why did he want it anyway? More abuse?

In late November the prison general manager and a few of his superiors called him in for a meeting; they were abrupt and wasted no time getting to the point: they found Brondo too soft for the position. He was devastated. Actually, he was crushed. He wasn't sure how much more rejection he could take, and he left the prison feeling heartbroken and defeated. He didn't want to have to go home and deliver the news to Sheena and face her wrath, so he drove out to the lake instead, and went to sleep in his car.

Eventually Brondo realised he would have to go home and face the music; he dreaded having to tell Sheena the bad news, and he knew it would negatively impact the relationship. Sheena heard him come in the door; she had gone to bed early and had been in bed for hours already, ahead of him.

"Come to bed, I've been waiting for you," she sang out from the bedroom.

Brondo climbed into bed; it was well after 11:00 pm and he cuddled up to her, thinking that if he did, she might go easier on him when he delivered the news.

Sheena rambled on about her day, never once asking how his day was. Brondo finally cleared his throat and spoke up:

"Well, my day didn't go as well," Brondo began, preparing her for the worst. Sheena sat upright in the dark.

"Why, what happened?" She asked, inquisitively. He had to have courage now.

"Well...I was informed by my superiors today that they think I'm too soft and not assertive enough to hold down this sort of job."

Sheena was furious. "What? They fired you?" She shouted angrily.

"Well, not fired, just let go..." Brondo said, devastated.

"God, Mother fucking Jesus Christ, Brondo! That's another job down the river! How many is that now? Six? Let's see..." she began listing all of his jobs, one by one, counting them off on her fingers. Brondo felt low. He felt so low he wanted to die.

"That's seven jobs, Brondo! Seven! This is your fault—I blame you for all this mess," she said, and then she went off at him, telling him that she was fed up with his constant careers and job changes, and that he changed jobs more often than he changed his clothes. Brondo didn't need to hear this. He realised that she revelled in kicking a dog when it was down. In his mind he switched off from her rantings, counter-arguing in his mind that *she* should be one to talk; she was always taking sick days off work, had taken multiple days off over the years, and, as sneaky as she was, would fudge the work attendance sheets and lie about how many days she had missed. He had counted that she had missed at least twenty-four days of work in the last year alone, but had never claimed them for sick days. Sometimes she would only go into work for half a day and pretend she had a doctors appointment and go shopping instead, so she had no right to throw stones at Brondo now or get on her high horse. But Brondo didn't have the energy to fight, nor was he in the mood. He could feel his depression kicking in, like waves washing in all over his body until he felt like he was drowning in it. The feeling was so overwhelming it was all he could do to close his eyes and will it to go away. Instead he tried to imagine himself floating on a life raft, drifting out to sea, waiting to be rescued by a rescue helicopter, watching the blades of the chopper circle as it hovered overhead, waiting to carry him to safety. It left him with a nice, if temporary feeling, far far away from Sheena's annoying voice as she raved on about his failures.

The next day at work Sheena messaged Brondo and told him that she hated him for losing his job and that he had better fight for his job, because this was their livelihood at stake; and if he didn't get his job back then they would be finished. For good.

Brondo was crushed, because he knew there was absolutely no chance of getting his job back; but he put in the call anyway to the general manager David Tuck, as well as the senior manager Terry Fiend and challenged their claims that he was unsuitable for the role. He reminded them of his reliability, that he always showed up on time for work, and always stayed late whenever it was necessary, and was always able to cover for other guards in their absence. He reminded them that he was a hard working, loyal employee and had back up character references to prove it; he argued that he was good enough to work the prison system, and that he had endured many hard knocks and hard blows in life and was up to the task when it came to dealing with hardened criminals. He had had to deal with people in the drug scene and had a lot of experience in dealing with drug addicts too; he knew how to handle them. Boy, did he know how to handle them. They had no idea how much experience he'd had. They thanked him for coming in and presenting his case, but it was a unanimous decision; they shook their heads and told him they had no choice, and the decision had been made. Brondo was beaten and he had to accept it; he would now have to go home and deal with Sheena one last time. Rather than face her, he decided it was better if he told her over the phone, at least then he wouldn't have to deal with her screaming at him.

"I spoke to them, I challenged them with all the reasons why I believed was a good hire, but they were resolute in their decision to let me go. I did the best I could, Sheena—but at the end of the day, they said no."

"Look, Brondo, I know you aren't a tough guy; I knew you weren't like Seedy, and your soft character, that was the very reason I fell in love with you—but you've got to toughen up now, you're not a baby anymore."

So now she wanted him to change. *Brondo be soft. No, wait, Brondo be tough. Now be soft again. No, tough. No, soft.* Jesus. Was it any wonder why men were always left confused by women? They could never make up their minds on what they wanted, he thought. One minute they wanted the big tough man who could go off into battle, fight wars. The next minute they wanted their man to be soft, effeminate, serve them breakfast in bed, light candles and go shopping at the mall with them.

Brondo knew he wouldn't be Brondo anymore should he change in any way for her; he also knew he couldn't be Brondo—the real Brondo—and be loved and accepted, just for being himself. Sheena was a hypocrite; for the many times she told Brondo he couldn't stand up to her boys and was too much of a softie, and when he did stand up to them she had screamed at him for being a violent brute.

Brondo had lost the spark and the passion to argue, even in a healthy manner; it had all just drained him to the point that he no longer cared. It was pointless. He decided to give up, give in and let her win, because he felt worthless enough as it was; there was no need for Sheena to twist the knife in any further. But twist it she did; for Sheena jumped at any opportunity to belittle him, verbally abuse him, and he knew she was relentless and would not stop.

The year ended badly and now they were back to one salary and struggling financially as Brondo started cold calling places with his resume looking for several positions, chasing down advertised jobs through the paper and using websites to apply for anything from retail and supermarket jobs back to his old security job days. He was determined to get his life back on track and renew his belief and confidence in himself and that he was capable of great things, despite Sheena's constant putdowns.

At the start of the new year it was Brondo's thirty-fourth birthday. Sheena announced she was going to have a party, despite the fact that they still had little money and mounting debts. He had realised long ago that Sheena was never good at money management, it was like many things in her life; she was always seeking the reckless path, preferring danger to stability, cheap thrills and drama to the quiet home life Brondo yearned for. Still, once she had an idea in her head, Brondo knew there was no stopping her. After the prison job Brondo's health had taken a hit; he no longer felt like working out at the gym and had gone on anti-depressants for his mounting depression. It was just another reason, Sheena said, why they should have a party. So Sheena began to organise a party for him, and she would write down a list of who she was going to invite: there would be Brondo's brother, Vito and Sonia with their two kids, his friend Tanya and her girlfriends and their partners; there would be his longtime friend Juan, Yaya and Uncle, whom he had not seen in forever, Maria and Joe, Max, Chloe, and baby Charlotte, Thomas and Lauren.

"This is going to be such a great party!" Sheena squealed with delight. Brondo tried to feel excited about it, though it felt more like a party for her than for him. Sure, it would be a great occasion to see his family and catch up with them, although he dreaded them knowing that he'd lost the prison job, because he couldn't bare to face the pitiful looks and free judgment that was always overflowing. But, he let Sheena have her way once again, because Sheena always got what she wanted. And what she wanted now was a great party.

And so it was a great party; everyone was there and it was a good turnout. The sun was shining and Vito and Chloe arrived early to help with setting up in the backyard. Chloe was now pregnant again, this was their third baby and they were hoping for a brother for Alicia and Jane; Brondo was so thrilled for his family, but somewhere deep inside he felt a pang of regret for what he had missed out on, for all he had sacrificed for Sheena. Yet she hardly seemed aware of it, and never even mentioned it. It was like the invisible marriage plans that had also faded into dust. The brothers set up the barbecue; they would have the barbecue firing up while they talked about the footy, and in the background the women arranged the main table, putting out plates of salads and glassware. Max was lurking around inside in the kitchen, feeling uncomfortable, so Sheena went out to have a word with Brondo.

"Max needs help," she whispered, pulling Brondo out of earshot of Vito.

"So, what's the deal? Why is he uncomfortable?" Brondo asked, baffled. As far as he was concerned he was on good terms now with Max.

"Well, you know...the whole *war* thing."

"But that was five years ago now, Sheena," Brondo assured her. "This was all sorted and resolved, surely he knows this."

"Maybe. Maybe not. I think you should go talk to Max," Sheena said, nudging him forward.

So Brondo went inside to talk to Max. He was sitting by the kitchen counter, doing nothing. *Go talk to Max*, Sheena had said. But Brondo couldn't see anything wrong with Max. Still, he got the ball rolling on the conversation, asking how Max was doing, if he'd been going to the gym lately, because Brondo admitted that he'd been slacking off. Everything seemed polite and pleasant enough; laughs and pleasantries were exchanged and Max's daughter Charlotte awoke from her nap and he then excused himself to go attend to her. What a turnaround, Brondo thought. He never thought he'd see the day when Max became a proud and doting father, and he was genuinely thrilled and proud of Max in this moment. Vito's two girls ran in the house playing chasey around the dining table. It was a beautiful thing to watch the kids having so much fun together. It warmed his heart. Yaya and Uncle sat outside under the shade of an old Oak tree talking to Maria and Joe, reminiscing on the old days, and Brondo got drunk on his birthday and started making a fool of himself with Vito as together they tried to dance the Greek dances, the Zorba and the Hasapiko. Vito, in trying to squat at one point heard a loud rip go, as the crotch of his pants split in two, which sent everyone into rounds of laughter. Everyone except Sheena. She told him it was stupid music and to turn it off. But the day ended well and had been just what Brondo needed, some good old fashioned traditional family fun. Eventually they all called it a night and everyone left; the last to leave was his good friend, Juan, who had been working overseas and living on luxury yachts in the south of Greece.

"Ah Brondo, I cannot believe it's been two years since the last time we saw each other and you came down to do security with me that night, remember?"

"Yeah, God that feels like so long ago now," Brondo nodded, feeling sentimental. His friendship with Juan had spanned decades, ever since they'd done an electronics traineeship together; yet through all the ups and downs, twists and turns in both their lives, he had always remained a constant in his life, kept him grounded.

"Things seem to have worked out for you and Sheena, still together, I see," Juan hinted; he knew Brondo too well though, knew something wasn't quite right. That glow, that passion he'd had always in his eye was gone, replaced by a dull, muted kind of star that was trying to come out and shine but was stuck somewhere behind a cloud.

Brondo shrugged. "Just tumbling along, ya know?" He said, not wanting to say more. "So how long are you in town for? Wanna catch up for a quick beer tomorrow before you head off? I'm not doing anything much."

"Yeah, sounds good—I have to head back to Greece on Wednesday; from there I'll head to Malta to work on the boats and yachts, it is truly one of the most beautiful parts of the world."

"You look like you're happy there," Brondo said, wistfully. Happy. What was that? What did it look like? He'd forgotten.

Brondo drove Juan around Scarborough the next day; they went to a chocolate apple factory and then visited the butter factory before stopping for lunch at the local pub. They said their goodbyes and eventually parted ways; Juan to Malta and Brondo to looking for new work. Part of him secretly wanted to climb in Juan's suitcase, fly to Malta with him; how exciting would it be to work on boats, smell the fresh sea air. It sounded like paradise. But Brondo could never leave his family, he was too big of a softie, too sentimental—he would miss his brother's family, his nieces, Yaya, and his parents too much. Strangely, the unexpected thought came over him that he might not miss Sheena, and fear engulfed him that the relationship was doomed. They still shared the same bed but the sex was diminishing;

Sheena was enjoying more time with her girlfriends, while Brondo's confidence had taken a big hit; Sheena pressured him about not working, and he felt terrible about himself; his guilt ran amok that perhaps it was all his fault all along; he had driven her to this point. He had failed her, failed to protect her, failed as a man; and now they were like two pieces of driftwood floating out to sea, just drifting, going in different directions.

CHAPTER EIGHTEEN
Heartbreak Hotel

Ecclesiastes 7: 26
And I find more bitter than death the woman, whose heart is snares and nets, and her hands as bands; whoso pleaseth God shall escape her; but the sinner shall be taken by her.

The insurmountable pressure that had been building on Brondo had taken its toll; he felt constantly depleted of energy, fatigued and just generally down. His depression had hit an all-time high and he was using antidepressants to cope with the overwhelming anxiety and darkness clouding his heart. He thought about the story of Sisyphus, then; a Greek mythological figure who was punished by Zeus, the King of the Gods. Sisyphus' punishment was that he had to spend eternity rolling an immense boulder up a hill, only for it to roll down again every time it neared the top. Every day he had to do the same thing; roll the boulder up the hill, until it became too great for him to push; eventually it would roll back over him, nearly crushing him, and then continue all the way back down the hill, forcing Sisyphus to have to start all over again. Brondo felt that this had been his whole life. He was Sisyphus; he had always been pushing, trying so hard to get to the top, but he always ended up being crushed before he got there, always having to start all over again.

Brondo had run the gamut when it came to his career; he had done everything, from security to maintenance man to cleaner to aged care worker; he'd even briefly had stints working for McDonald's and SPC and Rebel sport warehouse, and even as a support worker for troubled youths. He had worked hard to get his final Certificate Four in Aged care, but that had led to nowhere as he had been shunned by his co-workers, no thanks to Seedy who had spread rumours about him. Sheena suggested that Brondo join the Army Reserves, though he now felt that this was her attempt at pushing him away. Why would she want him to go into the Reserves, when it would mean that he'd be gone, probably for months at a time? Brondo told her he didn't think the Reserves would be a good place for his anxiety, either, though she refused to listen to him and dismissed his anxiety as nothing but fluff.

"You really should consider it, Brondo—it's good pay, and now that the boys have gone to Perth to work in the mines I don't need as much help around here with you playing referee between them, like you used to," she said and held firm to the decision. In the end, he sent his application off at her insistence but he didn't hold much hope for it.

In the meantime, Max had informed him that they were seeking truck drivers all around Scarborough; while it was a great idea, he reminded Max that he couldn't afford to pay the thousands of dollars it would cost to get his truck license. Max mentioned that in Laverton, just outside of Melbourne, if he didn't hold anything higher than a Certificate 3 then he could apply for government funding to get the training for the forklift license; he had already looked into it, Max said, before he'd chosen to go to the mines instead—he had to get the medium rigid license, plus the back and handling rope tying test; if he could pass those two tests he would be all set.

Brondo knew he had to act quick if he wanted to sit the test; but he was already in the middle of completing his Certificate Four and partial diploma in community services, therefore he would need to enrol quickly and put his name down for it. Brondo jumped on the phone that afternoon to make enquiries and was pleasantly surprised to find that there was a vacancy and that he would be able to enrol for both the forklift license and the truck license. Sheena was quick to retort that he didn't seem well suited to being a truck driver and Brondo was slightly annoyed by her negativity; he was trying so hard to get himself on track after losing the prison job, and here she was delivering yet another body blow, cutting down his abilities again.

Sheena was now calling the shots in every aspect of their relationship; where, once upon a time it had been she who had always been terrified that Brondo would leave her for a younger woman, it was now she who held a tight and powerful hold over him, and he had been slowly weakened over time by the fact that she had used all sorts of tricks and played all sorts of games to get at him. Brondo was her punching bag, her doormat, and he knew it.

"I'm going to punish you for losing your job like this," she said callously. Brondo now felt like a lost little puppy; he didn't want to lose her and had become so co-dependent on her in always seeking her approval, that he pressed on and did what she wanted, applying to the reserves and pursuing his forklift license; he also went for and got his reversing test and rope and pulldown test with the truck license, too. On the day he was due to take the truck driving license he was nervous; his casual work had interfered with his plan to sit the test the first two times, so this was his third and final chance, and he had a lot riding on it.

Brondo met with the instructor and they went out on the road together. He was carrying a long load, and the truck wasn't easy to manage. He manoeuvred the first two corners well, and was starting to feel good about it all; he put his head down and tried to stay focused. At the third corner he failed to stop at the red light in front of him with just minutes remaining on the test; he slammed the brakes hard, but knew he had gone over the line. The instructor got out of the cab to see for himself, but came back shaking his head, no; he told Brondo that he was over the length of the car distance required to call it a pass. Brondo had missed his third and last chance at taking the test, and was devastated as he realised he had failed. He had blown it again. The instructor reminded him that he had passed his forklift licence and that this was a good start for him; he would be able to get working casual positions with this at least, but he was having more trouble finding permanent work anyway, as employers were only wanting experienced forklift drivers.

Brondo had also driven out to the Albury Wodonga office of the Army Reserves to sit the initial interview; he had passed all the written and maths tests required, and now all that was left was to pass the medical test and the physical. Brondo was nervous though, as he knew that his anti-depressants might be an issue, having started back on them again. In the end he was knocked back for exactly this reason; as predicted, his being on medications cost him a shot at working in the Army Reserves. He was so despondent at receiving the rejection letter he told Sheena, but when he saw her face, her expression said it all.

"The boys are in Perth working in the mines and making good money, in fact fantastic money to be honest—meanwhile we're scraping by with your dead end forklift job," she said coldly.

"I'll give it one more shot with the truck licence; I'll go back to Melbourne and make a plea that I want to make a go of it, that I deserve one more chance—I was so close and all, maybe they'll waive it, Sheena..."

"...and if they don't?" She said, her eyes boring through him.

"Well, I've got Certificate Four and a partial diploma in community services, and that could further advance me in the aged care spectrum, allow me to move to a higher level, possibly move into different areas..." he said, his voice trailing off unconvincingly. But Sheena was now calling him a good for nothing loser, which really hurt him, because that was exactly how he felt.

It was simple science, really. Sheena and he had drifted apart.

It wasn't a good month when Brondo received word from Yaya that his father had been diagnosed with bowel cancer. Furthermore, he had apparently been admitted to the Royal Melbourne Hospital and was now awaiting surgery as the cancer could be terminal; she urged Brondo to hurry and go see him. Brondo thought about his strained relationship with Bill; it was not easy and they had never been close, but for the sake of making peace with the man he had to give him one last chance. He would do it for Yaya. Was this was a calling from God to make things right with his father, he wondered? Was the cancer terminal? He called Sheena to tell her that he was going to Melbourne to see his father in the hospital, and she only sent a curt response, informing him that she and Ally were going to Perth to see Max and Thomas. She was cold and emotionless, only commenting that *'healthy partners should usually travel and take holidays together.'*

Whatever that meant, Brondo thought. She was always trying to make him feel guilty. He knew he was delaying the inevitable with Sheena; after everything he had done for her, and this was all she could give him?

Brondo spoke to the kind Asian nurse, asking after his father's condition.

"He in good stable condition, Sir; visiting hours now close, but you come tomorrow, yes?"

"Yes, I'll be there tomorrow," Brondo replied.

"You *wery* good son, you come all time, yes? I see you yesterday, I think."

"Oh, no, I haven't been to visit him yet," Brondo corrected her, thinking it must have been Vito she had seen, "but I will be there first thing in the morning."

"No no—it definitely you—your father Bill, yes? He say to me that he only have one son—so it you, yes?" the nurse replied, sounding confused.

Brondo felt insulted and slighted, but he tried not to react. "No, he has *two* sons, and I am the elder, Brondo." There was a crackle on the other end of the line as he could hear the nurse say, *'wait, wait—you wery naughty boy, Bill; you tell me only one son.'*

Brondo called up Yaya and told his grandmother that his father was a fucking idiot, and that he was done. But Yaya in her dominance insisted that he still pay his visit. Brondo told her what had happened and that he thought it was all a bunch of lies, the old man wasn't terminal—but Yaya stayed firm, insisting that Bill did not have long to live and that Brondo needed to go. Brondo didn't need to be told twice, and so reluctantly he planned to go the next day.

The next morning he got up and showered, shaved and headed out to the truck depot first to see if he could chase down the possibility of obtaining his truck licence; but it was to no avail—they shook their heads no and Brondo left in a huff and puff. From there he drove on to the hospital, not looking forward to the visit with his father.

He located his father's room on the third floor and checked in at the nurses' station. Upon walking into his father's room, he saw his father lying there still under a white sheet, eyes closed. His father didn't waste any time chastising him though, as soon as he spied Brondo standing there.

"Who told you I was here, and why are you here, why did you come?" Bill blurted in a scathing and nasty tone, despite his being in obvious pain.

Brondo immediately felt sick and stressed in his stomach; he couldn't believe the level of disrespect that this pig of a man still delivered, even from his deathbed.

"What's your problem? I heard from Yaya and my brother, that's who," Brondo replied, caught off guard. If Bill were not so sick in this moment Brondo would so dearly have loved to break his father's face right then and there; this man Brondo knew, had been a worthless and vile human being to him since his childhood, and he had been a witness to the years of hellish abuse he had put their mother through. Instead, Brondo took a deep breath; he knew he had to try to do the morally right thing, even though he despised him with every bone in his body.

Bill could see his son was annoyed and said nothing, and both men just stared each other out, each one on the defensive. There was too much bitterness, there had been far too much water under the bridge. Eventually Brondo broke the silence between them.

"Look—I fucking came to see you, because I heard you were dying, you fucking moron," he snapped in an aggressive tone.

His father was speechless. Yaya. It had to have been her spreading the rumour that he was dying.

"Why, if I ever see that manipulative witch of a woman again—" he said, referring to Brondo's grandmother, "I'll teach her a lesson for meddling and speaking lies."

Brondo was done; he loved Yaya, and as he watched his father spew venom about her, he knew he was finished with him for good. He had lost all respect for the man who not only shunned and disowned him as his son, but had no respect for anyone else in the family, either. Brondo had been abused and put down by him for years; and now, as he lay there, Brondo saw his father in his true colours—he was nothing but a lowlife.

Brondo left without another word and drove back to his grandmother's house.

"Yaya—how could you interfere like that? Manipulate and guilt me into going to see him! He told everyone in there that he only had one son, too! And then he blasted me for coming! You should have known it would end badly," he said, infuriated with her.

"I only did so Brondo because I didn't want you to have to live with any regrets," Yaya countered. But Brondo was furious.

"I am done with this family and its manipulations! It's the reason I left for Scarborough in the first place!" Brondo yelled, storming out of the house. Yaya ran after him, pleading with him not to leave on angry terms, like he had done so many times before. He spun around on Yaya, feeling vengeful.

"The fact that he went around telling people that he only had one son...THAT should have been your first clue! He is not worth my time. Leave me alone, Yaya. I'm leaving," Brondo shouted back, and drove off, feeling angry and hurt with his grandmother. He was so done with all the games they played in his own family that he was just happy to be away from them all.

Brondo was still angry when he returned home; he stormed through the back door, past Sheena and Ally who were now back from Perth, but he said nothing to either of them and instead marched to the fridge, snatching a beer from the shelf. Sheena had been cold in the bedroom for months and uninterested in him, but tonight he would throw her down on the bed; Sheena, taken by surprise, was all for it and Brondo launched himself on her; it was wild and angry sex, lacking any passion and entirely physical, like two wild beasts in a forest, and like nothing he had ever had. Sheena was impressed by his display of manliness, but Brondo was just disgusted by her; he had finally used her in the same ways that she had always used him.

He then left her lying on the bed and got up to shower; he could still feel the anger pumping and coursing through his veins, adrenaline pulsating through his being. If she wanted to be treated like a piece of meat, a whore...then fine, that's how he would treat her.

By late June Brondo had landed the perfect job while continuing with his studies in community services. It was working with Calvary Community Care, and he would be responsible for the personal and home care of outpatients. His soft nature was appreciated and he was well suited to the role of caring for his clients as he cooked and cleaned for them, assisted them with showering and day to day activities, transporting them to and from appointments. Sheena, of course, was instantly negative.

"Brondo, Calvary Care have a bad reputation," she said, but Brondo was not interested in her and her stupid opinions anymore, he just wanted to work, and Sheena never listened to him anyway, so why should he listen to her? She had never been supportive of his pursuits, this he knew well. If sex was the only way to please her now, then he would use her, use and use and use her, just the way she liked it. Something had indeed snapped in Brondo, and it was visiting his father in those final days that did it; seeing his father still abuse him from his deathbed was the last straw, the straw that broke the camel's back—Brondo was sick and tired of being abused and mistreated, sick of never being respected, and now finally the tables had turned, and he would treat everyone exactly the same way that they treated him. *Do unto others as they do unto you? Or—do TO others what they do TO you!* He had to chuckle at the thought of it, wondering why he hadn't thought of it before; but in all truth he had never felt more empowered in all his life as he did in this moment.

Brondo pushed for intimacy over the coming months but Sheena was uninterested, preferring to read her fifty shades of grey rubbish instead; so Brondo spent more and more time on Facebook as Sheena ignored him more and more. The growing distance between them was palpable, even their fighting had disappeared into nothingness. Even the fighting, Brondo thought, had been something—anything was better than this silence.

In August 2014, Sheena came home and announced to Brondo that she wanted a tummy tuck; since the birth of the twins some twenty years ago she had been stuck with all the extra leftover, flabby skin from the birth and her stomach had been stretched beyond all comprehension. Since she had had health care at the time of their birth, Sheena was told she would be eligible for a free tummy tuck when the time came. She admitted she had never gotten around to it in the past because she had just never found the time; but now she wanted to research facilities that performed the procedure, because now it had become important to her to get her body back and feel good about herself.

Though Brondo thought it was odd that she had never mentioned it before, Sheena now admitted that she had always been self conscious about it; she had felt ashamed of her physique, never wanting to go to the beach in the summertime, or have anyone see her flabby tummy.

"I honestly never noticed anything wrong with your tummy," Brondo assured her, being completely frank.

"But, haven't you noticed that I have always kept my stomach covered during sex?" Sheena asked, incredulous.

Brondo didn't know what to say; first off, he felt disgusted that she thought he would judge her like that, but it also showed how little she understood about men and what they thought about when they were in the throes of passion. What man would care about a stretch mark here or there, when the promise of getting laid was right before him? But he did not say any of this to her, he only nodded sympathetically, remembering that he had only ever seen her stomach twice before, and Sheena would quickly cover it up again, feeling embarrassed.

Much to her disappointment, Sheena's insurance came back saying she would have to pay the entire $10,000 for the procedure now, as she had waited too long to have it. She was devastated, and kept saying over and over that it was her dream; it was all she ever wanted, and now her dreams were shattered.

"We will figure out a way," Brondo offered her in the way of support. He could see how much this meant to her, and if the most he could do was to be supportive, then he would do it.

There was talk of a surgeon in town that was a known

abdominoplasty specialist; he performed tummy tuck procedures, though Sheena was cautious to go to him as she'd heard that he was a body butcher who'd done some dodgy work. One day after work Brondo drove out to Sheena's work and picked her up; while he was waiting outside for her he noticed Jane Murray, a good friend of Sheena's, who looked like she had lost a lot of weight, almost to the point that Brondo didn't recognise her.

"Get a look at Jane," Sheena pointed as she climbed in the passenger seat.

"Wow, yeah—she looks amazing! I almost didn't recognise her, babe."

"That's the butcher surgeon I was telling you about, he did her tummy tuck and she thought he was the best," Sheena said, glancing back again at Jane, impressed by her results. Perhaps the work he had done on Jane wasn't that bad and Sheena decided that maybe he wasn't as bad as people had made him out to be.

"It's decided," she announced emphatically. "I want to go through with the surgery; Jane even told me today that with this particular surgeon his services are free, apparently you only pay an amount at the end once you are happy with the result. If you are not happy, it's simple—you don't have to pay."

Brondo was suspicious, though. *Nothing was ever free.* Free was what Sheena wanted him to believe, and usually Brondo was gullible enough to believe her.

Sheena had been busy juggling another big case in her life; the molestation she had suffered at the hands of her stepfather over forty years ago. She had forgotten to tell Brondo the rest of the story, so she revealed all to him now.

"Well, you know how after it happened, and I didn't tell Varma until I was fifteen? Well, that's when we took him to court, pressed charges. My sister and I had to go before the Judge and make a statement; it was nerve wracking, we were only young and we were afraid of seeing him again, we dreaded even having to lay eyes upon him in the courtroom. Well, apparently our individual testimonies didn't match up, and so the Judge voted against the case, and it was thrown out. We felt so let down by the whole judicial system, that a man like that, a pedophile, could walk free of his crime, never to be punished. I wouldn't give up though; three years later I decided to appeal it; this time I had to go before three Judges, and I won. Varma then pushed us girls to fight for personal damages, and we decided to pursue personal injury and compensation claims. And we were granted this, too. I won some money, being a victim of crime," she said, though Brondo could see the monetary gain had done little to erase the years of her psychological pain.

"So, what happened to the money?" Brondo asked, curious.

"It's been sitting in a term deposit for twenty years, and it's finally coming due," she said gleefully, rubbing her hands together. "I'm going to use it for this tummy tuck—and buy myself a new car!" She announced ecstatically.

For a split second, Brondo was happy for Sheena, for the fact that she had finally served retribution and justice upon the man who had caused her so much pain and lifelong anguish. *But, hang on a minute: hadn't Brondo scrimped and scraped and saved all this time, only just getting by, and all the while paying all the bills, feeding everyone, carrying the load by himself? Why had she never told him about this?* But he decided to drop it; it was in the past now, and he just didn't have the energy anymore, couldn't be bothered making waves with her, because it would just end up in a full blown verbal war.

Max drove Sheena out towards Croydon to pick up the car;

Sheena now had sporty and flash new red wheels, plus another court case loomed on the horizon; she gloated that she was going to chase her stepfather's superannuation as well; she was not finished with the bastard yet.

"I'm going to destroy him just as he destroyed me," she seethed, venom dripping off her tongue.

Sheena was discussing this all with Varma a few days later, who suddenly said something quite unexpected.

"I'm still torn over this man—and I don't know if it's because I share kids with him, or not."

Brondo looked over at Varma Parrish, and all he could feel for her was utter disgust; then he looked over at Sheena, trying to gauge her response. Sheena just sat there, motionless, her face crestfallen.

What kind of mother could love a pedophile? Only a sick, twisted and unstable one, Brondo thought. Sheena looked as though she'd just had the wind taken out of her sails; as though being punched in the gut wasn't enough, Varma had driven the knife straight through her heart. Sheena bled. She looked over at Brondo, not knowing what to say. Brondo felt sorry for her. He could see in that moment that behind all of Sheena's nastiness was a deep gash, a wound so deep it had never healed, and in large part it was because of Varma. She had never been validated by Varma, vindicated of any wrongdoing. And Varma didn't have a backbone, she knew her mother had allowed what had happened, to happen, which made it all the sicker.

You allowed your daughter to be violated, molested, raped—and not only did you do nothing, you served her up to him on a plate, like she was nothing more than a piece of meat, Brondo thought. No wonder Sheena had a warped sense of intimacy... she could never truly trust anyone; so she abused them instead.

Just as she had abused Brondo. Let the cycle of abuse continue, he thought. That's how it seemed to go in all families. It seemed to him that the patterns of abuse would always be there, would always exist, to be handed down from generation to generation, and this, sadly, was just the way of the world.

Brondo could see the anguish in Sheena's eyes and decided to drop the topic. Instead, he reminded her of the upcoming surgery, and how fabulous she was going to look. This made her face relax, her jaw unclench, and her mind went off into her vain, supermodel fantasies.

The day arrived and Sheena went into the hospital with Brondo, ever supportive, by her side. After signing some legal forms Brondo watched as Sheena was wheeled off into the theatre. Ever the worrier, he paced around the waiting room letting his nerves get the best of him; Varma told him to go home and chill; she would call him when she heard anything. So Brondo went home and had a shower then put some TV show on, but he couldn't focus on anything.

"Have you heard anything yet?" He messaged Varma. After not receiving any reply from her, he messaged again. And again. Finally Varma responded.

"I have not heard anything yet—it is a three hour surgery!" She replied coldly.

Finally Brondo got the call that she was out of surgery and resting, recovering from the anaesthesia. By all accounts the surgery had been a success; he was relieved that Sheena was Ok, but for the next two weeks she would recover in hospital to protect her from any chance of infection and Brondo would be at Sheena's side every day, morning and afternoon, while juggling work and life. It was a crazy time, and he ran back and forth from the house constantly, getting things for her that she had wanted; more toiletries, the pink nightie with the flowers, not the blue one because that made her skin itch; then she wanted chocolates as a treat, flowers to brighten her room—no, not irises, they were too dull, something with a pop of colour to fight the monochrome hue of sickly white hospital walls. Then she needed soda, because they only served juice and water.

"Please, Brondo, can you just rub my feet please, they are screaming out for a foot massage, and you know how I love my feet!"

So Brondo gave her a foot massage while she lay there, bored and flipping through magazines. Sheena wasn't much of a reader at the best of times, and he noticed how quickly she would tire of things, as she tossed the magazine to the floor and let go an insufferable sigh. When he couldn't be there, and when he finally found a minute to himself, she would message Brondo, asking him where he was. *'Where are you babe, I miss you,'* and *'come see me, I'm bored,'* as well as a dozen other messages which filled his inbox. When he did go in to sit with her, he felt that Sheena was distant with him, though he tried in vain to support and provide and protect her at his best and with all that he had. But he would no sooner leave, happy to get home to peace and quiet and there she would be, reaching out and messaging him again. As frustrated as he was, he couldn't see it as anything more than her trying to reach out, and so he would answer her call, hoping this would bring them closer again.

Brondo was there every day without fail, loving and tending to Sheena and Sheena's needs; what he could not have known was that she had already made up her mind about a lot of things, and, unbeknownst to him, she had already been laying the groundwork for other plans.

The two weeks were over, and Sheena came home to an ever

doting Brondo; he would get up early, make her breakfast in the mornings, run for her pills and make sure she had everything she needed and was all set for the day before heading off to work, himself. The district nurse came every day to dress and tend to her wounds to make sure she was healing. Sheena told Brondo one night that she wanted to go to Melbourne as soon as she was able, and that Brondo was to show her off, give her a night on the town as her big coming out party. It was to announce "the new and improved Sheena" to the world, and she couldn't wait.

As promised, and when she was sufficiently healed, Brondo took her to Melbourne; first they went by to visit Yaya and Uncle, whose eyes boggled at the sight of Sheena's transformation.

"Yes, she is beautiful now, but why, oh why?" Yaya asked, puzzled.

Then they went to visit Vito and Sonia, who were also blown away by her new appearance. Brondo told his brother how panicked he had been for her during the surgery, and the relief that it was all over, and Vito suggested they go for a drive and leave the two women alone to chat for awhile.

"I mean, I'm happy for you, for her, really Bro, I am; but, why did she do it? Why didn't you tell me?" Vito asked, genuinely shocked.

"She wanted it to be a surprise, you know, the new and improved Sheena," Brondo shrugged, explaining that she had hated her body after the birth of the twins.

"Yeah, I get that, Bro—but why *now?*" Vito asked, silently suspicious.

But Brondo didn't read into it being anything more than her wanting and needing a boost in confidence; after all, he said, Sheena had suffered years of putdowns and abuse at the hands of Seedy, had suffered a multitude of abuses he would not disclose to his brother, but just leave it at that: it was just that now it was finally her time to shine.

After the weekend in Melbourne they drove back out to Scarborough, stopping in Echuca on the way and paying a visit to the district nurse, who finished dressing her wounds; Sheena was given a clean bill of health and was told she could return to work the following Monday.

In the week that followed, Sheena had become a brand new person; her confidence had sky rocketed, and she was now getting more male attention than ever before—especially from younger men, much younger than Brondo. Brondo, however, was not the jealous type and Sheena knew this, but he did feel the need to say something because Sheena was drawing more and more attention to herself now and it was changing her; if she had been vain and selfish before, now she had become the overgrown monster of vanity. Having lost two dress sizes, she spent thousands on a whole new wardrobe for herself, too; it was like she was re-inventing herself, having some sort of identity or mid life crisis, and she was starting to look out of control.

"I'm just worried that you...you might be losing a bit of focus about it all," Brondo gently suggested, but of course any of his suggestions only came across as wrong to her.

"My God, Brondo—I'm finally doing something for myself after raising three kids and getting out of a hellish marriage, and now you're starting in on me? Why can't anyone be happy for me? I thought you of all people would understand how it felt to be kicked down so many times you no longer knew how to get up," she barked angrily at him. Sheena dismissed his concerns completely, brushing it off as a sign of his own insecurities.

Sixteen days after her surgery, seventeen days after their conversation, Sheena delivered her last blow.

"We're over," she said, as blank as a wall. "I want out of the relationship. End of discussion."

Brondo couldn't believe what he was hearing and he just looked back at her, stunned. He couldn't speak, he couldn't cry, he couldn't feel...anything.

"What do you mean?" He said, for something to say.

"The spark is gone," she replied flatly. He searched himself to try and find the right words.

"I still love you, Sheena—yes, things have been hard, but we've survived impossible odds...look at all that we've been through..."

"The passion has gone," she said, numb.

"I beg to differ; two weeks ago we were at it like wild boars," he argued. But he could feel himself starting to lose his dignity, even as he said it. Because the truth was, she was right. The sex had been robotic, unfeeling. Awful. In that moment, Brondo fell to Sheena's feet, kissing them and crying like a baby. He begged.

"You have to give me one more chance," he cried, his heart breaking in two.

"Ok, I'll give you one month to find the spark, but that's all," she said coldly.

Brondo began to rewrite the poems he'd once written for her; he knew she loved his ability to write her romantic, loving ballads, as he had such a way with words, had the ability to pour his soft heart on the page for all to see. He tried to work harder at foreplay, too, wining and dining her, but Sheena shut off like a cold fish; it felt like an uphill battle he was going to lose. The month came and went like lightning, and Brondo knew his time was up. The relationship was dead. It was so dead that even a set of spark plugs couldn't have helped them. Sheena walked out into the living room in a tight fitting black dress that hugged all of her womanly curves. She had painted her nails firetruck red and Brondo couldn't stop looking at her. She was smoking hot. She sat him down on the couch.

"I love you Brondo—but I'm not in love with you; I just don't want it anymore. The age difference, it's always been a problem, and I want more from you, but you're too soft, too nice, too gentle, too..."

"But once upon a time you said the age difference *wasn't* a problem, remember Sheena? And you said you loved me for my gentle ways, because Seedy had abused you so much..." Brondo tried to remind her. He didn't really even know why he was still fighting for the relationship, even now. He just was.

"Well, it bothers me *now*—I want you to be tough, I want you to hurt me a little, dominate me," she said flatly. "But you can't. You just can't."

"I can do that," Brondo said in complete desperation, though inside he felt sick. All of his dignity had by now flown out the window, and it was he who had thrown it away. But he didn't care. He just had to have her now. But Sheena just shook her head, said that it wasn't in his character, it wasn't natural for him.

"We don't do anything together," Brondo quickly asserted. "Let's go to the movies, let's watch a movie, let's go for a walk, or try a game of bowling again..." he said, grabbing at straws.

"What's wrong with the movies at home? My God," she laughed, "you truly don't get it."

And in that instant he knew that for once she was right. He didn't get it.

"Where are you going tonight?" He asked, hoping she might reconsider, change her mind like she always did, perhaps ask him to come along too. But she was just a cold fish.

"I'm going out dancing with my sister Lisa and her friends," she stated, matter-of-factly. "And don't wait up for me, I'll probably just crash at Lisa's tonight because it will be a late night." Brondo just sat there, feeling defeated. She had been staying at her sister's house more and more these days, too; he should have seen the signs. He let go a defeated sigh, and with that Sheena got up and walked over to the table, collected her car keys and left.

Brondo sat on the edge of the couch, on the edge of his life and could swear he felt his insides shattering into a million pieces. He imagined he could see his whole body crumble, smash like fine china all over the cold tile floor. He though of the passage in the Bible, maybe it was Ecclesiastes: *that which is crooked cannot be made straight,* and he turned to God's words to try and take comfort in them. This, he realised, was what it must feel like to be walking around in the grounds of Heartbreak Hotel; it was a haunted old place and the rooms were like the four chambers of his heart, all cleared out and empty.

CHAPTER NINETEEN
Redefined

Ecclesiastes 7:3
Sorrow is better than laughter; for by the sadness of the countenance the heart is made better

They still shared the same bed and the same house, but Brondo's world had collapsed before his very eyes. Sheena said that they would soon move out and start new lives, but he couldn't believe how cold and heartless she was being; he had given her everything she wanted, and she had always wanted the best of everything, but now she claimed he had given her nothing.

"How can you say that, Sheena? I worked myself to the bone, paying off debts, paying for all the damage your sons caused me—the $6000 in speeding fines, the tax fraud, my broken jaw, smashing my car; I paid for not one, but two houses that you just had to have, remember? And what about the furniture, all the things you wanted? You've bled me dry," he said out of sheer frustration.

"Yeah? Well we are going nowhere financially, and we never

even go on holidays!" Sheena yelled back at him. Brondo was fuming.

"That's because you *spent it all!*" He yelled back at her.

Sheena shrugged her shoulders and simply said, 'end of discussion' and walked out of the room. Internally he blew a fuse, and in that moment he thought he wanted to kill her.

Brondo was at the end of his rope and he finally gave up trying to fight for her; if she had made up her mind that this was the end of the Brondo and Sheena story, so be it. Sheena, however, wasted no time informing all of her friends and family that they were over, and for the next week Brondo began waking up in the middle of the night weeping as he looked upon Sheena sleeping there, next to him, so close and yet so far away.

Brondo tried to remind himself that, as painful as this was, perhaps he was being primed for something much greater; but these thoughts quickly disappeared as he lost his appetite, his ability to sleep, and could feel himself falling back into a deep depression. People bombarded him with messages expressing their sorrow and offering their prayers, but he was hurting too much to talk to anybody. Words could not describe the dark, lost and lonely pit of despair he now found himself in, and he questioned himself and his life, wondering what on earth was the point of it all.

By years' end, Sheena had moved in with Max and Chloe; ironically, both her boys were emotional, especially Thomas when they heard the news; Ally too, was crushed, as she had come to love Brondo a great deal. But in Sheena's mind she was just glad to be rid of Brondo's controlling, nasty family, stating that she wanted to be with someone whose family could accept her.

But Brondo couldn't get past the feeling that he'd been used, and it began to gnaw at all his senses. His intuition was talking to him as though on loudspeaker now; he couldn't believe how he had just done everything for her, too; the surgery, doting on her, helping her day in, day out...and now this? This was how she repaid him? It sickened him that Sheena had won her court case despite its being a hung jury, and was now driving around in a fancy car, while her stepfather was serving a jail sentence, put behind bars for life. It felt like after all the money she'd won as a victim of crime had freed her, and she no longer needed him—while now it was Brondo who struggled financially and psychologically, picking up the pieces of his life.

Sheena fed him even more rubbish and bullshit about her sexual fantasies, about having her needs fulfilled, and about the fact that she had to set him free, because if he was hers he would come back to her, and if he didn't come back, then he wasn't hers to begin with.

Rubbish, Brondo thought. He wanted to argue that it wasn't him asking to be set free in the first place—it wasn't him calling things off, but her—and it made no sense why she had always tested him, tested the relationship, questioned his love for her. Who was he trying to kid, anyway? The fact of the matter was, it was over. But, why call it off now? Why now? It looked to him like she had wanted to end it because she was hiding something. And this time he had to listen to his gut, because his gut instincts were always right.

Times were hard, and Brondo let go of himself as his entire world began to unravel; his anxiety went through the roof, his diet and cleanliness suffered as he moved into a new unit all alone, trying to face a life without Sheena. Nighttime was the worst, though; Brondo dreaded going to a cold and empty bed alone. He missed her body, her presence. He wanted to text her, ask if he could come and visit baby Charlotte; maybe if she saw him again she might change her mind. His unit became a pigsty, too; he became slovenly, unmotivated, and fell into a slump; he even lost the will to go to the gym. Most nights he cried himself to sleep, calling out to God asking, "Why me, God? Why me?"

But either God wasn't taking calls or emails that day, or Brondo simply couldn't hear Him.

On Australia Day he finally broke down, and in a deep depression he reached out to his brother and sister-in-law to tell them he and Sheena had ended things. Sonia was astonished that Brondo had kept this to himself, and had not reached out for help sooner.

"I just can't think clearly, half the time I'm in a daze, I just feel so alone," Brondo said, apologetically.

"Why don't you come down and spend the Australia Day weekend with us," Sonia said, reaching out to him. Brondo agreed; he had nowhere to go anyway, so maybe a weekend with his nieces would do him good. He finally opened up about Sheena's sexual fantasies, her money demands, her always wanting the high life. She was all about money, thrills and self gratification.

"Wow, Bro, we never knew it was that bad—why didn't you tell us?" Vito said, shaking his head.

"Because I loved her; I didn't want it to end, and I knew you would all look at me like I was a failure," Brondo muttered, broken hearted.

Vito told his brother he needed to pull his head out of the sand; she was no good, he had to let go, get on with his life. Maybe join a new church, put himself out there on dating sites.

So Brondo joined a new church; called the Encounters Church, and for a short time he would even bump into Max and draw him close as the two men talked about the breakup. He would ask Max how Sheena seemed, and if she was doing ok.

"Oh you know my mother, she's fine, she's always fine—she always takes care of *herself*," Max remarked bitterly. "You know, going out a lot, complaining about turning fifty, blah blah," was all he said.

Alas, Brondo wasn't anywhere near being over Sheena, though, and his every waking thought was of her and their life together. He felt couldn't move away from Scarborough no matter how much he wanted to—because he felt that, as long as he was somewhere in the vicinity of her, she might still change her mind down the track, give him another chance. Foolish thinking, he knew, yet it was the last thread of hope he clung to, and he just could not let go.

But as much as Brondo didn't want to go back to Melbourne, back to his mother's mind games and guilt trips, he also knew that staying near Sheena was wrong for him, too; and staying there was hurting him, and holding him back from being able to free himself of the memories of her; it was the wrong town, and as much as he didn't want to admit it, even the new church was proving not to be enough for him.

He thought then about what Max had said, that she was going out a lot. Was she thinking of him, missing him too? It didn't sound like it. It stung Brondo to think of this. It sounded like Sheena was having no problem with moving on. He decided to spy on her Facebook page, to see if there were any pictures that would tell him what she was up to. He did notice one guy's name consistently appearing in the comments section of her posts, and wondered who he could be. Sheena knew a lot of people, though, and her wild, gregarious and daring personality naturally drew people to her.

By November, Brondo had regressed into deeper depression; his hours at the Cavalry Community Care had been slashed, his gold Commodore was acting up as it sounded like it was on its last legs and he had a severe ear infection and migraines that just would not go away. He had tried to go on a few dating sites, but his heart just wasn't in it, because he couldn't stop wondering about Sheena and what she was doing. He tried to get himself motivated to return to the gym, and made friends with a new guy there called Shane Farrant. One night after gym he opened up to Shane about his troubles, and Shane told him about how he and his wife had just survived a house fire and were struggling to make ends meet; they had to work but had no one to look after their two kids.

"Well, I happen to be great with kids," Brondo said, honestly. "If you need me, I'll be happy to help out."

Shane invited Brondo around to meet his family, and he immediately bonded with Shane and his wife, Tanya, and he hit it off with the two kids. Brondo started coming around three nights a week, and would help out with the kids, while Shane and Tanya would help Brondo out with food and groceries. Shane and Brondo even did a day trip to Echuca where they bought pet rabbits for the kids and had a lovely day out, which really raised Brondo's spirits.

"You know, you're one hell of a great guy, and you've been a real lifesaver for our family when we thought we had no one," Shane said that afternoon on the drive back. "Any woman would have to be completely insane to let go of you," Shane said, matter-of-factly.

"Well, maybe you've just hit the nail on the head—maybe she *is* insane..." Brondo remarked with sarcasm, and the two men laughed. For a couple of months the two worked out regularly together, supporting each other through tough times. Brondo's migraines and earaches persisted though, and Shane kept reminding him to get it looked at. Eventually the insurance for the house fire and property damage came through, and Shane and Tanya had enough for a downpayment on a new place; the only problem was that the new place they'd found was too far away from town. Brondo promised them he'd come and visit one day, and the Farrant family moved away.

Brondo tried to stay motivated, really he did; but without Shane around to pick him up, he quickly spiralled downwards again into loneliness and depression.

Then came another crushing blow; the landlady and owner of the shared apartment complex sent him a letter stating that Brondo had just four days to move his belongings out. He was being evicted. Brondo was thunderstruck. How could they do this to him? Not that it was a great place to live, anyway; he was sure there was some elaborate drug laundering operation going on at the back of the units that she'd been running on the sly. He argued with the landlady that she had to give him more notice; but the mean woman bit back, saying he had never signed a lease agreement, and then told him to 'get the fuck out' or she'd be calling the cops on him.

By Thursday Brondo found himself homeless and on the streets, sleeping in his car or on park benches. He was suffering even more migraines as the world whirled around him; he felt lost, disoriented and more alone than he had ever felt in his life. He thought about calling Sheena, or Vito, but his pride wouldn't let him; so he lay down on a park bench and cried the hours away. The severe earaches returned, and he noticed a new discolouration of his skin; so Brondo went to see a doctor, who told him he needed to have his wisdom teeth pulled.

Brondo became hysterical; could things possibly get any worse, he wondered? He spent several hours at the 24-hour gym though he didn't have any energy to workout; he saw his reflection in the mirror for the first time in weeks and was alarmed to see that he looked like total shit, so he hung around until late, until all the other patrons had left, then he used the facilities to shower there, tried to clean himself up a bit. He sat for a long time afterwards in the change rooms, trying to fight off and avoid loneliness, hoping and praying that someone, anyone would help him, but no one paid him any attention. He slept in his car again and went to cash converters, selling his watch and a few other items just to buy food; at one point he became so hungry he thought he was going to die. One night he sat on a park bench by a rubbish bin and the thought dawned on him that perhaps he was no better than a piece of garbage, because he felt truly worthless. Brondo was sinking further and further into debt now; it was by now January 2016 and he had resorted to borrowing money from a kind man at the church, because by now he had completely lost his care job at the community centre, too.

Alan Worthington and his wife were from the church and they brought Brondo in for a couple of nights and offered him their couch; Alan took Brondo to see an ear specialist, because Brondo was obviously in a daze, barely eating and not thinking clearly. He knew he had hit rock bottom as depression took him to a new low; it was so dark down there that all he could think about was how he could end his life, how he could remove the feelings of worthlessness from the pit of his stomach. Life held no meaning anymore, and he could no longer find any purpose in it, or will to live. The ear specialist was concerned with the colour of his gums and immediately booked him into the base hospital to undergo a brain scan and test for tumours. By this stage Brondo had pretty much given up, there was no way he was going back to fucking Melbourne either; so if it was cancer that was going to be the thing to take him down, so be it—then he would give up altogether.

Within twenty-four hours of his scan at the hospital, Brondo received a phone call from a woman who was the receptionist to the specialist.

"Dr. Bartholomew has asked me to inform you that you will need to return to the hospital; he wishes for you to begin treatments in both radiation and chemotherapy in the oncology department, and strongly recommends you start the program right away."

Brondo stopped dead in his tracks; he froze and everything around him went silent, as though he had already entered into death itself, but while still in life. It was weird. He struggled to comprehend any of the words as they circled around his periphery; they had just become a bunch of moving, indecipherable letters to him. Was he already dead, he wondered? He could faintly hear the girl's voice on the receiving end, repeating that he needed to come in and see the specialist, but he couldn't answer her, he couldn't say anything at all.

Brondo went to the hospital, and on his way he thought about how he had given his heart and soul for Sheena, how he had stood by her through thick and thin; while her boys were on ice and out of control, he'd been there for her; when she'd had problems and needed his help, he was always there, had always bailed her out. But where were they now? Max and Chloe were living the high life and had their wonderful little family with babies Charlotte and Lara; Thomas and his girlfriend Lauren had their new baby, Evelyn, too; meanwhile, Brondo had...

nothing. How ironic that they had made Brondo's life a living hell for years, had stripped him of everything—and now he had nothing, and they had it all. He just couldn't understand it. His suffering and misery had become too much to bear, and his heart ached with a sadness so deep that he thought that it might just stop, altogether. He got out his phone. He called Shane, he desperately needed help, needed somewhere to go; but sadly they could not offer him a place to stay, and he hung up the phone on him, feeling hurt. He tried calling Alan and his wife, but they didn't answer. He hung up. He thought about all the times he had helped others, had always been the person to be there, been someone others could rely on. And yet, when he needed help, no one was there for him. Ok, ok, he had to gather himself now, he thought. He would have to call his brother. He could imagine Vito crying, Yaya and Uncle in shock when he delivered the news. He walked around in a daze, feeling directionless, and began contemplating his funeral and where he might be buried. In sheer desperation he fell to his knees and looked up at the sky and cried to God. He called out to Him. Of course, he didn't expect any answer, because nobody ever answered him.

"Why God, why? What is my purpose? I've served you no purpose; I've done nothing to give you glory, I'm nothing but a pathetic, miserable joke." He sobbed.

John 16: 32 I am not alone, for my father is with me came whispering to him then through a rustling in the leaves. He looked up. Was he imagining things? Was someone there?

All of a sudden, as if on cue, his phone started ringing. He got to his feet to answer it. It was the receptionist girl again.

"Hello, am I speaking with Brondo Violaris?" She asked politely.

Brondo sighed and cleared his throat, preparing himself for

the worst. He could feel his heart sinking even further into his chest cavity as he braced himself for more bad news.

"Yes," he said, "This is Brondo," he answered flatly, fighting back the tears in a near emotional breakdown.

"I'm sorry to trouble you, Sir; but it seems we got your results mistaken with another patient. I am so sorry for the stress this must have caused you. Mr. Violaris? Are you there?"

Brondo went silent again; all the colour had washed from his face as he stood there under the moon and the night sky; he just couldn't believe his luck. He felt dazed and confused, but in a good way; he couldn't comprehend how the mix up had happened, and he let go a stream of emotions as relief took over him. The girl kept apologising somewhere in the background, explaining that it was an honest mistake, but Brondo felt no need to say anything; he didn't need to say anything at all, because in that moment he realised he had just been given a second chance at life, and that was all he needed to hear.

Suddenly it was as though the air around him became lighter, cleaner, too, and he could breathe again. He hung up the phone and his mind whizzed along at a thousand miles an hour as he realised that, just moments earlier his whole world had crashed; now, by some strange stroke of luck or fate or whatever kind of miracle one could call it, he had been blessed with a clean bill of health. It was incredible. He started jumping up and down on the sidewalk, jumping for joy, until a passerby looked at him like he was an idiot. But he didn't care. He was alive again! He just couldn't believe it, but in that moment all his other worries faded into insignificance, because nothing else mattered. He walked down the road with a renewed pep in his step as his mind began planning things.

First, he would set about finding a job. He picked up the

local paper and saw an opportunity to run a carpet cleaning business. By the end of January he had a new job and started earning money again. After a month he had enough for a lease deposit on a dumpy little studio at the back of a shop; it wasn't much, but it got him off the streets and out of sleeping in his car. With each small step forward he prayed to God and thanked Him. After the second month he was finally able to get his car fixed and running properly. Each tiny baby step was still a step forward, and although he missed Sheena he tried to focus on just staying grateful in the moment, for each new small thing he had. The carpet cleaning business was booming, and he felt his life was finally getting back on track, and he was learning how to be truly alone for the first time in his life, too, even learning how to enjoy his own company. He thought about Sheena, and missed her, but he didn't miss her selfishness, or how she had dominated his life. He did try his hand at a few dates but decided against it because he was still on the rebound and he had no desire to share himself with anyone.

Things were finally looking up for Brondo for the first time in a long time, and he was content because he had finally found inner peace; he was working hard, saving hard, going to a good church, a peaceful church that was filled with love and acceptance and was free of judgment, free of scams; and slowly, ever so slowly, Brondo could feel he was getting back on his feet.

It was on Good Friday when Brondo's boss, Paul Neely called him and sent him out on a cleaning job to the Coomb family's residence. Brondo had heard rumours about the Coomb family around town; they were a notoriously dodgy family in Scarborough with questionable connections. Brondo had figured they were probably involved in the drug trade, as Max had once been. He wondered if he knew them. He knocked at the door and was greeted by Shelley Coomb, one of the daughters. She was cute in a way, with sandy brown hair pulled back in a ponytail and a face full of freckles. She had to be about twenty something, he thought, and she smiled at Brondo but he immediately sensed something not right in his gut; something felt off. He went back to the van to collect his carpet cleaning equipment, and decided to call his boss. Paul Neely told him not to worry and to go ahead with the job because they needed the business and the Coombs were regular clients. So Brondo ignored his intuition and went back in to start cleaning the carpets.

Brondo entered the premises, and gave a respectful nod to Shelley and her mother as he proceeded to go about his business, cleaning the floors. Her mother, he noticed, was a rather aggressive, manly looking woman, and she scowled at Brondo as he set about his work. He started up the water pump and was connecting the hoses when he heard a loud scream and ran to the back of the unit, where he found Shelley Coomb with half her clothes off, complaining her foot had been bruised, caught up by the wand Brondo had been using to wash the floors. In a panic, Brondo raced to the van to retrieve the first aid kit from the back. He knelt down to attend to Shelley's foot when she produced a sly and sheepish grin, and Brondo began having flashbacks; he couldn't help but think this girl was toying with him, playing him. He had seen that look before. It reminded him of Sheena.

Brondo suddenly stopped what he was doing, apologised for the accident and quickly returned to his work. He didn't appreciate being played and wanted to focus on just getting the job done. When he was finished, Shelley and her mother offered him a coffee.

"What a wonderful job you have done, Brondo," her mother commented, buttering him up, "we've had other cleaners before, but *none* were as good as you," she crooned.

"Thank you," Brondo replied, accepting the compliment, and feeling bashful.

"Have you heard about our family before? Some people like to spread nasty rumours in this town, but we are all right, really; Shelley's brother has gone to jail for a petty crime, but we really are nice people. Everyone makes mistakes, you know? Look, we can't pay you the full $360 upfront today, but we can pay you the money tomorrow, if you'll come by then, ok? Here, have some more coffee," Shelley said, pouring him another cup. Brondo felt his uneasiness return, and he excused himself, saying he needed to call his boss to see if their making a late payment would be alright.

Paul Neely told Brondo he didn't like doing business with them and to just get the money from them in any way he could, even if it meant returning the next day. They had shafted him of payments in the past and were unreliable about making good on the money. Brondo assured Paul in good faith that he would get the money back; Brondo respected Paul and wanted to repay the trust Paul had instilled in him to run his business; it had been Paul's generosity that had saved his life and gotten him off the streets, and Brondo felt indebted to the man.

Brondo returned to the kitchen and his cold cup of coffee. "That will be fine, Mrs Coomb; my boss has instructed me to return tomorrow for the full payment," Brondo said, and packed up his equipment and made his goodbyes.

Brondo went home that night and after a long work day, settled in to watch some TV on the little portable TV unit. At 11pm Brondo's phone rang; it was an incoming call from a private number.

"Who's this?" Brondo inquired, suspicious.

"It's Shelley, honey—you came to my place today and cleaned my carpets? I owe you some money; come around, I got the money for you now," she said sweetly.

Better to go get it now, he thought; it was Easter and the long weekend, and he knew Paul would be pleased if he got it straight away, instead of having to wait the whole weekend. When Brondo arrived, he could hear more voices inside; there were five other girls there now, including Shelley's sister, Jen, the mother, and two other women and their kids. Brondo felt immediately uncomfortable and cursed himself for once again not listening to his gut.

"Come in, Brondo," Shelley smiled warmly, inviting him in as she played with her hair. All he wanted was the money that was owed to him, but somehow he felt he wasn't going to get out of this situation easily.

"I'm just here to collect the money," Brondo announced, trying to remain as polite and professional as he could.

"You hungry, babe?" Shelley asked. "Sit down a minute, make yourself comfortable," she said, moving to the kitchen to get snacks.

"You got the money, girls?" Brondo asked again.

The girls all looked at one another and back at Brondo, "Yeah, babe, of course we do—why don't you just hang out awhile here, we'll cook you something and watch a movie; we like you, you're cool, sit with us, we'll have the money for you soon."

The footy was on TV, and Brondo realised he *was* hungry; so he sat down and tried to relax; the girls came and sat next to him and he noticed that they smelled good and were all dolled up with their best cute outfits on, so he thought there was no harm to staying for a bit. Besides, he was getting pretty sick of the loneliness and being home alone all the time. As long as he got the money and left in an hour or so, because he didn't want to let his boss down or lose his job.

So Brondo ate and sat with the girls; they put on a horror movie called Wolf Creek, and each time a horror scene played out the girls would all cling to Brondo, especially the two sisters.

"Aren't you hot?" Jen, the younger one asked. She was taller than Shelley, and a fiery redhead. "It's boiling in here; here, take your jumper off. Would you like a drink, babe? We have everything here, beer, wine…"

"Oh, ok yeah, what have you got?" Brondo replied. One drink wouldn't hurt; he hadn't had a soda in ages, he thought, even though he really just wanted to get back home to his own place, his comfort zone. He just couldn't think of a reason to leave, and he didn't know how to be assertive enough to walk away.

Jen returned with the soda, trying to look inviting, pouting duck lips at him with a look of desire. He tried to ignore the way she was eyeing him up now, as though she wanted to devour him. He took the soda from her, thanking her; he had always had a love of soda, and he gulped it down fast, enjoying the refreshing fizziness. The girls laughed and giggled into the background, then broke into full on hysteria; he looked around, not understanding what was so funny, when he suddenly felt his head growing heavy and dizzy at the same time; he tried to get up but fell back into the couch. Just before he passed out Brondo saw the final scene of the horror movie playing before his eyes, as well as the live horror scene before him. He struggled against the urge to close his eyes just long enough to hear the girls' conversation in the room.

"He's gone, he's gone—yes, yes it worked," he heard one of them say.

Brondo awoke late the next morning and felt extremely groggy; where was he? He looked around the room, figuring it was Shelley's bedroom, and suddenly remembered where he was. He went to move but saw that his left hand had been pushed into the bed frame and his arm tied with string around the metal rod; his right arm was numb with pins and needles and his eyes were bloodshot, too, and his mouth was dry, so so dry.

He looked across at the girls who were both crashed out in the bed next to him and noticed he'd been stripped down to his boxer shorts. Jen walked in the room.

"How did you enjoy your sleep, Brondo?" she asked, sporting a sinister smile. Brondo was horrified as his mind raced.

"Fuck—what are you doing to me?" He asked. He tried to breathe, but anxiety and panic overwhelmed him. *Try to think smart, think smart, Brondo, just get yourself out of this...*

"Can you just untie me please, I need to use the toilet," he said, trying to sound cool with it all. Inside, every cell of his body was screaming out in fear.

The girls just laughed. "Shelley, can you go get the bottle from the kitchen," Jen said. "Just piss in here, Brondo," she instructed calmly.

"*Please*? I just need to use the toilet?" Brondo pleaded. He had never felt more vulnerable in all his life.

"Here, here's a bottle—just piss in that, babe," Jen coaxed him again, removing his boxers for him as she did.

Brondo pissed into the bottle. He felt like crying. *I'm trapped! I'm never getting out of this place...Oh fuck! How do I get out of here? Oh dear God—if there is a God, help me now; dear Lord, give me strength,*' he prayed to himself, though his mind was racing. He couldn't believe how powerless he now felt; how could this be happening? Things like this only ever happened in TV shows, right? There had to be a way out of this, he just had to keep his wits about him, and *think*.

The girls left him lying there on the bed in a daze, only Shelley came back in the room.

"We know all about you babe—we know your ex girlfriend, Sheena, and she told us all about you, stupid idiot," she spat at him. "And your name's unique, there's only one of you in Scarborough, so it was only too easy to find you."

Brondo went to speak, but thought better of it. These girls had the upper hand right now; he was just stumped as to what they wanted with him.

The girls laughed. "Suffocate him, Shelley! Suffocate him, Jen!" they laughed menacingly. Brondo was near tears and couldn't defend himself if he tried. Here he was again, a sitting duck and victim of his own life. Shelley reached forward with her hand and pinched Brondo's nose, trying to force him to pass out. Brondo angrily pushed at her, kicking her with his foot to get her off the bed. Shelley shrieked and Jen blurted out, "Kick him in the head! Slap him, slap him, Sis!" and the girls punched into Brondo with all their might. He tried kicking them again even though he thought he might pass out at any minute.

Shelley screamed. "We're gonna knock you out and fuck you one at a time and make you sore, you cunt," she said as she straddled him and spat in his face.

Brondo realised he was defeated; he couldn't beat them all and so he submitted to their will. He tried to plead with them instead, to ease up.

"Look, why don't we all just have some fun here," he said, trying to sound cool and casual.

"Lie back down—don't move, you wog cunt," Shelley ordered, and Brondo took a deep breath and lay down, calling out to God in front of them.

They all laughed at him. "Sheena said he likes legs and feet, but she never said anything about him being a religious freak!" Jen said, laughing. Shelley smirked and lay back down next to him and as she did she raised her leg and pushed her foot in Brondo's face, cutting off his air supply. Brondo tried in vain to free his face from her foot, shaking his head aggressively side to side.

"Fight it all you want, it's just gonna tire you out more, you idiot," Shelley retorted, with an evil laugh.

Within seconds Brondo felt too fatigued to fight, he had used so much energy with his anger that he dozed off again.

Hours later Brondo came to, drunk and sore. The girls were all standing there and smirking, having had their way with him.

"Are you sore, babe? Did you enjoy your sleep, babe?" Shelley said, smiling.

Brondo was mortified; no one knew where he was and his phone, wallet and keys were gone. He felt so vulnerable and scared. He had to think of something, quick.

"Shelley," he said, "Why do you need to do this to me? Surely a beauty like you could have any guy you want—why me?"

"Because you're hot 'n sexy, stupid and nice, just like Sheena said you were—and we especially like the stupid part, right girls?" She said, and they laughed. "Plus, payback's a bitch, and that dumb whore of yours owes us, yeah?"

"Ok, ok, cool babe—" Brondo said, trying to play along with it, "but, I mean I liked you the minute I saw you, right? And when you asked me to come over I came running straight over, right? And what does this have to do with Sheena anyway? We broke up months ago…" he said, trying to play Mr. Cool. Brondo had to admit, he was impressed by his own act now, he could be cooler than he thought, when necessity was the driver of it.

"Haha, you didn't want me, babe, you only came running for the money just now…you're no better than Sheena. And, as for Sheena—you mean you don't know? She used to take us out all the time, Man—I mean, she used your credit card to pay for our hotels, food, partying, you name it, we went cruisin'—" Shelley said, bragging. "We lived it up, all on your dime, babe—the shopping, the jewellery—until she ran off with our stuff, the fucking bitch."

"Haha, remember the night she crashed the car, too?" Jen chimed in. Brondo's eyes widened. He was stunned. Sick in the stomach. "Yeah, and how she was cheating with that guy, who was he? Derek? for months, messaging him, going off to meet him, making out she was going to her sister's place or Perth? It was all a fat lie—and he believed it!" They laughed. He winced at the thought of how he had been lied to all along, but there was no time to think about that right now; he didn't care about Sheena, he just had to get out.

"No, you're wrong, please, look—I'll prove it to you… please, I'll do whatever you want," Brondo said, looking innocent, playing the game with them now.

The two sisters looked at one another. Brondo wondered where the other women were; he had to get past the two sisters first, and just hope there wouldn't be a second trap waiting to ambush him. He was full on paranoid now, but he didn't care; he could feel his willpower and determination growing and he just had to get out of there. *Fucking Sheena.*

"*Ok, cool, let's get to it,*" both girls said. Brondo told them that he would need both hands released, if he was going to have a two on one deal, so Shelley produced a pocket knife and held it to his neck.

"I will fucking cut you and make you bleed if you try anything," she whispered sickly.

"I couldn't think of a more desirable way to die," Brondo said, and kissed Shelley gently.

Revelation 2: 10 Do not fear what you are about to suffer; be sober-minded; be watchful.

Your adversary the devil prowls around like a roaring lion, seeking someone to devour.

"Rougher," Jen said. "Rougher, rougher!" She demanded. "My God, he kisses like a fucking soft pussy! No wonder Sheena dumped him for that other guy!" they mocked.

Brondo's ears burned; he couldn't believe what they were saying, yet it had to be true. Sheena had been cheating on him. It all made sense now; her dying interest in him, the lies, constantly saying she was staying at her sister's, the guy sending her the plane ticket. How Sheena complained that he was too soft, too this or that, never enough. He realised how pathetic he looked to them in that moment; it was the same way Sheena had looked at him, and his anger grew and he upped the ante, and felt Jen release his arm. He knew he could have broken free earlier, but he was fatigued and worn out; he hadn't eaten in over God knows how long and right now he just had to play the part, make no sudden moves. Be patient, he thought; make them think he wanted to be there, even though he so desperately wanted to throw both girls off him right then and make a run for it. He seriously doubted how much strength he had in him; they had sufficiently drugged him enough, and he knew they would be wary too, prepared for him to escape. And these girls were crazy—one wrong move and things could get bloody.

Sometimes, you do what you gotta do to survive in this big bad world, he thought to himself.

"Where's my loving cunt?" Jen asked, holding the switchblade to his throat. Brondo submitted; he moved over to her and began kissing both girls at the same time, gagging inside as he did. He felt so disgusted and ashamed of himself, but he held his breath so he wouldn't vomit all over the them; he was walking on eggshells, and he knew it. There was nothing to do but give them what they wanted, so he rammed them until they were full and lay back on the bed, satisfied. He could hear the other three women just outside the room watching TV, and the girls enticed him to come lie with them, and so he did. The girls were impressed with him, and started rambling on about him being a big hot stud and a great lover; that he was theirs now, not Sheena's. Brondo just lay there in the dark, looking at the ceiling and praying to God to get him out of there.

Saturday night rolled into Easter Sunday morning; the girls said they were going out, but for him not to get any ideas because he wasn't going anywhere; they were locking him in the house, they said, until they returned. He thought it was the dumbest thing he'd ever heard, but he played along with it. He wondered where they could be going on a Sunday morning anyway, and had to laugh to himself because the only place open was church, and they definitely wouldn't be going there.

"And you'll be here waiting for us when we get back, our darling Brondo—and then we'll have more fun!" they both said, laughing, walking out the door and locking him in. He pretended to be half asleep, and they left; but Brondo knew he wasn't tied up, even though he was trapped inside the house. As soon as they were gone, he moved from room to room like a caged animal; it was deadlocked inside and the windows were shut, but his energy levels were rising. He found his clothes, wallet and keys and got dressed and checked his phone; the data was all used up and the phone was dead, but he didn't care—he desperately wanted a shower, but raced around the house instead, looking for a way out, panicking at each second of the clock he wasted. He found the laundry; just past that was a small toilet, and an even smaller window. But the window was not dead-bolted, so the only way out, he thought, would be to climb through this little window. Only Spiderman could fucking get through here, he thought to himself.

He returned to the bedroom and pulled the leg post off the bed, leaving the bed falling to one side, and raced back to the toilet, climbing on top of the seat. He got the post and smashed the window with it, cringing at the noise it made; he cleared the shards off its edges and quickly climbed through, worried they might all return before he got out of there. He got through unscathed and ran to his work van and started her up. She stalled. *Fuck, fuck, shit, shit,* he swore until she finally ticked over.

Brondo drove home in a panic like a madman. He breathed a sigh of relief when he ran inside the unit and bolted the door; he was home. He sat down with his back against the door and put his head in his hands and started to cry. He couldn't break free of the psychological shackles of torment he had endured; over and over he kept reliving it in his mind—the rape, the abuse, the things they had said about Sheena. Was any of it true? Well, it had to be, he reasoned; how else would they have known so much? It would prove to be the last mistake Brondo would ever make when it came to women, because in that moment he swore he would never trust another woman again.

He charged his phone and checked his messages, quick to block their numbers. There were about a dozen messages from

Paul Neely, asking 'Mate, are you ok, where have you gone? Please call me.'

Brondo knew he had lots of explaining to do, but how could he look his boss in the eye with all this? He couldn't tell Paul; he would just have to say that he had done the best job he could cleaning their carpets, and that he tried and couldn't get the money back off the Coombs.

The Coomb girls were not about to let go, they started sending him threats from a private number and he knew he had to be wary; Scarborough was a small town and they might find a way to get to him again because they were so cunning. He wondered whether he should involve the police; but who would believe him when it just looked like it had been a fun night, a threesome? He didn't think the police would believe him, either, because of his past associations to Sheena. *Oh, you poor bloke, we feel sorry for you,* the coppers had said to him, once upon a time.

But, he still couldn't believe what they'd said about Sheena, and it was so incredibly painful having to learn the nasty truth about it all. He knew the day was coming, he could feel it in his bones; he would call Sheena, he'd have it out with her. Just not yet.

By late March the carpet business was going dry; too many competitors meant the company was struggling to stay afloat, and Paul decided that he was going to take over the business and quit his day job. Brondo knew he needed to start looking for another job, and he was distraught about having to start over yet again. Paul put him onto a steam cleaning business for tiles and grout, and because of what had happened with the Coomb's, Brondo decided it was best to move for his own safety, since they knew where he lived. He saw an ad for shared accomodation and decided to give it a go. He met Ben Hill on a Tuesday afternoon after work; Ben was returning to Scarborough and needed a flatmate. Within five minutes of meeting him, Ben admitted that he was battling clinical depression, and Brondo took an instant liking to him. They moved in together and became fast friends, Brondo even talking Ben into joining his gym. They would train together in the gym, then hit the spa and sauna afterwards, and between the two of them, they made things work. Ben helped Brondo with resources in terms of understanding and conquering homelessness, and his background in HR proved to be invaluable in teaching Brondo what to do and how to better present himself in an assertive way in the workforce and everyday life.

Brondo, in turn, would teach Ben how to be street smart and how to fight depression, stay motivated, get fit and eat well, because the depression had sent Ben into serious weight gain. They lived together, trained together and enjoyed each other's company, becoming healthy allies. But Brondo could see that Ben still battled serious depression. Sadly, Ben was constantly a downer and a cleric personality, which meant that he was one of those types where everything had to be perfect (even though he was far from perfect and struggled with a gambling addiction), and he was driven solely by money and success (the source of which also fed his gambling addiction). He was permanently stuck in a loop. While Ben was intelligent, even savvy, he wasn't a particularly friendly person, and was even harder to live with. Still, Brondo remained optimistic that he could pull Ben out of the darkness and into the light. He told Ben some of his own dark tales of the past, and Ben's eyes widened as Brondo's story got worse and worse.

"My God—you've been through some real shit, man," Ben

said, shaking his head. Ben told Brondo that he too, had reached a point where he felt he couldn't handle life anymore and had even contemplated suicide, and Brondo sat up all night with his friend and evangelised the word of God with the young man. He convinced Ben to come try his church; they were good people there, and they would open their hearts to him, welcome him. Brondo felt he had finally reached Ben, when one Sunday after church, Ben came out smiling for the first time in a long time. He could see the young man was drawing closer to God, and Brondo felt he had done good and saved a soul from taking his own life, and this gave his life a sense of purpose and satisfaction, too.

"Sorrow is better than laughter, my friend; it may sadden your face, but it sharpens your understanding…check it out—says so in the Bible," Brondo said humbly. He of all people knew a lot about sadness; it seemed to be the one constant in his life.

The next couple of weeks Ben drifted apart from Brondo; they would see less of one another as he saw Ben withdraw further and further into himself. Brondo felt helpless, but there was little he could do; he would just try to remain a constant, steady presence for the young man, thinking that would be what he would want for himself, if it were him. In late May, Brondo stepped out of the shower to find Ben curled up on the couch, crying uncontrollably.

"I'm not well, Man," he said as Brondo sat down next to him.

"What can I do to help?" Brondo asked, reaching out to the man in his time of suffering, as though it were his own.

"Well, I don't want you to be angry, but since I became a Christian, I've been doing a lot of thinking—and I think it's best if I move back in with my parents for awhile."

Brondo just looked at him, speechless.

"I knew you'd be upset, that's why this is so hard—but I have to break the lease; I know I'm not well right now, and I have to be honest about it...I need to be on my own. I'm so sorry, Brondo."

Brondo was furious, but he tried not to show it. He wanted to tell Ben to stay, that it was he who had brought him to God, and that he could be the one to help him. But he could see the kid had already made up his mind. Fuck, he thought. He wouldn't be able to keep the lease on his own; the cleaning job simply didn't pay enough for him to be able to afford it. Ben promised to repay him what he owed, and Brondo begrudgingly knew that he would have to go ahead with it, he would have to let him go. But he wouldn't turn his back on Ben because he knew he'd lost friends like this in the past; he was a good kid, he was just messed up. Now he would need to sit down and look over his finances right away, do some serious number crunching and figure out what he was going to do, how long he could possibly last there on his own.

On Saturday morning Brondo pulled out the manila folder to go through his finances. He wasn't too good at keeping up with his bank statements, he usually just filed them away, because it depressed him too much to see how many debts he still had owing. He had finally paid off the thousands of dollars he owed VicRoads for the speeding fines without any help from Max, and he knew he'd lost the bond money, too; but he still had quite the insurmountable credit card debt that, no matter much he tried to whittle it down, it just seemed to climb back up again. He couldn't understand it, because he had been trying so hard to save, for himself.

He looked at the list of bank charges, running his finger down the debits column. Petrol, supermarket, phone bill, electricity. Nothing seemed out of the ordinary. Then he came to see one charge he didn't recognise; a hotel charge for $570 at the Hilton Hotel in Melbourne. Well, that must be wrong, he thought; he'd never even stayed at that hotel before; he was sure of it. It must be a mistake. He took a closer look at it; it was dated January 26, Australia Day. That couldn't be right, because he knew that he'd spent that weekend visiting Vito and Sonia. He looked at the statement and saw there were a few other charges around that time, too; restaurant dinner at the Crown Casino, and another for an in-house dining room charge. What the fuck? He'd have to call the bank and report the charges and cancel his card.

On Sunday morning Ben had gone out for a jog and Brondo was in the kitchen making eggs on toast when his phone rang. He went to pick it up, and saw that the incoming call flashing at him was Sheena. Sheena! His heart skipped a beat; just seeing her name light up on the screen made his palms sweat. What did she want? Why on earth would she be calling him, after all this time? In the beginning Brondo had tried to reach out to her several times just after the breakup, asking if he could see Charlotte, asking how everyone was doing, but she had just been a cold fish, pulling away. He knew she just wanted to get back out there and play the field in her sporty new car and skinnier frame; she hadn't been single in twenty-five years and she just wanted her freedom, so he'd let her go. But Sheena had been cruel, slowly cutting her ties altogether from Brondo, afraid of the truth ever coming out. He wondered if perhaps she knew about the Coomb girls, maybe they had said something to her to rattle her cage. He picked up.

"Hello," he answered, trying to sound normal, nonchalant.

"Brondo—we have to talk." No 'hello, hi, or how are you.' Typical Sheena. It was just all about her.

"What about," he replied coolly, in a couldn't-care-less kind of way. He wasn't about to make this easy on her. Why should he go easy on her, after all she'd done to him.

"I'm in trouble, Brondo—I'm financially strapped, and I lost my job, and I crashed my car, and, well, yesterday you cancelled the card on me. You have to unblock the cancellation." Brondo couldn't believe what she was saying.

"Sheena—do *you* still have *my* credit card?" Brondo said, incredulous, trying to remain calm and hide his complete shock. God damn it. The charges were from her. These were *her* charges. He just couldn't believe it. She still had the card. She was still *using* the card. User.

"That's not the point, I need it—I'm stuck in Sydney right now, and if you don't fix the card, I can't get—"

"Are you fucking insane, woman? I am NOT paying for you, you crazy bitch!" Brondo screamed at her. "Get your *fucking* boyfriend, whatshisname, Derek? to pay your way! Don't worry; I know all about him, you were seeing him when you were still with me. Weren't you?" He challenged. Brondo's eyes were turning red, the vessels in his cheeks burst and he thought he was going to have a heart attack. But Sheena was cunning, oh, she was so coy, he thought as she quickly went on the defensive.

"No, Brondo—I wasn't seeing Derek then, I was..." but he could hear her hesitation, he thought he might have even heard a slight shakiness to her voice, a slight stutter as she tried to regroup; he had never heard her sound so uncertain about herself, so weak. He had to hand it to her, she was good at misleading people; she always knew how to play it smart, how to twist things, play things to her advantage in that underhanded way she had.

"You were what, exactly?" Brondo demanded to know.

"Brondo, I swear on Charlotte's life, on my kids' lives—"

"Stop lying, Sheena, I know all about it—Shelley told me everything," he said, calling her bluff. All of his past hurts were coming back to haunt him right now, but he was in no mood to be his charming self. And he was enjoying the moment too, finally pulling her up on all her own crap.

"I give you my word," she said and started crying on the other end of the line.

"Save your water works, Sheena," Brondo said, "the game is up. And your 'word' has never meant much to you anyway, you've never held those paths to truth dear—they're just cheap words to you. Everything about you is cheap; I know you Sheena Baxter—I know you better than anyone...even better than your own kids, or your mother...you can't fool me anymore, I know the painful, nasty truth about you; it wasn't Max who crashed my car, it was *you*; it wasn't the boys racking up my credit card debt, it was *you*; I know you lied and took the bond money; I know you went to hotels with the girls and partied on my dime, and I know you never went to Perth, and about the guy who sent you the plane tickets, and now I know that you've been messaging him since November 2014. The bottom line is that you have played God with my life for far too long, but thank God I finally woke up, because I only answer to one God now—and it *isn't* you! You thought I was weak, you thought I was soft and stupid, you thought I was too nice...and so you thought you could use me. And I am all of those things. But being nice isn't about being weak, or soft; being nice is a strength, a *choice*. It takes *strength* to be nice. Being bad is easy. I've ignored my gut instincts for so long about you—even your sister-in-law Michelle warned me about you at the beginning, told me you were a user; but, like a fool, I didn't listen. I didn't listen because I wanted to be your *"Good Little Greek Church Boy,"* as you put it. Well, listen to this:

You're nothing but a dirty whore—a lying, cheating USER."

Brondo hung up on Sheena for the last time; he'd got the last word. He was livid, but God it felt good to offload on her like that. *In the beginning was the word, and the word was with God, and the word was God.*

In that moment Brondo saw how good he had been at saving others, just never himself. Now, for the first time in his life, Brondo was discovering what it truly felt like to be *saving* himself. And it felt good. The Truth shall set you free.

Acts 2: 21
'And it shall come to pass
that everyone who calls
upon the name of the Lord
shall be saved.'

EPILOGUE
God Awaits

Romans 1:16
For I am not ashamed of the gospel, for it is the power of God for salvation to everyone who believes, to the Jew first and also to the Greek.

"The lord is my Shepherd, I shall not want. He maketh me to lie down in green pastures," Brondo whispered to himself and lay down under an old Oak tree in the long grasses listening to his instincts; he watched the leaves of the tree dancing in the breeze, the sounds of swallows singing a tune high above him. He could hear his gut speaking to him now, and it was telling him that today was going to be a good day.

Brondo was adamant he wasn't coming back to Melbourne; there was no chance in hell was he coming back to what he had left behind years ago. He had wanted to stay in Scarborough and fight it out—so he was frustrated with God as all signs pointed him back there, back to Melbourne, because apparently it was *The Place To Be*. But why would God want him back in Melbourne?

Brondo couldn't understand it. By July he had moved in to a new place; a six bedroom expanse that was empty and only $150 a week until October, when the backpackers arrived and the place would be full again. Brondo even brought some Greek boys over on a working visa from his native homeland to help out the local Greek priest, but then the rent went up and within weeks their visas expired, and Brondo was unable to afford the rent alone. Within days the landlord was asking him to leave and once again Brondo faced the prospect of homelessness. He felt as though he was cursed, but these were the cards God had dealt him, for whatever reason; he just couldn't understand why these things kept happening to him.

Brondo was about to swallow his pride, call Vito and ask for help, when out of the blue he got a call from his old childhood friend, George Harman. They talked and talked for hours; there was so much to catch up on. George asked to meet him out for coffee, and though he was strapped for cash, Brondo agreed to it. They went to a little place in Brunswick on the corner; it was his old haunt and they served the best Greek coffees in town.

George was ecstatic to see Brondo, and for the first hour they reminisced on their childhood together, reigniting the friendship from years past.

"Listen, I don't know if you'd be interested, Brondo, but I have a spare bedroom I'm interested in renting out, if you're keen? Sure would be great to have your company," George said fondly.

Brondo said he'd do some soul searching and get back to him; moving back to Coburg, back to his old stomping ground was something Brondo didn't think he wanted. He'd moved on, and needed to start afresh; he didn't want to keep dragging the same old bags around behind him. Finally he agreed to it, and

George said he had a truck and would help with the move.

Brondo didn't have much, he'd lost nearly everything because of Sheena; so it was a tearful journey as they rode in the truck together down Sydney Road a week later. The truck slid over tram tracks as memories great and small flashed in Brondo's mind. Brondo felt empty, and he looked out the window and upon the clouds, gazing and asking God quietly, "What now, Lord?"

The next six weeks were difficult and Brondo struggled to adapt back to city life. He missed his church friends, the infinite space of the countryside. But he needed a new outlook on life, too, and getting away from Scarborough felt good. And he knew he was slowly forgetting about Sheena, too, and that was really good.

"I know we are both men of God, George, but I've been thinking of ending my quest with Christianity," Brondo said, out of the blue.

"Why is that?" George asked, genuinely confused. In his eyes, Brondo was one of the most Christian men he'd ever known.

"I don't know; I just feel at a loss after all that has happened, you know?"

"I don't know; I can't begin to imagine the horrors you've been through, or how you survived it all—mentally, too. I would have fallen apart if it had been me. By the way, I know we've known each other for decades now, right? Yet I never knew how you got your name. It's so unique," George said, cleaning his plate.

"Have you ever heard of the cartoon from the 80s, Astroboy? The little boy robot who was a hero? Well, in the final episodes there's a robot called Brondo; he's a fierce, fighting robot dedicated to justice who's destroyed—but he fights gallantly and nobly to the end."

"Ha! No, I've never seen it, but that suits you to a T," George said with conviction.

They ate dinner together in peace; he and George would go out for a walk afterwards to stretch their legs, as the Greeks often liked to do; it was the customary thing to do after meals. Just then Brondo's phone began to ring; he wasn't going to answer it, he was enjoying the solitude too much, but it was Vito.

"Hey Bro—I don't know why I had to call you just now, but it has been on my heart to mention this to you, because it came to me yesterday in a dream," Vito said, sounding weird and excited.

"What?" Brondo asked, surprised.

"Well, I dreamed you were sitting in this church, see, and I could see the name of it, in big, big letters..." he said.

"That's weird," Brondo said, "because I was just talking to George about quitting the church for awhile," he relied soberly. How strange, it was like his brother had overheard their conversation, or something.

"Well, where was this church, Bro? The one in your dream?" Brondo asked.

"I don't know; all I know was that it had a big sign out the front, and it was called "Centrepoint."

George looked at Brondo, and his face turned pale; he pointed at the street sign directly overhead. They were standing on Centrepoint Road. Brondo gasped.

"My God Vito, it's a sign—I've gotta go, I'll call you back," he said and hung up.

Over the coming week Brondo would pray to God and read the word again; he would attend the gym and start running again, motivating himself to get back to work in the aged care and community services, which he truly loved. He reconnected with his family and saw more of his brother and his nieces than ever before. He was not sure what life in Melbourne would bring for him; he wasn't entirely where he wanted to be in life, but he was relieved and happy that at least he was no longer where he once was. New doors were opening everywhere around him, letting the fresh air in.

On Sunday morning, late in August of 2017, Brondo drove out to Sharps Road in Tullamarine; he sat there in the carpark and looked around, it was 10:35 or so and he was the last one to arrive. He felt apprehensive, but he was dressed for the occasion, and despite his nervousness he knew he was far stronger and far more assertive than he'd ever been in his life. His self-love and self-confidence had grown tenfold, and he had found himself once again, could feel he was growing in a positive way, in the right way. Change to him had always been a scary prospect, yet now he was beginning to see change in a new light, and it was beautiful; it was a place full of hope and promise.

Brondo turned off the car radio in the car; it had been playing Tony Scuito's 80's hit song, *Out of the Darkness and Into the Light*. He got out of the car and walked into the church and sat quietly in one of the back pews, wondering what relationship encounter he would have with God today. It was a mystery. Life, he'd learned, was a mystery. Brondo was uncertain about many things, but there was one thing he was certain of, and that was that God was always with him; God had never left his side. All his life, Brondo had always been trying to fit into what he believed others wanted him to be, when all the while God had silently been working on him, moulding him into the perfect fit of who Brondo should be for Brondo. As he sat there, a strange feeling overcame him; he could feel himself moving into a new place, because, through God's good grace, something was pulling him forward, moving him into the light, into a new lightness of being. He smiled to himself as he sat there in the Centrepoint church, surrounded by abundant peace and contentment, knowing that, for all his pain and heartache, for all his struggles in life, he had finally found his true centre point.

Brondo prayed silently thanking God for everything He had done for him. He looked up, smiled and closed his book in prayer.

Amen.

John 14: 6

Jesus saith unto him, I am the way, the truth, and the life: no man cometh unto the Father, but by me.

About the Author

Fivos Panayiotou grew up on the outskirts of Melbourne in the 80s in a traditional Greek family. As a first generation born of AustralianGreek heritage hailing from Cyprus, he was raised in the multicultural area of Brunswick and ate meat pies and was a devout fan of Carlton football club like any normal kid in Melbourne's eastern suburbs. He has a particular interest in working with the elderly in aged care and is a dedicated uncle, family man and man of God. He is a survivor of domestic violence and strong advocate against psychological abuse and wishes to speak out on this largely unrecognized aspect of men's mental health. Fivos is currently at work on his second novel, due for publication in 2021.

www.ingramcontent.com/pod-product-compliance
Lightning Source LLC
Chambersburg PA
CBHW030253010526
44107CB00053B/1684